# MODERN FRENCH DRAWINGS

MODERN

# FRENCH DRAWINGS

IN CZECHOSLOVAKIA

GABRIELA KESNEROVÁ
AND PETR SPIELMANN

PAUL HAMLYN

LONDON · NEW YORK · SYDNEY · TORONTO

## EDITORS' NOTE

We wish to express our thanks to the National Gallery, Prague, to the National Museum of Literature, Prague (formerly the Karásek Gallery), to the Moravian Museum, Brno, to the Gallery of Fine Arts, Ostrava, and numerous private collections throughout Czechoslovakia for permission to reproduce the illustrations shown in the present work.

First part of text and catalogue up to Cézanne written by Gabriela Kesnerová, second part by Petr Spielmann
Translated by Enid da Silva

Designed and produced by Artia for
THE HAMLYN GROUP LTD
Hamlyn House, The Centre, Feltham, Middlesex



Printed in Czechoslovakia by Polygrafia, Prague
S 2313

# GENERAL INTRODUCTION

The drawing of French artists in the nineteenth century is astonishing in its immense diversity. In no other century in the history of art has drawing developed at such a pace. It was in this particular body of work, especially during the last thirty years of the century, that modern graphic art found its form and became crystallized. French drawing of this period did not grow out of one dominant style, but combined new departures of every kind linking up all the trends and successive phases of nineteenth-century French painting. The conditions for such a development were a result of the new distribution of social forces following the French Revolution and their resultant influence on European thought in the search for social and individual freedom. The century which laid down the principles of the Declaration of the Rights of Man upheld two fundamental principles: historical objectivity and a respect for the individual. The unity which had governed thought and artistic creativity in bygone times was superseded by a liberalism. The solidarity of one dominant style gave way to the work of a number of trenchant personalities striving to express their own feelings and responding in their own way to the new and burning issues of the day. In so far as drawing was an immediate and direct expression of the personality of the artist, it was able to interpret this endeavour with sensitivity and a wide variety of ways and means.

The function of drawing changed. From the private working sketch, the studio aid, it became a supreme artistic expression in its own right, translating the artist's ideas as completely as on canvas. Until then drawing had only attained this status in the work of great artists, such as Leonardo da Vinci, Rembrandt or Claude Lorraine. During the nineteenth century works based on linear principles, in which drawing was as important as painting, appeared. Ingres, Degas and Toulouse-Lautrec are among the greatest masters of drawing in the nineteenth century, even if they are not the only ones. The artistic concepts of Ingres, expressed primarily by line in drawing, counterbalanced the opposite tendency represented by Eugène Delacroix, who expressed himself fundamentally through colour. These two opposed artistic tendencies, known as classicism and romanticism, determined the development of French art at the beginning of the century.

Drawing, as an ancient means of representational art, is in itself an abstraction of reality, of nature, of events lived through, of the world as experienced through the senses. Whatever its functions or the material used, a drawing interprets three dimensions on one plane, showing natural colour by a range of monochrome shades, or by colours which have a largely symbolic value. As a quick and direct means of artistic expression, drawing has always been an instrument of research, a means of making contact with objective reality. At the same time it remains the direct interpreter of an inner world of images, sensations and impressions experienced subjectively. Drawing, therefore, does not imitate reality but transcribes or accentuates its essential features as projected through the personal vision of the artist. In a few moments it can capture a sensation or an image, whereas painting is a longer process, being gradually developed and built up towards the final result. Drawing uses its own language of abbreviations and graphic signs as its means of expression. It demands a minimum of technical skill and goes beyond the limitations of style more easily than any other art-form.

Delacroix, a painter of great freedom and emotional energy, found in drawing a means of liberation. He wrote in his journal: 'The difference between literature and painting is relative to the effect which can be produced by the sketch of an idea, in short, to the impossibility of outlining something in literature in such a way as to present it vividly to the mind with the same force as in a sketch or primitive drawing.' The sketch, for Delacroix, was 'the best possible way of expressing an idea, not in the suppression of details but by their complete subordination to the broad strokes which first grasp the essential'. In the spontaneous emotional style of Delacroix drawing had primarily an expressive role, springing from his innermost feelings. Through his drawing Delacroix freed himself of creative tension, making it interpret his impressions, like Rembrandt or his contemporary, Honoré Daumier. His immensely rich manner of drawing changed according to his needs and the subject represented. His particular style is achieved by dynamic execution, an exaggerated expressiveness and an abbreviation of form, using pencil or more often a pen, which could be more sensitive and animated. In the drawings in his travel sketchbooks the rapid pencil sketches are strengthened by watercolour and enlivened by a touch of colour applied with a brush.

Even though drawing can stand on its own without colour, the romantic painters, Delacroix and Géricault, explored the use of reverberating colours in connection with drawing. Tradition cut by classicism gave art new impetus to attain forms capable of further development. The watercolours of Géricault demonstrate how far he had travelled from his early wash-drawings. The immediacy of his realistic studies of horses and horse-racing anticipate the drawings of Degas and Guys. The passionate ideas of Delacroix are expressed with increasingly free and luminous colours.

Whereas to Delacroix, as to Rembrandt, drawing was a personal confession, and transmits to us his inner impressions and thoughts, the graphic legacy of Ingres, Delacroix's great adversary, retains a classical purity and grandeur of style. 'In Paris,' said Baudelaire, 'we know of only two men who draw as well as Monsieur Delacroix, one in a similar way, the other with a quite different technique. One is Monsieur Daumier, the caricaturist, the other Monsieur Ingres, the great painter, whose secret idol is Raphael.' The art of Ingres consists of capturing reality by means of reason, harmony and order; his means of expression is the purity, discipline and melodic flow of line. Whereas Delacroix translated his emotion into colour, which he transmuted into the living fabric of his paintings, Ingres imprisoned reality in clearly-defined form, delimited by fine decisive strokes. Ingres' sculptural style also involved the abstraction of natural forms; he portrayed reality seen as a whole, leaving nothing to chance, making modifications only in the interests of pure and ideal beauty. Drawing was the basis of his creative work. 'The purpose of drawing is not simply to reproduce an outline; drawing does not consist simply of strokes; drawing also conveys expression, inner form, structure and form in the round. See what is left after that! Drawing constitutes three-quarters and more of what painting comprises. If I had to put a sign above my door, I would put "School of Drawing", and I am sure I would produce painters... Form is the basis and essence of everything; even smoke must be shown by a line.' Hundreds of studies, portraits of unsurpassed perfection, are the personal legacy of this artist. Thanks to these, we have a picture of both the artist and his period. Unlike the tempestuous Delacroix, this born draughtsman did not like changing one technique for another, he preferred the classical methods of drawing with pen or pencil.

Artists of succeeding generations have returned to the clear metallic tones of the drawings of Ingres whenever they needed intellectually based form as opposed to sensual and emotive inspiration. The Ingres tradition was taken up again by Chassériau and its dignity re-established by Edgar Degas, one of the greatest modern masters of classical drawing. The same tradition enabled Renoir to counter Impressionist sensualism by the imposition of a new discipline of composition and form. Its echo reverberates in the silence of drawings by Puvis de Chavannes, just as it is discernible, even at the close of the century, in the attractive modernity of Lautrec's graphic work and in the purity of contour of Picasso's classical drawings.

The most direct interpretation of nature, during the nineteenth century, was found in the drawings of the Barbizon artists, who at the beginning of the 1830s sought to achieve directly through nature a realistic portrait of the countryside, which they showed in every detail as a part of life in a perpetual state of change. Like the great Dutch landscape painters of the seventeenth century, they set out to capture nature's monumental and inner aspects. They sought and discovered its secret life, finding the most exact way of expressing every detail—the form and movement of a tree, a rock formation, a heap of stones or stream of water—but they were also able to observe the general character of the countryside in its relation to the atmosphere which complements it and forever gives it life. Their drawing, however, was not restricted simply to objective representation but also interpreted the feelings and moods which nature aroused in the artist. The romantic sensibility of Diaz is expressed by a soft and modulated stroke made with charcoal or chalk. Diaz preferred thick pencils rather than pencils with a fine point or a pen, which, for instance, Théodore Rousseau used.

The unique richness of feeling, harmony and beauty in Corot's drawings, confirm the exceptional place of this great lyrical painter of nature among French landscape painters. The development of his drawing, linked with his artistic maturity, led him from the careful observation of the countryside to its poetic and spiritual interpretation. Camille Corot described the emotions awakened in him by the sight of a landscape, with a range of tones and a freedom of stroke in brush or charcoal which heralded the filtered light of the Impressionists. It is for this reason that the painters of succeeding generations turned to his work as to a refreshing spring.

Many painters who devoted themselves to landscape and its atmospheric interpretation, favoured the lightness of the pencil sketch heightened by watercolour or simply watercolour by itself, as the most atmospheric and immediate technique. This is borne out by the magnificent watercolours of Jongkind and the spontaneous landscape pictures of the Normandy coast by Boudin.

The Impressionists made visual perception the sole point of departure for pictorial representation. They did not show the physical tangibility of objects but represented them as purely optical phenomena of which the solid form was dissolved by the action of light and air. Any constructive function of drawing was thus entirely absent. The Impressionists could best produce the luminous surface of objects or the effect of disintegrating colour with watercolours or pastels. They did few drawings, and those by Manet, Pissarro or Sisley are comparatively rare. These painters did not study nature in detail nor did they compose or borrow from the countryside. Rather they strove to grasp by means of sensations of colour and light the infinite permutations of nature and to fix one fugitive moment of passing time. They painted the subject direct, having no need of drawing as an intermediate stage between spontaneous impressions and the subsequent creation of the picture.

Nevertheless, drawing did play a role of importance in the work of Auguste Renoir and, to an even greater degree, of Edgar Degas. These two artists, under the influence of Impressionism, enriched and liberated the forms and nuances of their expression even while branching off into other directions. Renoir went beyond the Impressionist technique with his new sensuality and fullness of forms, while Degas balanced harmoniously the intellectual and sensory elements in his pictures, emphasizing the function of drawing as the constructive element. His figures of dancers and ballerinas woven out of lightly applied coloured chalks, perfectly express the special atmosphere of the theatrical world–its excitement and concentration, its suspense and emptiness, the glitter of the footlights and the darkness of the auditorium. The drawings of Degas can justly be connected with Impressionism because of the extraordinary richness of colour, the luminous quality of his pastels and plasticity of movement.

The relationship of Rodin's drawings to Impressionism can be understood in similar terms. He was also able to capture in his innumerable studies of the human body momentary varieties of posture and action, seizing every fleeting gesture or movement.

The Neo-Impressionists used Impressionist techniques to explore the divisions between tones, but their *pointillist* or 'divisionist' technique led them to produce quite different results. They provided an exact construction of the picture within strict spatial relationships, with a harmonious and balanced composition of line, form and colour. Drawing was again an essential and prominent part of their work. The contrast between the personalities of the two leaders of this movement, Seurat and Signac, emerges more strongly from their drawings than from their paintings, where it is submerged by the demands of style and the discipline of pictorial composition. The drawings of Seurat, in gently blended charcoal or pencil, astound us by their grandiose conception of simplified forms set within distinct spacial limits, modelled by gradations between contrasting tones. They have the same emotive and meaningful tension as his pictorial works, with the same elaborate colouristic effects. Signac, bolder in style, used *pointillist* techniques in his atmospheric and luminous watercolours.

It was the artists of the 1880s and 1890s, who after 1884 were centred around the Salon des Independents, who determined the new directions in which French painting was to go. In their work the admirable variety and richness of French drawing surpassed everything that had been done before. Paul Cézanne, Van Gogh and Gauguin, although very different from one another, all used Impressionism as their starting point. The results, very different as they were, together created a new basis for pictorial representation opening the way for modern painting.

Paul Cézanne did not emphasize the independent function of drawing but considered it as an integral part of pictorial expression. His drawings are inextricably linked with his work as a painter. They are the means whereby he sounded out the depths of things, and went beneath the surface of visible forms into the actual structure of the landscape. He drew in order to unveil the substance of its phenomena and to this end moved the subjects depicted into new relationships of volume and space. On this basis, he constructed a new vision of the world.

In the broad context of the creative movement in French drawing at the end of the nineteenth century, the drawings of Vincent van Gogh are dramatically individual and communicate with a power which cannot be equalled. In the drawings following the Arles period, Van Gogh expressed his feeling of fatality by fevered sketches, all done in parallel and hatched wavy lines. It was the same feeling which made this emotional artist embody his tragic view of the world in painting.

Paul Gauguin, third of this great trio, discovered the visual power of the symbol. This means of communicating content by allusion led Gauguin to break through the frontiers of artistic language. His images build up, and his line and coloured planes become the interpreters of his graphic and pictorial expression, their role being as much expressive as decorative.

The programme of the artists of the School of Pont-Aven, who were grouped around Paul Gauguin, was adopted by the Symbolists. Its principles were also the point of departure for the painters known as the *Nabis*, Bonnard, Vuillard and Maillol, whose interest in decoration was reflected in the *Art Nouveau* movement.

The true significance of drawing during the years of creative turmoil at the end of the century can not be properly appreciated if one does not remember its importance for graphic art which, towards 1890, underwent rapid developments both from the technological and artistic point of view. Examples of this include not only Gauguin and Toulouse-Lautrec, remarkable painters who laid the foundations of modern graphic art, but also the Symbolists, Felicien Rops and Odilon Redon, and the works of Bonnard, Vuillard and Denis.

Alive and flourishing throughout the whole of the nineteenth century, was a tradition of book illustration and caricature which had no equal outside France. The topical genre picture and the caricature with its wit and satire, was closely linked with everyday life and reacted instantaneously to political and social occasions. Events and opinions were reflected in these drawings, which were at the same time a chronicle and a popular and widely used weapon in the hands of the increasingly powerful press. In them is reflected a general picture of the time, depicting human relationships whereas the mainstream in the development of French painting reflects these same conditions in a much more complex manner. The Napoleonic period was chronicled by some of the most eminent lithographers and by the drawings of romantic artists like Raffet, Vernet, Bellangé, and above all Géricault. They celebrated, in a romantic spirit, the heroic onsurge of the French nation. The revolutionary atmosphere and the growth of society galvanized into activity the satirical artists grouped around the revues *La Caricature* and *Le Charivari*, which attacked the shaky foundations of the July monarchy. Even if these artists, apart from Paul Gavarni, did not step beyond the limits of their own time, the work of Daumier, by contrast, is a unique example of art which is socially committed, transcending time and attaining the highest ranks of art and ethics.



If the analysis of French society made by Daumier may be compared with the greatness of *Comédie humaine* by Balzac, the picture of Parisian society during the Second Empire, as represented by Constantin Guys in his wittily drawn observations, is comparable to the novels and short stories of Guy de Maupassant, Edmond de Goncourt and Emile Zola. Daumier and Guys influenced the work of artists, who in the course of the last thirty years of the century held out a mirror to the corruption of the ruling class. The barbs of their satire were aimed at the heart of the political and social life of the Third Republic. The realistic sketches of Rops, Forain and Steinlen had a more far-reaching significance than that of the political journals which they illustrated.

## CLASSICISM AND ROMANTICISM

During the nineteenth century, French classical drawing reached its climax with Ingres who, at the beginning of the century, was the bridge between the past and the future. He gave new life to the ancient legacy of purity of form and to the heritage of the Renaissance. His romantic sensibility and realistic conception of life lend tension to his clean line and classical feeling. The artists of the succeeding generations were able to draw on his work as from a source of living tradition. Ingres himself admired ancient art and the Italian Renaissance. His main ambition as a young man was to follow Raphael: 'Forever adored by me are Raphael and his century.' Later he declared: 'Yes, even if I am accused of fanaticism for Raphael and his contemporaries, I can feel humility only before nature and their works.' The drawings by him which are illustrated here are directly linked with these two sources of inspiration. *Venus Wounded by Diomedes* (plate 1) is a variation of the composition on which Ingres was already working in 1802 for a state commission. The style of this precocious work stems from Greek vase painting and displays a static character and severity of line. The drawing, dated 1844, differs from the composition of the painting chiefly in the element of movement which is infused into the group. The drawing of the scene and the dramatic conflict introduced by its sense of movement are the unmistakable marks of mature artistic development. Furthermore, it was Ingres' usual method to build up the final form of his large compositions over a long period, usually using studies of the individual parts. Later, especially towards the end of his life, he copied them again. He did this with the *Odalisque*, *Stratonice* and in the large mural painting, *The Golden Age*, in the château of Dampierre. Not only the date, therefore, but also the whole conception and way of drawing leads to the conclusion that the Prague version was executed later than the canvas. It shows an intimate knowledge of Greek sculpture which Ingres saw in Italy, and studied chiefly during his stay in Florence from 1820–24. There is a harmonious flow of movement through the central group, billowing through the folds of the drapery, imparting rhythm to the action of limbs and curving bodies picked out by a fine, sinuous line. The light brush of the artist gliding over their contours gives his bodies a fullness and shapeliness. 'The great painters like Raphael and Michelangelo always emphasized the outline. They restated it with a fine brush, thereby reanimating the contour and imprinting their work with verve and vigour.'

If the drawing of *Venus Wounded by Diomedes* (plate 1) recalls by its firm composition and relief the delicate carving of an antique cameo, the second work, *The Infant Jesus and St John the Baptist* (plate 2), reminds us of a statement Ingres made to his pupils: 'Draw with simplicity but with grandeur: these are the qualities of drawing and of art.' This particular drawing, probably done during the course of Ingres' second stay in Italy (1835–41), displays his understanding of the masters of the Italian Renaissance, his profound admiration for Raphael and for the grand style, with much more directness than his complicated pictorial compositions. Grandeur of conception is combined with purity of visual expression. The simple gradation of his lines, ranging from a hair's breadth to an accentuated contour, the marked contrast between empty spaces and areas cross-hatched, lends the drawing a purposeful and great graphic purity.

'I am a preserver of good doctrines and not an innovator,' wrote Ingres in a letter to his friend, Gilibert. But the 'grand style' of Ingres does not depend solely on his admiration for Raphel and antiquity: his admiration for tradition is counterbalanced by his interest in nature, his emotions, sensuality and innate curiosity. This is why the differences between Ingres and the artistic innovator, Delacroix, are not irreconcilable. Their characters, seen in the round, are also made up of opposite and contradictory elements. If Ingres, combining the discipline and purity of classical expression with romantic sensibility has justly been called by Focillon 'the Romantic of Classicism', Delacroix, on the other hand, aims at classical discipline wherever his violent temperament needs to be moderated by the necessity for a monumental of decorative scene in his mural frescoes.

In one of the numerous studies for the cycle of murals for the Palais Bourbon, *Cicero Accusing Verres* (plate 3), one can observe how Delacroix subjected his natural artistic fervour to the classical theme and the needs of mural decoration. He did not represent this dramatic scene of conflict with baroque, agitated strokes, as in his studies for the decoration of the Chambre de Députés, which are characteristic of his romantic drawings. In a calmer way, *Cicero Accusing Verres* impresses one with its representation of space which emerges and makes the principal figure stand out against the static background. He also expresses this contrast by modelling the central figure with short vigorous hatching and suggesting the rest of the auditorium of the Roman Senate by light strokes. Measured against the personality and exclusiveness of Delacroix's drawing, this restrained study is a more interesting milestone in the artist's development than a picture showing him as one of the chief leaders of the romantic movement.

Among his contemporaries, it was Géricault (plates 4, 5) whom young Delacroix most respected and admired. Géricault brought together with an extraordinary sureness the penetrating vision of realism and the rebellious doctrine of romanticism. Like his paintings, his first graphic works echo the glorious past of the French people. They are concerned with the heroism and suffering of the French soldier, and are more human than the heroic canvases of Gros, or the battle scenes by Raffet and Bellangé. Already during this period (1818–19), one can observe in Delacroix's choice of subject the democratic attitude of Géricault. For the first time unknown people became heroes of important dramatic events. *The Return from Russia*, *The Ammunitions Carriage* and *The Artillery Changing Position* rank among the major works of contemporary lithography. Their visual impact lies not only in the forcefulness of the expression but also in the imposing reality of the monumental drawing. The dramatic character of the battle scene is expressed by a sustained stroke with a soft pencil, which changes in intensity under the guiding hand of the draughtsman. The realistic figure of the grenadier (plate 5), bears witness to the sculptural sense of the artist.

While Géricault concerned himself with the destiny of an individual warrior, Auguste Raffet (plate 6) depicted the army of Napoleon as a sea of people without names, hurled *en masse* onto the implacable roundabout of war. In this collective struggle the individual could not prevail, the ordinary soldier was not distinguished from his commander. In this sketch the anonymity of war-time heroism is underlined by the romantic nature of the drawing. This would be unthinkable without the example of stimulating vitality in Gros'drawings.

## CAMILLE COROT

The beginning of modern landscape painting in the nineteenth century coincided with the emergence of Camille Corot, who had assimilated not only the advances made by the romantics in the use of paint and colour, but also the classical tradition of seventeenth-century landscape painters. Those drawings which can be dated to the period of his first stay in Italy present a certain analogy with each other by their firm, fine line, their precise contour and form. They can be traced back to his drawings of Italian architecture and to his grandiose studies of the countryside near Cività Castellana, dating from 1826. It is as if Corot had wanted to confirm the thesis propounded by Ingres that 'drawing represents the honesty in art'. The examples shown here (plates 8–12) reveal the way in which the painter used drawing to penetrate the character of the landscape, first sketching the whole panorama in pencil, then emphasizing in ink its structure or some interesting natural feature with clear and precise strokes. 'I know by experience,' wrote Corot in his Italian notebook in 1825, 'that it is a good idea to begin a picture with the utmost possible precision by drawing on the white canvas after having previously sketched out the general impression on grey or white paper.' The purity of form and the clear atmosphere of the early Italian pictures, *Castel Sant' Angelo*, *The Bridge at Narni* (Louvre, Paris), *Roman Landscape with Aqueduct*, *Fountains at the Pincio*, are the result of this great creative discipline to which the artist subjected himself. Like so many of his predecessors and contemporaries, Corot confirms once more how the French mind in an Italian environment is always directed towards producing work of classical guise. The style of Ingres, drawn from the very source of antiquity and from 'renascent' Italy, is echoed in the linear purity of Corot's studies of Cività Castellana (plate 8). In *Landscape near Naples* (plate 9) one can follow traces of this tradition right up to the baroque classicism of the drawings of Claude Lorraine. The dynamic flow of his pen, its swirling circles, hooked lines and biting strokes conjured up the image on the paper. The drawing was no longer simply a landscape study but a means of imprinting the expression and impression on the memory of the artist before he translated it into a picture. In the 1850s Corot made a few more of these spontaneous sketches with landscape features such as *Landscape with a Bridge*, 1855. The easy-going simple line is the unique expression of the personality of the artist. Corot's post-Barbizon period with a style stemming from romanticism is characterized by the free and poetic representation of nature in drawings impregnated with a strange atmosphere of their own. He expressed his aims thus: 'I am seeking to portray the pulsation of nature.' In his early drawings the smooth surface of the paper acts in conjunction with the soft pencil line and sharp line of the pen as the sole source of light; later, however, Corot preferred the possibilities offered by charcoal or red chalk to render light by the interplay of both tone and intensity of colour. Only rarely did he show the contour of form by a tone outline. More often, he models form by gradations of the same colour. Thus in *Town on a River* (plate 10) he uses charcoal as a colour. This landscape with its small boats, a typical subject, has links with the 1850s when Corot was drawing riverside landscapes at Ville d'Avray and Douai. He expressed the atmosphere of a cloudy day with a rich scale of tonal values ranging from the dark, velvety colour of the black water to the greyish colours of the sky where he intentionally used the charcoal to reveal the texture of the coarse paper. In *Landscape* (plate 11) he expressed the light and colours by shades of the red chalk. The transitions between the tones conjures up the countryside with the light gliding over it.



In plate 12, *Landscape with Tall Trees*, his latest work in the Czechoslovak collection, the Arcadian countryside with the misty tops of tall trees, introduces us to his late period of the 1860s and 1870s and exhibits points in common with his engravings. In this drawing with brush and charcoal, Corot treated the landscape in the manner of a painter. His etchings and lithographs are the equivalents of his late classically lyrical pictures. At the height of his creativity, he elevated drawing to the autonomous area of dreams, memories and nostalgia which equals poetry and music in its emotive power. No one, no successor, has been able to produce from tones of white, grey, and black a melody of such sweetness and penetrating conviction.

## THE BARBIZON SCHOOL

Compared with Corot's large-scale drawings, the pencil sketches of his Barbizon companion, Théodore Rousseau, are little landscape studies, tinged with romanticism, drawn from a rough sketchbook. The main purpose of Rousseau's lines is not constructive but emotional, they interpret the atmosphere of the countryside and convey his wish to reveal through the countryside a complete picture of life and nature. The subject of the solitary tree in a landscape (plate 13) is not only a frequently depicted and characteristic feature of nature, but can also act as a symbol of nature itself. 'I listened to the voice of the trees: their sudden movements, the variety of their shapes and their peculiar attraction for light revealed to me all at once the language of forests... Though they were dumb, I guessed their signs and could discover their passions. In watching with all the religion in one's heart, one experiences and enters into a real world where all happenings surround one.' In the same way, a person alone in a landscape is not seen as an isolated figure, but as an expression of the inextricable human participation in nature.

## HONORE DAUMIER

Unfortunately, Honoré Daumier, the greatest draughtsman of the middle of the century, is represented in the National Gallery, Prague, by only one drawing. The gallery has a more adequate selection of other aspects of his work: his famous painting, *Barricade*, and a version of *The Washerwoman*, a work of sculpture and numerous lithographs.[1] The drawing in plate 16 is closely linked with the picture of the same subject in Prague. Nevertheless, it is only a rapidly sketched composition establishing nothing more than the fundamental relationship between the figure and space. It is scarcely possible to make out the qualities of Daumier, the draughtsman, but one can recognize traces of his sensitive style. Through distant associations, this work recalls drawings by Daumier in which his expression is less restricted and more personal. With these drawings one could, for instance, link those in the Claude Roger-Marx collection in which, out of the fine fabric of strokes moving swiftly and animatedly over the page, suddenly emerge form, image and expression, movement stirs and light streams forth. Where 'there is one line, there is an infinity of lines', is how Baudelaire described Daumier's work.

## CONSTANTIN GUYS

Daumier's gifts and his way of drawing from memory is shared among his contemporaries only by Constantin Guys. This impassioned observer of life walked tirelessly for days on end in the streets of Paris and sat down at his table in the evening to capture, in thousands of drawings, the life of the Parisians, the rich and the poor, in all their poses and guises. At first artist-reporter while a soldier in the Crimea, he developed in the course of his war-time experience his capacity for observation, his memory and speed in drawing. After settling in Paris in about 1860, he was irresistibly attracted by the brilliance of Second Empire high society, giddily encircling the enticing light of wealth and power. Painter of the dandy, he followed with equal enthusiasm the morning rides of men and women in elegant carriages in the Bois de Boulogne (plates 15, 17, 19), and the dancing and festivities of the ordinary districts of Paris. Everywhere he discovered women, from the elegant women of high society reigning in their salons to those of the streets of Paris. There is contrast both in Guys' method of drawing, described exactly by Baudelaire, and in the innumerable variations on his subjects. His method combines the graphic effect of line with the luminous qualities of wash-drawing. Drawings, in which the swift, light, precise strokes faithfully render the outline while the brush follows the form, alternate with expressive engraved works where the form is created out of the scratched surfaces or else with broadly conceived watercolours. The rapid technique of the watercolour drawing fully satisfied the facility of Guys for catching the moment, seizing a quick gesture, a characteristic movement, a silhouette. In this way, Guys uncovered the true character of this society, summing up the people and the style of the age. Just as his horsemen resound with the rhythmic hammering of their horses' hooves, the body of his works pulsates with the life of the time. In this respect they are modern.

## GUSTAVE DORE

Among the mid-century painters of Parisian society, the fantastic world of Gustave Doré, the famous illustrator, makes itself felt as an antithesis to the monumental epics of Daumier or the witty reporting of Constantin Guys. His work, too, bears traces of the ever-widening gulf which was opening between the inner feelings of people and their behaviour. Whereas Daumier transposed political and social dramas on to the general plane of moral conflicts, and whereas Guys follows contemporary society as an outside participator and impassioned spectator, though with some reserve and a shade of irony, Doré evades its various aspects and turns towards the past, to a world of dreams, games and fantastic illusions. The illustrations by this late romantic encompass a wide variety of subjects, beginning with the romantic tale of the Chevalier Jaufré and the realism of Jerrold's London, passing through the genial interpretation of Cervantes' *Don Quixote* (plate 20) and Coleridge's *Ancient Mariner*. Though he constantly changed his style, it is his drawings which best exemplify his extraordinary capacity for invention and the witty content of his artistic approach.

## IMPRESSIONISM

A single drawing in coloured chalks by Sisley (plate 22) is the sole representative of the Impressionists in the Prague National Gallery. It can be dated to about 1873 when Sisley was painting on the banks of the Seine on the outskirts of Paris at Argenteuil, Bougival and Port-Marly. The pictures from this happy and productive period during which Sisley first exhibited with the Impressionists, in 1874, already bear all the creative qualities of an artist at his peak: a lyrical atmosphere, an aerial transparency of sun-lit space and luminous shadows, as well as a range of clear soft colours. His brush strokes portray the vibration in the air, the ripples on the water and the movement of the waves, he noted the play of light and the reflection of the sky on the calm surface of the river, but beyond the objective observation of Impressionism, he found poetry. It is his capacity for feeling for the countryside which links him to the tradition of the Barbizon school, particularly with Corot's riverside scenes of Ville d'Avray, Douai, Gouvieux and Mantes. 'In each picture there is a corner which we love particularly. It is this which creates the particular charm of Corot and also of Jongkind', said Sisley in a letter to Tavernier. In the Prague drawing (plate 22), where Sisley replaces monochrome drawing by coloured pastels, one feels his kinship with Corot. On the surface of the paper his pure and fresh colours create a space of extraordinary depth and impact. The bank of the river disappearing towards the horizon emerges from the blended strokes of his pastels, while the foreground is sketched by short coloured lines, independent of each other, only uniting in their final impression in the eye of the spectator.



## AUGUSTE RENOIR

In about 1880, the classical tradition which based its visual expression on the eloquence of pure and precise line, originating from the work of Ingres, was still alive. It was diametrically opposed to the driving forces of Impressionism. The studies of young girls by Renoir dating from his classical period bear its stamp most distinctly. The drawing in plate 23 forms part of the series of studies for the canvas *Young Girls Playing at Battledore and Shuttlecock* (Institute of Arts, Minneapolis), painted by Renoir in 1887. A drawing from the Majovszky Collection, now the property of the Museum of Fine Art, Budapest, also belongs to this series and probably the pencil study of young girls in the Albertina, Vienna, which is similar both in subject-matter and style to the work illustrated here. Renoir, who even during his Impressionist period did not lose sight of the tradition of his predecessors, and admired Rubens, the Venetian painters and the emotional colouring of Delacroix, after 1880 broke with Impressionism in an awareness of the onesidedness of any principle founded exclusively on optical empiricism. He sought afresh lasting values, a logical order and the solid form of objects. He found them during his journey in Italy as much in the work of Raphael whom he admired as in the frescoes of Pompeii. His great compositions, painted towards the end of the Impressionist period, already show a glimpse of the direction in which the artist's interest was to turn. The effect of such pictures as *Luncheon of the Boating Party* (Phillips Memorial Gallery, Washington), *Dance at Bougival*, *The Umbrellas* (National Gallery, London, or Municipal Gallery of Modern Art, Dublin), and *Lunch in the Garden* comes not only from the pictorial arrangement of the figures, but also because of their relationship in space within the precise confines of contour and volume.

As part of his reaction against Impressionism, Renoir drew with energy; his pictorial compositions were based on classical drawing. If, during this period when he painted his great picture *The Bathers* (Museum of

Art, Philadelphia), he was led by a severe discipline of composition and form to a certain dryness which did not correspond with his nature (see the canvas *Young Girls Playing at Battledore and Shuttlecock*), the drawings of these years nevertheless retain a special simplicity and purity. It is possible to find the originals of these young girls and nudes among the many women painted by Ingres, but the delicate tenderness and the particular charm of youthful vitality are incontrovertible qualities of Renoir's personal art. Where Ingres uses simple lines, Renoir builds up his contours with fine parallel strokes. These merge in the eye of the spectator into a soft and continuous contour, giving his works a sensuous charm (known as *nacré*—mother-of-pearl), which was developed to the full in his drawings the following period, and in his pastels.



## PUVIS DE CHAVANNES

Puvis de Chavannes also derived his inspiration from the tradition of Ingres. In his calm studies for his late mural compositions at Paris and Rouen (plates 24 and 25) he stated a wish for order and harmony. Puvis found his inspiration not only in Ingres but also in Chassériau whose masters were the Umbrian primitives. Puvis regarded drawing as an important rational element of a work. Comparing a completed fresco with an opera, he underlined the compositional function of drawing: 'The preparatory drawing is the libretto, the colour is the music itself.' The symbolism and modelled linear style of Puvis de Chavannes was much admired by the post-Impressionists.

## GEORGES SEURAT

The pictures of Georges Seurat also go beyond Impressionism. They represent a triumph over the subjective visual impression and a return to the objective understanding of reality, expressed in pictures where form and space are subjected to the control and logic of order. What Seurat brought to his art was a capacity for expressing his own individual impressions and feelings within a harmonious composition of coloured surfaces in which forms were strictly defined from a linear point of view. The communicative and expressive nature of Seurat's pictures brings them much nearer to a visual manifestation of Symbolism than to the direct optical recording of the Impressionists. Paul Signac, friend of Seurat, co-inventor and theorist of Neo-Impressionism, remained nearer to the Impressionist school.

## PAUL SIGNAC

The striking watercolours of French and Mediterranean ports, done during the first twenty years of the present century, shows Signac's loyalty to his principles till the end of his life. The open-air watercolour landscape has, since Boudin and Jongkind, been associated with a direct description of the atmosphere of the sea coast. Signac's drawings, fairylands of light and colour, express the ephemeral quality of the atmosphere and the collusion of all the changing natural elements: light, air, wind and water. These spontaneous records were the basis for his pictorial compositions of which the principal subjects, forever presented in different combinations and with modifications, were the sea, ships in harbour at anchor and the architecture of ports. Signac always used watercolour on a ground first drawn in with pencil or charcoal, bringing out the interplay of dark lines with the pure tones of the watercolour as the element of construction, since this palette completely avoided any shades of black. He worked with the brush, first over whole areas, later in patches and with light touches of pure transparent colour. He never watered the colour down and did not use it for modelling but let the contrasting and complementary colours act in juxtaposition with the whiteness of the paper to achieve great brightness. Later his irridescent tones were replaced by more constant shades which lost their transparency and took effect through contrasts of sharp bright colour. This is apparent in plates 29 and 30. The coloured Divisionism of Signac's paintings and watercolours led to the objective recording of an impression of light and colour, rather than to an inner and emotive expression of a reappraisal of nature.

## THE PAINTERS OF EVERYDAY LIFE

The work of the late nineteenth century is represented in the Czech collection by the drawings of the last great masters of the century: Félicien Rops, Jean-Louis Forain, Théophile-Alexandre Steinlen and Henri de Toulouse-Lautrec. Their common denominator is the interest they took in social problems. The art of Rops, Forain and Steinlen was born in the social environment of the Third Republic, in a conscious reaction against its restrictions, but it crystallized into emphatically individual works, each different from the other. In the symbolic work of Rops, he dramatically expressed the scepticism of the end of the century; the social satire of Forain lashes out primarily against the financial oligarchy of Paris, the corruption of its public institutions as well as of the private lives of the rich. The militant humanism of Steinlen has its roots in the conviction of his social ethics, and is closely linked with the struggles of the proletariat.

## FELICIEN ROPS

The subjects of Rops, gleaned from the cafés of Paris (plates 34 and 35), reveal in the way they are done the engraver's experience of dry-point. This Belgian, settled in Paris after 1876, confessed, in a letter of 1879, to the enchantment of city life to which he had succumbed: 'I am caught up by modern life and I believe that anyone who wishes to paint it must seek it out in London or Paris where it manifests itself with the greatest intensity, and in order to understand London, they must move in the tide of English life.'

## JEAN-LOUIS FORAIN

Forain's studies of the streets and cafés of Paris, contemporary with the sketches of Rops, show how much this shrewd observer was indebted to the discoveries of Manet and Degas, and the influence on him of the Impressionists, with whom he later exhibited. His rapid drawings summon up in a few strokes the physiognomy and characteristics of the subject. In watercolour, he relies intentionally on the eloquence of the white paper. A lightness and sureness of touch accompanies his biting wit. In a form simplified in the extreme, he expresses all the complexities of the environment and psychological situations in which modern man is placed. *The Orator* (plate 33) recalls Daumier and classical Japanese woodcut-engraving.

## THEOPHILE-ALEXANDRE STEINLEN

In the field of political and satirical drawing, Forain's irony is surpassed by the true heir of Daumier, Steinlen, whose fierce attacks knew no compromise. His penetrating analysis unmasks the inhumanity of society; his sense of reality can be felt even in drawings of nudes in which, through the expressive emphasis of their features, the social background of the subject is apparent.

## HENRI DE TOULOUSE-LAUTREC

From the social environment of a modern metropolis also emerges the art of the greatest draughtsman of the end of the century, Henri de Toulouse-Lautrec. His work does not have the character of conscious protest, but of a profound knowledge of life. His *Sketch of a Rearing Horse* (plate 37) is one of his earliest works. It does not yet have the inimitable and disturbing rhythm of his later drawings which evoke the feeling of the Parisian *demi-monde* in such a fascinating way. This drawing dates from the period of about 1860 when the adolescent Lautrec was passionately drawing caricatures and sketches of the people around him and making studies of the movement of animals. His early sketchbooks have been assembled at Albi by his cousin, Mme. Tapié de Céleyran. The drawing illustrated here has the same dynamic tension of line; it displays Lautrec's uncommon capacity for capturing a fleeting movement with complete visual summary as well as in all its character. His talent, till then without anchor, only found fulfilment in the atmosphere of Montmartre, guided by his own perspicacious intelligence and the sophisticated drawing of Degas.

## AUGUSTE RODIN

The discovery of the drawings of Auguste Rodin had the same significance for Czech artists as the revelation of his sculptures. First exhibited at Prague in 1902, they caused a wide stir by their revolutionary conception of statuary drawing, their pictorial expression of sculptural values by means of paint and light, their absolute freedom of line and spontaneous expression of movement. The three drawings illustrated (plates 38–40) come from the same series of works as those which amazed the cultivated Czech public at the end of the century. As in sculpture, Rodin created his own representational methods in drawing. He made hundreds, perhaps thousands of sketches of moving models. These researches ceased in Rodin's maturity, becoming a mere shorthand. First he swiftly established the outline of the body with an extraordinarily expressive and alive line. His strokes, often brutal in their disfiguring abbreviation, follow the tension, relaxation and movement of the body, and register the innumerable variations in their expression. Absorbed by observation, he did not correct the flow of line, nor use his brush for modelling but for catching, on surfaces and patches of pure colour, the reflections of light and depths of shadow by alternating bare places with rich areas of colour. Rodin expressed the psychic content with concrete visual symbols, giving sculptural movement a new function. A secret life emanates from his works, moving from within towards the surface and extending itself through movement into space. The drawings showing movement are precisely those which are the evidence of the inner study which Rodin achieved with the expressive potentials of the human body. He aimed at reality and its expression, not ideal beauty.

## PAUL CEZANNE

The influence of Paul Cézanne was not felt in the development of French art until a few years after his death, in 1908–10. Only then did the principles characterizing his work become fully appreciated. In his classically pure landscapes of Mont-Ste-Victoire he arrived at the fundamental and invariable features of the subject so as to portray its artistic equivalent with moving humility, expressing with planes of colour all the relationships of space and volume. He derived from all forms in nature single geometric solid shapes, as he wrote to the painter Bernard on April 15th, 1904: 'Consider nature as a cylinder, a sphere and a cone, and put everything in the right perspective so that each facet of a solid shape or of a surface is directed towards the centre. The parallel lines at the horizon determine the cross-section of nature, or, if you prefer, the scene which the Pater omnipotens aeterne (sic) Deus brings before our eyes. The lines perpendicular to this horizon give the depth. Nature is now for us, human beings, more deep than a horizontal surface whereby arises the necessity for mixing into our vibrant and luminous interplay of tones of reds and yellows sufficient blue to arrive at an impression of the atmosphere.'

The will for clarity and purity won over his temperament. A long journey, however, was needed for this, bringing him from pictures such as *Washing of Christ*, *Portrait of the Painter Achille Empéraire* or *Zola and Alexis* (all between 1886 and 1870) to *Bathers* (Museum of Art, Philadelphia), *Views of l'Estaque*, *Montagne Ste-Victoire* (Museum of Art, Philadelphia), *Black Castle*, painted towards the end of his life. The three pictures purchased in 1923 for the Modern Art Gallery at Prague belong to this last period. Although Cézanne concentrated on problems of colour, he nevertheless affirmed that 'for the painter, however, drawing is colour. If colour reaches its maximum intensity, form is excluded. For the painter there are no curves. For him there are only the contrasts of colours. These contrasts do not exist only for black and white, but are all-important in appreciating colours. The modelling develops our true relationships between the tones.' Cézanne did not, however, disregard drawing, but considered it a continuant part of the work of the painter. 'Drawing and colour are never really separated. As far as one is involved in painting, one is also drawing. The more harmonious the colour, the more precise the drawing. When colour is supremely rich, form attains its supreme perfection. Between the contrasts and harmony of tones lies the secret of drawing and modelling.' The drawings at Prague illustrate this statement. Unlike the pictures and watercolours which are, in fact, very close to these drawings (such as *Landscape near l'Estaque*, a watercolour painted in 1882–5, now in the Kunsthaus, Zürich), the contrasts of tones are here restricted to black, white and a few shades of grey. On occasion the problems of the construction of forms and space are excitingly expressed by allusion alone, this is particularly the case in *Landscape* (plate 43). The drawings and pictures of the National Gallery of Prague anticipate further development by their way of conceiving space and volume and convincingly explain why the Cubists turned to Cézanne. From these works leads a direct path to the landscapes and watercolours of Derain, painted at Cagnes in about 1910 (plates 44, 46).



## ANDRE DERAIN

For Derain, originally linked with Fauvism, a leaning towards Cézanne signifies his nearness to Cubism. His sketch for *Still-life with a Green Jug* of 1910 (plate 45) shows this conclusively.

## PICASSO

Picasso's work is the focal point of the group of modern French drawings in Czechoslovakia. The collection of Picasso's drawings begins with a study for his portraits in coloured chalks (plate 48) which is reminiscent of the work of Toulouse-Lautrec, not only on account of its atmosphere and theme, but also because of its method. It is as if the drawing was a diagram of the form's dynamic lines, the line assuming immense importance as a means of expression. Line plays a similar part in a drawing of a rearing horse by Lautrec in the Karásek Collection. In these two drawings it is the line which introduces dramatic tension: here a pressure of the hand gives it density, there a light almost imperceptible touch barely hints at form. During this period, Picasso was living at Barcelona and drew a great deal; his sketch-books are full of sketches describing with a melancholy poetry the life of the poor. When in October, 1900, a few days before his nineteenth birthday, he left for Paris, he was ready to meet the circle of men, Cézanne, Renoir, Pissarro and Toulouse-Lautrec, who were to be the dominant influence on his future. According to A. H. Barr, it was Picasso's fellow countryman and senior, the painter Ramon Casas, who had introduced him to Steinlen and Toulouse-Lautrec long before Picasso saw their works in Paris. In the review *Arte Joven*, founded at Madrid, with Picasso as the artistic head, a number of his drawings appeared, which seem to be influenced by Toulouse-Lautrec. In Paris, Picasso discovered the art of Degas, Van Gogh, Gauguin and Toulouse-Lautrec. Under the patronage of the latter he painted, between October and December 1900, *The Can-can* and *Moulin de la Galette*. Gertrude Stein, in her book on Picasso, also underlines the importance of Toulouse-Lautrec on his work at that time. His influence is recognizable by the subjects chosen: some of them, horse-racing, for example, were borrowed from Degas; a picture of an interior betrays the influence of Vuillard; scenes of Parisian society are reminiscent of Lautrec, as the drawing in plate 48, a sketch for portraits of a man and a woman wearing a hat in the fashion of 1900. But although it recalls Lautrec the drawing already bears Picasso's own stamp, a particular spontaneity of expression coupled with a sense of order and discipline.

Only a few years separate this drawing and the next one published in this book (plate 49). In the meantime Picasso had gone through his important blue phase. In the following period, not only did pink replace blue, but sustained expression ceded to a contemplative calm and to poetry sometimes fringed with mystery. The subjects are generally derived from circus life. A picture which displays all the characteristics of this period is *The Family of the Saltimbanque*, dating from 1905. Its tender poetry served as a source of inspiration for Rainer Maria Rilke, native of Prague, who had seen the picture during his stay in Munich in 1915. On this occasion he noted:

'While I live with this entrancing Picasso, who has so much of Paris in him, I forget for a moment...' Inspired by the picture, he wrote in the fifth of his *Duineser Elegier:*

> 'But who are they, tell me, these wanderers, these men fleeing somewhat more even than we ourselves, hard-pressed, tormented–for whom, for love of whom? –by a forever unsatisfied desire? It twists them into a tight coil, bends them in two, binds them up, hoists them, tosses them away, takes them up again but like oily air, smoother still, they slip back down on to the worn carpet, threadbare with their eternal striving, the lost carpet of the universe.'

The gallery at Prague also contains a Picasso nude of a young girl reclining, which is connected with this period when the painter was striving to attain a transparent purity of form. He drew these works with the clean unshaded line which he used for the classical portraits of between 1910 and 1920. The example illustrated is a nude, standing side-view, dating from 1905–6 (plate 49). A pure line outlines the form of a woman whose beautiful head is of Grecian type with a high forehead and a straight nose. The laurel wreath, which frames the drawing, puts it in striking relief. It contains a clearly stated expression of Picasso's relationship with antiquity, and, for the first time, the influence of the classical, which has subsequently played such an important role in his work, is apparent. The tradition of classicism, so general in France, which can be traced back to the Middle Ages, is one of the supports on which the work of Picasso rests. He met the classical ideal in the work of David and Ingres. What united him with them is not only his concern with form but also his desire to link art with society and its ethical values. During a holiday spent in Spain in 1906, Picasso discovered the ideal of classical beauty still alive in the peasants of Gosol who seemed to be descended directly from the inhabitants of ancient Greece. In a comparatively short time, he painted a great number of pictures of outstanding brightness, done from drawings radiant with sunshine. Besides the painting *Seated Nude*, Prague possesses a beautiful drawing of an Andorran peasant of a type recurring time and time again in the Gosol works.

Back in Paris, in autumn 1905, Picasso completed, or rather repainted, the portrait of Gertrude Stein, at the same time finishing *Self-portrait with a Palette*, an important canvas in his development towards a bolder, more concrete form, which he had already embarked upon in the summer in Spain. This also emerges from the picture *Woman's Head in Red*, painted in the winter 1906–7 in memory of the Spanish peasants. The planes determining the form are more and more strictly contoured, this becoming even more apparent in the *Self-portrait* of 1907, in Prague, in which the planes meet at sharp angles accentuated by broad lines.

The next phase in Picasso's work shows the influence of the expressionism of Negro masks on the forms in his canvases. Balanced proportions and grace disappear. The contours now seem roughly carved as if by a sculptor. In the spring 1907, Picasso expressed these new tendencies in a large, swiftly painted canvas, *Les Demoiselles d'Avignon* (Museum of Modern Art, New York). Picasso encountered complete incomprehension on the part of most of his friends: Matisse was disgusted; the collector Leo Stein did not understand it; Braque rejected it, the collector Shchukin regarded it as a loss for French culture, and even Apollinaire had reservations about it. Only Picasso's German friends, Daniel-Henry Kahnweiler and Wilhelm Uhde, gave the work a favourable reception. Certain figures in this picture recall Catalan folk art or Iberian bronzes.

This brief glimpse of the development of Picasso's art is sufficient to show that it was not Negro art alone which caused Picasso to embark on a new path, but that the direction in which he moved was the logical consequence of his prior development. In Negro art he found only an echo to support his own endeavours.[2] From the same period and mood came *Female Nude* (plate 50), a drawing from the collection of František Čeřovský, done in 1907. The planes meet and intersect in solid pencil lines intensified by watercolour. But the lines, less angular than before, point to Picasso's next phase under the influence of Cézanne. 

Despite his long development since, Cubism may be considered as the most significant of Picasso's creations. With it Picasso led Cézanne's principle of the geometricization of objects to its highest peak; simplified geometric elements of forms are redistributed in the pictorial space which they create themselves by their relationships with each other. The fine drawing, *Still-life with a Bottle* (plate 47), is a product of fully developed Cubism. The classical way of constructing space as a closed logical summary is clearly evident. Cubism destroys this static relationship by representing objects in a series of positions which draw the spectator into the work. The picture brings together different elements, features of the external world, taken at certain points in time and towards the interpretation of which rational experience contributes a part independently of the optical sense. Time becomes involved in the picture as a creative spatial value and finds free analogy in the conception of time as a portion of space. It is interesting to note that what came about in art without conscious intent found similar expression in science and philosophy, in Einstein's theory of relativity which defines time scientifically as an element of space.[3] Cubism, however, although born in an environment of scientific progress, did not constitute a new scientific poetical method. It remained in the widest sense an artistic appraisal of the world which used different aspects of reality with supreme creative freedom, arranging them according to the laws of beauty into a way of thinking where rational objectivity and subjective feeling were amalgamated. Cubism therefore could be said to have been the cradle of new progress in painting and to herald the arrival of Surrealism.

All these problems and attainments are present in the gouache, *The Guitar* (plate 51). The motif of the guitar is typical of French Cubist painting, to Picasso it is a reminder of his native Spain. But more important than this, both Picasso and Braque represented guitars, clarinets, violins and pianos as objects stripped of incidental individuality, things of abstract form, already fashioned by human hand. This conception of still-life painting is very different from the Dutch one which consisted of an harmonious arrangement of fruit, flowers, fish and other objects, taken from nature, accentuating their richness of form and avoiding the ordinary. The lines of the guitar, emphasized by repetion and variation, are the central motif of this work. They provide the melodious element contrasting with the varied rhythms of the planes. The constructions of the drawing is distinctly contrapuntal and this association with time as an element of space brings to mind a striking resemblance with music where time as a rhythmical element is of fundamental importance. Vincenc Kramář, the previous owner of this work, alludes to this phenomenon: 'Picasso's pictures emerge, in fact, as monuments of counterpoint worthy of Bach. Picasso and Braque loved old contrapuntal music and its instrument—the organ—and detested by contrast, modern musical impressionism.' This relationship with music is much wider. Painting and music are brought closer together by the introduction by the Cubists of time into art, through the analysis and successive synthesis of reality by a multiplicity of views.



The most recent work of Picasso to be published in this book is the gouache, *The Sculptor's Studio* (plate 52), dated 18th July, 1933. During the summer of this year, Picasso spent several weeks at Barcelona, returning to France completely saturated with the atmosphere of Spain. One feels in this drawing both the burning rays of the southern sun, and also a classical tranquility and calm, with which he embraces the subject of the artist and his model, to which he so frequently returned. Picasso does not like making statements or supplying verbal explanations about his work, but in his pictures or drawings on this theme he makes a profound attempt to resolve through painting and through symbols the fundamental problems for the artist of the creative process. *The Sculptor's Studio* displays the method of stylized self-representation, often used by Picasso; true self-portraits are rare. One of his biographers, Roland Penrose, thinks that Picasso's habit of indirect self-portrait is probably motivated by his love of fancy-dress and of masks; he has represented himself on different occasions as a harlequin, bull, horse or Minotaur, owl or dove, lover, painter or sculptor, and even, in a mysterious etching of the thirties, as a child holding a candle.

## GEORGES BRAQUE

Whereas Picasso is well represented in Czech collections, the Prague National Gallery possesses only two drawings by his companion, Braque. They are variations on the same subject—a still-life of a glass and apples on a table—one of them also has a knife. The lines are the gentle lines of a painter, with a rich range of expression created by the pressure of the hand, the angle of the pencil, the imprint of his particular style. The two drawings give the impression of crystalline light and clarity. Plate 53 contains a feature of great importance to Cubism and to modern art in general: the table in this still-life is so palpable that one could mistake it for the real thing. It calls to mind the illusionistic *trompe l'œil* techniques used in Baroque painting of the Netherlands, later employed by workmen to imitate on wood marble and other materials. In his youth, to satisfy the wishes of his father, a painter and decorator in Paris, Braque had learnt to do *trompe l'oeil* work, although he soon abandoned this trade, he retained his skill. At the height of analytical Cubism, when Braque and Picasso began to use printed letters in their pictures, Braque started to include a plane of *trompe l'oeil* in his work. No doubt, he was attracted by the tension created by a contrast between a surface which seemed physically palpable and the abstraction of the picture as a whole. From there it was only one step to the actual use of real materials—various sorts of paper, carpet, etc. —to the technique of *collage*. Braque always kept a passion for tactile sensations and a desire for harmony. He persisted in an endeavour to attain a system which would correct feeling.

## PIERRE BONNARD

Other groups of drawings comprising the second stage in the development of French art are equally remarkable. A poetic drawing by Bonnard, *Reclining Nude* of 1909 (plate 55), anticipates the new decorative atmosphere of such works as the pen-drawings of Matisse, who, like Bonnard, created an atmosphere of calm and harmony.

## THE FAUVES

The Fauves are comparatively well represented in the Prague collection. Included here are two of the great series of coloured and gouache drawings by Maurice Vlaminck. Plate 56 is a coloured drawing from his Fauve period of about 1906–7, showing a landscape and a boat. The watercolour *Houses among Trees* (plate 57) bears the clear imprint of the influence of Cézanne, such as the picture in the Prague Gallery of 1914. Another Fauve, Othon Friesz, is represented by the watercolour executed in 1928, *Algerian Landscape* (plate 59). Such subjects, attractive in their picturesque and bizarre oriental character, occur quite often in French art after Delacroix.

## HENRI MATISSE

Strangely enough, Henri Matisse is only represented in Czechoslovakia by a single, although important, drawing (plate 58). In 1939 he wrote: 'I have always considered drawing not an act of extraordinary skill, but above all a means of expressing inner feelings and a description of states of mind, a simplified means of making expression more direct and more spontaneous, which should not weigh on the soul of the observer.' Matisse's drawings are painter's drawings in contrast to the more sculptural drawings of Picasso. But the two artists had in common their desire to attain a purity of means in drawing and to embrace the essentials of their subject. As Matisse said: 'The personality of the drawing is not created by the precise reproduction of the forms of nature or by a patient assembly of sharply observed details, but by the deep feeling with which the artist approaches his chosen subject, to it he gives his whole attention, and into it he enters completely.' The way the drawing illustrated here is composed is agitated, the impetuous strokes of the pen create a dramatic tension characteristic of Matisse's early period. This tension was later replaced by harmony and calm.

## RAOUL DUFY

A similar calm and joy permeate the work of Raoul Dufy. Line retains a prominence even in his paintings which, almost without exception, can be described as a 'draughtsman's pictures'. This particular quality, the lightness of Dufy's characteristic style and his frequent use of gouache makes the boundary between drawing and painting difficult to find. His drawing is mobile, alive and full of melodious charm and wit. His pen drawing *The Bay* (plate 60) has a crystalline purity and possesses the charm of the naive or of the unprejudiced eye of a child. In the gouache *Sea and Boats* (plate 61), Dufy's individual palette with its clear and striking colours is a dominant element. Line also plays a large part in the structure of the colouring; the work acquires vitality from the frequent noncorrespondence of the areas of colour with the drawn contours. Léger developed this idea to its conclusion in completely separating drawing from colour.

## GEORGES ROUAULT

Through drawings done mostly in 1914, Rouault emerges as an Expressionist of a social-religious character. One gouache, *The Inn* (plate 62), represents in a typical way the world of outcasts and the downtrodden, a frequent subject in his work. Rouault depicted them with neither respect nor irony, but with love and compassion. He captured in a masterly way the stifling atmosphere of an inn full of people. Another theme often treated by the artist is exemplified in the gouache, *The Crucifixion* (plate 63). The group of people—Christ crucified, Mary kneeling and John standing near the cross—completely fills the picture. The colour-saturated forms and the accentuated lines of the contours recall medieval stained-glass windows by which Rouault was no doubt influenced.[4] With his *Portrait of Verlaine* (plate 64), Rouault attained the height of artistic and psychological expression. Observation is combined with expressive drawing and rich colours in work of captivating poetry and profound philosophy.

## MAURICE UTRILLO

*The Church of St Peter, Montmartre* (plate 66) by Maurice Utrillo, executed in gouache and dated Christmas, 1930, is from his third period (according to the chronology of Francis Carco, in his book on Maurice Utrillo, Paris, 1921). The work of this period combines a subtle sense of colour with the naïve poetic quality of primitive painters, it also acquires a more graphic character, no doubt from the example of the artist Suzanne Valadon, Utrillo's mother. The delightful corners of Montmartre, which he painted mostly from memory, are crowded with characters. He used a wide range of rich colours, as well as the muted shades and fine tonal values which are possible with gouache. In his pictures Utrillo discovered the poetry of Paris which was later to be expressed in literature and the cinema.



## THE SCHOOL OF PARIS

An interesting aspect of the history of art is the role played by certain great cities as centres of art and international culture, bringing together the *élite* among the most progressive representatives of the artistic world. In the twelfth and thirteenth centuries, the forms and principles of Gothic art spread from France over all Europe; already at this time artistic personalities of every nationality gathered in certain centres. In the fourteenth century, the court of Charles IV, Roman Emperor and King of Bohemia, at Prague was one such cosmopolitan arena. In the second half of the seventeenth and during the eighteenth centuries, Versailles was the centre of European art and culture, it became the model for the kings and princes all over Europe and set the tone of fashion, art and customs. Towards the middle of the nineteenth century, Paris assumed the role of a magnet for artists. The atmosphere of the 'city of light' was extremely favourable for artistic conquests and experiments. The artists, who came from all parts of the world, felt liberated from traditional concepts. Coming from different regions of Europe, Jewish artists formed a special group. They brought with them individual cultural contributions and, never forgetting their native lands, created in the liberal environment of Paris works that were often extremely original.

## MARC CHAGALL

Marc Chagall, who came from the village of Liosno near Vitebsk, arrived in Paris in 1910 after studying at the Academy at St Petersburg and with Léon Bakst. He associated with writers, such as Blaise Cendrars, Max Jacob and Guillaume Apollinaire, as well as with the painters, La Fresnaye, Delaunay and Modigliani. As a young man, Chagall was influenced by the recently developed Cubism, although rationalist tendencies did not really suit him, there are neverheless numerous traces of Cubism in his work. In 1914 Chagall had a large exhibition at Berlin, which was welcomed with great enthusiasm, particularly by the German Expressionists. Back in Russia, which he could not leave because of war, Chagall found again in real life all the subjects which he had painted from imagination and memory in Paris. His models were now sitting opposite him, he walked side by side with them every day in the street. All this was reflected in his style: his work became simpler, more realistic, and the influence of Cubism, although not completely forgotten, was restricted. From this period dates the drawing *The Tailor* (plate 68), one of many portraits of those around him. In an oval frame, on a half-empty page, a bearded man sits wearing a hat, in his left hand he is holding a bowl resting on his knees and in his right hand a spoon. In the background, on the right, a house bears the inscription 'портно(й)' (tailor). Chagall respected the laws of graphic expression and skilfully exploited extremes of black and white. The direct relationship between the artist and his subject emerges distinctly from the drawing.

After the revolution of 1917, Chagall became Commissioner of Fine Arts in the Vitebsk area. He founded an Academy where he took on as professors El Lissitsky, Pougny and Malevich. But differences which he had with the latter led him to leave and go to Moscow in 1919. There he made the acquaintance of Efross and Granovsky; it was due to them that he worked on mural frescoes, scenery and costumes at the State Jewish Theatre. In 1922 Chagall decided to return to France. There he again painted and drew childhood memories. He refined his mode of expression in painting and displayed a sensitive feeling for colour. In 1927, in an anthology on Paris by Raynal, Chagall wrote: 'In short, I am indebted for all the success that I have had at Paris to France; her atmosphere, people and character were for me a real school of art and of life.' From this period dates the gouache *Woman with a Scythe* (plate 69) which bears all the signs of the painter's mature style. It astounds by the power cast over reality and the boldness of his unaccustomed colour harmonies. In a characteristic way, Chagall combined bold strokes with intimate details. This gouache has become painting and has left behind drawing and its problems. A little later originated the delicately coloured gouache *The Window*, in which Chagall returned to the motif of the view of Paris through the window from 1913.

## JULES PASCIN

Jules Pascin, whose real name was Julius Pincas and was a native of Viddin, Bulgaria, held a similar place in the School of Paris as Chagall. He arrived at Paris in 1905, at the age of twenty already a remarkably skilled draughtsman. Although a foreigner, he felt at home in the atmosphere of Paris, and depicted the scenes of its life with light frivolity. He liked to draw and paint the female body and created works which were subtly erotic under the guise of a carefree smile or an ironic grimace. The great melancholy which emanates from all his work may be due, to some extent, to his origin. An inner restlessness prevented him from remaining in one place. He left Montmartre to travel to Algeria, Germany, the United States and Mexico, making many remarkable drawings on the way. It is to the credit of Paris that both the malicious sarcasm, delicate eroticism, and exceptional virtuosity of his output, and also his private sadness, melancholy and bitterness were accepted. So profound were his grief and loneliness that on the opening day of an exhibition of his work in 1930 he committed suicide. The two drawings which are reproduced here are characteristic. The drawing *Englishman in Arab Captivity* (plate 70) is as much full of irony as the drawing *Three Young Girls and a Dog* (plate 71) is overlaid with sadness.

## CHARLES DUFRESNE AND MARCEL GROMAIRE

The works of other French painters are represented in the collection haphazardly by one or two drawings. A gouache by Charles Dufresne (plate 72), probably from the end of the nineteen-twenties, bears traces of Cubism and the Classicism that subsequently influenced him. Of the two drawings by Marcel Gromaire, *Woman in a Fur Coat* (plate 73), reproduced here, shows the ornamental style which is the dominant characteristic of Gromaire's work. He was one of the most eminent revivers of tapestry-making, which enabled him to exploit to the full his gift for grandiose decoration.

## FERNAND LEGER

By Fernand Léger there is a fine drawing of one of the heads from his famous picture, *The Constructors*, of 1950. It is an example of his late style which linked direct representation with abstract concepts. Léger expressed it thus: 'The object replaces the subject, abstract art has arrived as the perfect liberator and it has therefore become possible to regard a human figure not as an emotive element but solely as a compositional element.' In Léger's pictures, there is a complete division of purpose between the black lines of the drawing and the colour: the lines delineate the object, the colours unify and compose the planes. Léger called this phenomenon 'colour outside the object'. The contrast between representational and abstract art in his works gives them a powerful inner tension.

## DRAWINGS OF SCULPTORS

The modern sculptors, Antoine Bourdelle, Charles Despiau and Aristide Maillol, inherited a common legacy from ancient classical sculpture. The two drawings by Bourdelle (plates 75, 76), lightly coloured in watercolour, come from a series of studies of the free-expression dances of Isadora Duncan. They form an important part of four thousand drawings, watercolours, gouaches and pastels by Bourdelle.

The classical heritage is even easier to trace in the drawings and sculpture of Despiau. His drawings are densely packed with firm shapes. His line is neither sharp nor bold, but ambiguous, the same drawing being done many times in order to find the most satisfying form. The Despiau series of drawings were acquired for the National Gallery in 1923 at the same time as the purchase of two bronze statues. The artist is reported to have been astonished when the purchasing committee expressed their intention of buying the drawings as well, and to have said that it was the first time that anyone had been interested in his drawings.

The works of Aristide Maillol are the fulfilment of Hellenic harmony. They were created under the skies of the French Midi, so evocative of sun-lit Greece, where Maillol found calm, equilibrium and purity. He was an excellent draughtsman and during his lifetime made hundreds of drawings which have many of the same qualities as his statues, but his clean lines give his drawings and engravings their pure graphic form. He drew very rapidly, as he said: 'I have drawn hundreds of such sketches, very hurriedly and impulsively; I have seized any kind of paper, even wrapping paper, in order to set down the immediate sensation.' He also said: 'Now I draw. By drawing I can always learn something. Shouldn't a sculptor always draw before anything else? He should have piles of drawings and one fine day, when he has understood one of them, he should make a statue from it.' Elsewhere he wrote: 'I have done nearly all my drawings from memory.' From the rich harvest of drawings by Maillol, a few fine ones are to be found in Czechoslovakia. One of them, *Crouching Woman* (plate 80), recalls his statue, *Night*, of about 1902. The other is a study for the *Judgment of Paris* (plate 79) which bears eloquent testimony to the enchantment which ancient Greece had for the sculptor.

## THE ORIGIN OF THE COLLECTIONS IN CZECHOSLOVAKIA

The collections of French drawings in Czechoslovakia, despite their breadth and homogeneous nature, are far from able to reflect the richness of French drawing in all its diversity and development. These collections, which have been growing for more than sixty years, were assembled thanks to judicious purchases by national institutions and private collectors. This is why drawings of secondary interest hang side by side with remarkable examples, and works by outstanding personalities intermingle with those by minor artists. Although artists like Millet, Manet, Degas, Seurat, Gauguin and Van Gogh are not represented, and idea is nevertheless given of the continuous evolution of drawing during the nineteenth century.

It was in about 1890 that representatives of French and Czech cultural institutions began to establish relations which permitted the creation of this collection. At this time, Czech opinion was becoming aware in a more informed way of the direction in which art was moving in western Europe and Czech artists joined in the great innovating trends.



Many young artists were filled with the fervent desire to free Czech art from the stifling influence of the Austrian academic school and from the stigma of being considered merely a provincial manifestation of Austro-Hungarian culture. They wished to be taken seriously and to rediscover their rightful place in the mainstream of European art. So it was to Paris, city of the avant-garde, the only real alternative to Vienna and Munich, that they turned.

František Kupka, in particular, from the beginning of this century, threw in his lot, human and artistic, with French art. In Parisian reviews, such as *L'Assiette au Beurre*, Kupka published drawings and illustrations of social comment. His explorations in the field of Orphism took him among eminent representatives of abstract art. Other Czechs, Jiří Kars, close friend of Suzanne Valadon and Maurice Utrillo, and Otakar Coubine, who settled in the south of France, were also members of the School of Paris.

It may appear at first sight that this was merely a quarrel between Bohemia and Austria, but a more careful look shows that this was not so. Like Paris, Prague was a city with a long artistic tradition, and one where artists of all nationalities had found a home. In 1907 the Mánes Society of Prague held an exhibition of paintings by a group of its own members. This group, known as The Eight *(Osma)*, included Bohumil Kubišta, Antonín Procházka, Emil Filla and Otakar Coubine. Reaction to the exhibition was immediate. The general public was indignant, but many young artists joined the Society.

These young Czech artists, the generation of The Eight as it came to be called, influenced by the work of Daumier and Van Gogh, had discovered Cézanne and then Picasso and Cubism. Their reaction was immediate, in fact it came hardly a moment behind that of their contemporaries in Paris. Evidence for this can be seen not only in their paintings and sculpture, but also in the pages of current reviews on the arts and in the writings of the artists themselves.

The discovery of Cubism had immediate repercussions on Czech art. From now on it represented the new, modern style. It became a moral and spiritual issue of the greatest importance. Filla saw in Cubism the only real way of objective expression. However, he did not just copy Picasso, but brought to Cubism new, special Czech values. Procházka used Cubism to express his own personal vision,[5] while Otto Guttfreund applied its principles to his sculpture.

In 1911 a radical group within the Mánes Society formed a breakaway movement called The Group *(Skupina)*. In the following years they organized four significant exhibitions showing works by Picasso, Derain, Delaunay, Metzinger, Mondrian, Archipenko, Brancusi and Duchamp-Villon. By 1914 Prague had become one of the leading centres of modern art in Europe.



Parallel with the exceptional interest shown by members of the Czech public in modern French art, there was a growing interest on the part of the collectors. These men, who have now in the main bequeathed their collections to the national museums, have safeguarded their valuable treasures for the nation. The most important collection, apart from the magnificent group acquired by the National Gallery of Prague in 1923, is that of Vincenc Kramář. It is unique of its kind and permits Czechoslovakia to boast one of the most complete collections for retracing the origin and development of Cubism. Picasso's work occupies a dominant position, but the collection also contains works by Braque and Derain. In the field of drawing, Kramář's collection is entirely devoted to the work of Picasso whose artistic metamorphoses during the first twenty years of this century are well represented. Another valuable collection was acquired during the stay in France of Dr Zdeněk Macek. The greater part is made up of drawings by his friend, Jean Cocteau, and of rare editions of his books. Likewise, the collection of Dr František Čeřovský, in which Braque, Chagall, Picasso, Utrillo and Vlaminck are featured, now partly belongs to the National Gallery of Prague. Works collected by Václav Nebeský, art historian and picture dealer, should also be mentioned. All these collections have given a place of importance to French art in Czechoslovakia.

# NOTES

1 *Family on the Barricade* (National Gallery, Prague, inv. no. o 4782); *The Burden* (National Gallery, Prague, inv. no. o 4787); *Portrait of Mr. Viennet* (National Gallery, Prague, inv. no. P 1550)

2 'Picasso went among the Negroes just as one goes to the country: one brings back the regret of not being able to live there forever. He felt that their religious and mystic naivety had preserved a feeling for drawing and proportions; in this is to be found the best evidence that the return to linear discipline emerged from something primarily human.' M. Raynal, *Picasso*, Paris 1922.

3 'In this way one saw gradually entering into art the stimulating principles of science, whereas till then it had been only scientific methods which had been a determining factor in art.' M. Raynal, *Picasso*, op. cit.

4 Rouault said: 'I have heard said many times that my paintings resemble stained-glass windows. This is no doubt a result of my trade. When I left school, my parents placed me as apprentice to a master-glassworker. My task was to look after the mounting of the pieces of glass in lead and especially to sort out the missing pieces from leaded windows brought to us for repair. This is how my passion for old stained-glass windows developed, one which has stayed with me till the present.'

5 'Let us consider Cubism which has had a profound effect on Czechoslovakian art but which, instead of being the spiritual speculation which it is with most of the Parisian artists, particularly those who invented it, becomes an agreeable sort of game for dealers in prints. Popular art proceeds apace with its lively rhythms, crude artifice, puerile and charming inventions.' R. Cogniat, 'Modern Czechoslovak Art', in *Život*, XVI, 1937–8, p. 13.

# BIBLIOGRAPHY


A. H. Barr, *Picasso. Fifty Years of his Art.* New York 1946

Charles Baudelaire, *Curiosités esthétiques (Oeuvres complètes).* Paris, Calman-Lévy 1889

Charles Baudelaire, *Constantin Guys: le peintre de la vie moderne.* Geneva, Editions La Palatine 1943

Anthony Blunt, *Picasso, his life and work.* London 1962

Boyer d'Agen, *Ingres, dessinateur des Antiques.* Paris, Delagrave 1926

Pierre Descargues, *Fernand Léger*, Paris 1955

*Journal de Delacroix.* Paris, Plon 1932

František Dvořák, *Twentieth-century Painters. The Paris School.* Prague, Artia 1959

Frank Elgar and Robert Maillard, *Picasso.* Paris, Hazan 1955

Raymond Escholier, *Daumier.* Paris, Librairie Floury 1930

René Huyghe, *Millet et Rousseau.* Paris, Skira 1946

René Huyghe, *Le dessin français du 19ème siècle.* Lausanne, Editions Mermond 1948

*Ingres raconté par lui-même et ses amis. Pensées et écrits du peintre.* Geneva, Pierre Cailler 1947

Miloš Jiránek, 'Les dessins de A. Rodin' in *Volné směry*, no. 5, Prague 1901

H.K.C. Jaffé, *Pablo Picasso.* London 1964

Jacques Lassaigne, *Lautrec.* Paris, Hypérion 1946

Henri Matisse, *L'art de l'équilibre*

Henri Matisse, *La précision n'est pas la réalité*

Jiří Padrta, *Picasso, le charmeur de formes.* Preface by Jean Cocteau. Prague, Artia 1960

Denes Pataky, *Dessins du Musée de Budapest.* Paris, Editions Cercle d'Art 1960

Roland Penrose, *Picasso, his life and work.* London, Gollancz 1958

Maurice Raynal, *Picasso.* London 1953

Jaime Sabartés, *Picasso. Un éventail 1905–1914* (Preface). Paris, Leda 1962

František Xaver Šalda, 'Luttes pour le lendemain – Méditations et rhapsodies 1898–1904' in *Volné směry*, Prague 1905

František Xaver Šalda, *Le Synthétisme dans l'art moderne.* 1892

Alfred Sisley, 'Lettre à son ami le critique Tavernier' in *l'Art Français.* March 18th, 1893

Gertrude Stein, *Picasso.* Boston 1959

Christian Zervos, *Dessins de Pablo Picasso, 1892–1948.* Paris, Editions Cahiers d'Art 1949

# LIST OF PLATES

AUGUSTE RODIN

38 Study of a Standing Nude
39 Nude Kneeling Woman
40 Study of a Crouching Nude

PAUL CEZANNE

41 Sketch of a Tree
42 Sketch of a Landscape
43 Sketch of a Landscape

ANDRE DERAIN

44 Landscape
45 Still-life with a Green Jug
46 Cagnes Landscape

PABLO PICASSO

47 Still-life with a Bottle
48 Portrait of a Man and a Woman
49 Profile of a Female Nude
50 Female Nude
51 The Guitar
52 The Sculptor's Studio

GEORGES BRAQUE

53 Still-life with Apples and Knife
54 Still-life with Apples

PIERRE BONNARD

55 Reclining Nude

MAURICE VLAMINCK

56 Landscape with a Boat
57 Houses among Trees

HENRI MATISSE

58 Study of a Nude

OTHON FRIESZ

59 Algerian Landscape

RAOUL DUFY

60 The Bay
61 Sea and Boats

GEORGES ROUAULT

62 The Inn
63 Crucifixion
64 Portrait of Verlaine
65 Still-life with a Table-lamp

MAURICE UTRILLO

66 The Church of St Peter, Montmartre

MARC CHAGALL

67 The Window
68 The Tailor
69 Woman with a Scythe

JULES PASCIN

70 Englishman in Arab Captivity
71 Three Young Girls and a Dog

CHARLES DUFRESNE

72 Three Women in a Garden

MARCEL GROMAIRE

73 Woman in a Fur Coat

FERNAND LEGER

74 Head

EMILE-ANTOINE BOURDELLE

75 Plate from the series: The Dances of Isadora Duncan
76 Plate from the series: The Dances of Isadora Duncan

CHARLES DESPIAU

77 Seated Nude
78 Reclining Nude

ARISTIDE MAILLOL

79 Study of *The Judgement of Paris*
80 Crouching Woman

# PLATES

## JEAN-AUGUSTE-DOMINIQUE INGRES

### 1 Venus Wounded by Diomedes

Pencil and wash, partly coloured, $37.4 \times 32$ cm. Marked bottom left: J. Ingres, inv. et fac. 1844. National Gallery, Prague (K 13 941), acquired 1923, formerly Countess Carolyne Sayn-Wittgenstein collection.

The drawing done in 1844 is a later variation of a subject which had pre-occupied Ingres since 1802. The pictorial version of it, known from the sketch belonging to P. Rosenberg, precedes this drawing.

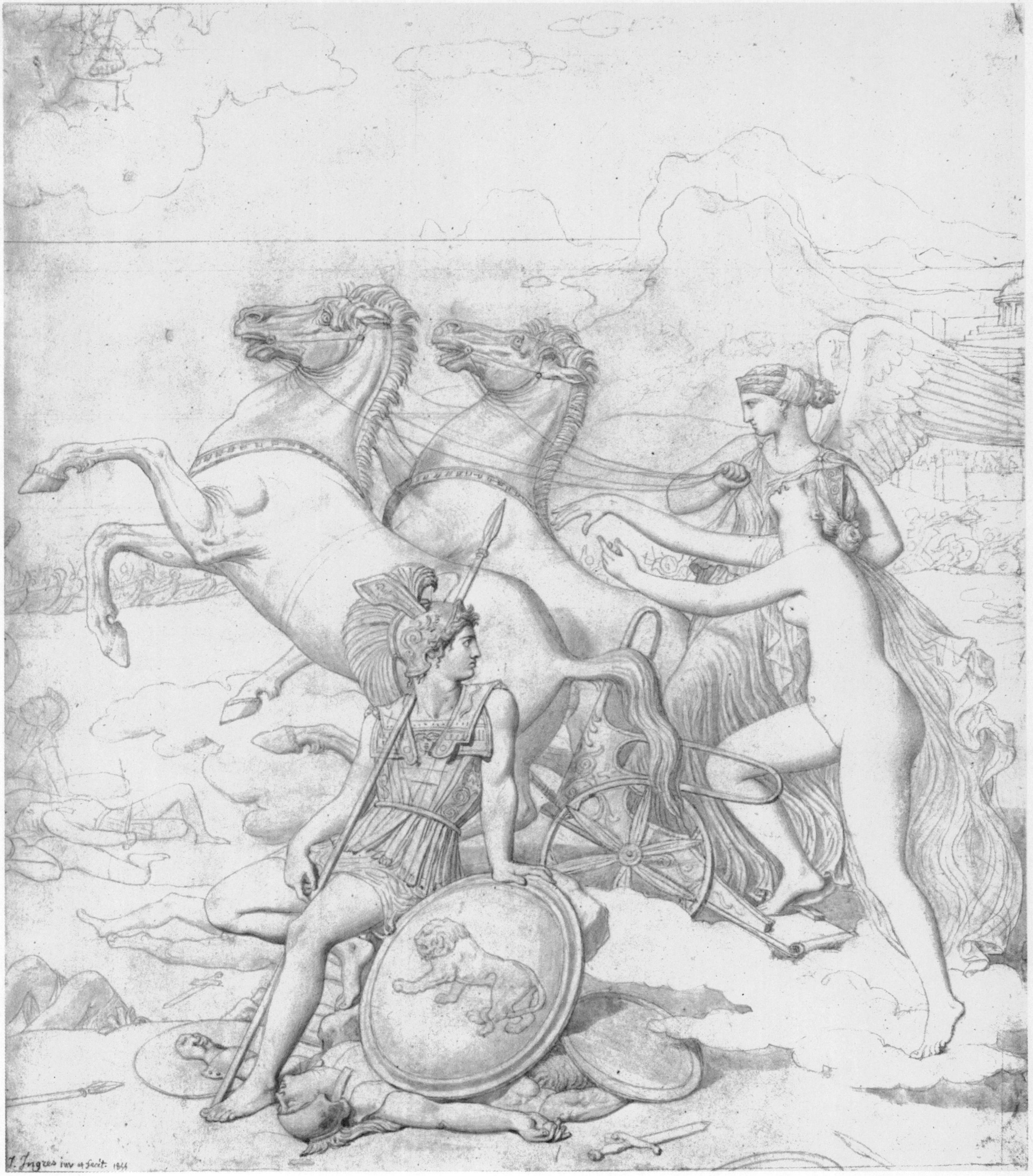
J. Ingres inv et fecit. 1844

## JEAN-AUGUSTE-DOMINIQUE INGRES

2 The Infant Jesus and St John the Baptist

Dark brown ink (bistre) on paper, 23.1 × 33.3 cm. Museum of Czech Literature–Karásek Gallery, Prague, formerly Marquis of Chennevières collection.

The drawing bears indications of the close artistic ties between Ingres and Raphael, not only in the general arrangement of the composition but also by the placing of the scene in an Italian-style landscape. This drawing can be dated to between 1835 and 1841, the period of Ingres' second stay in Italy.

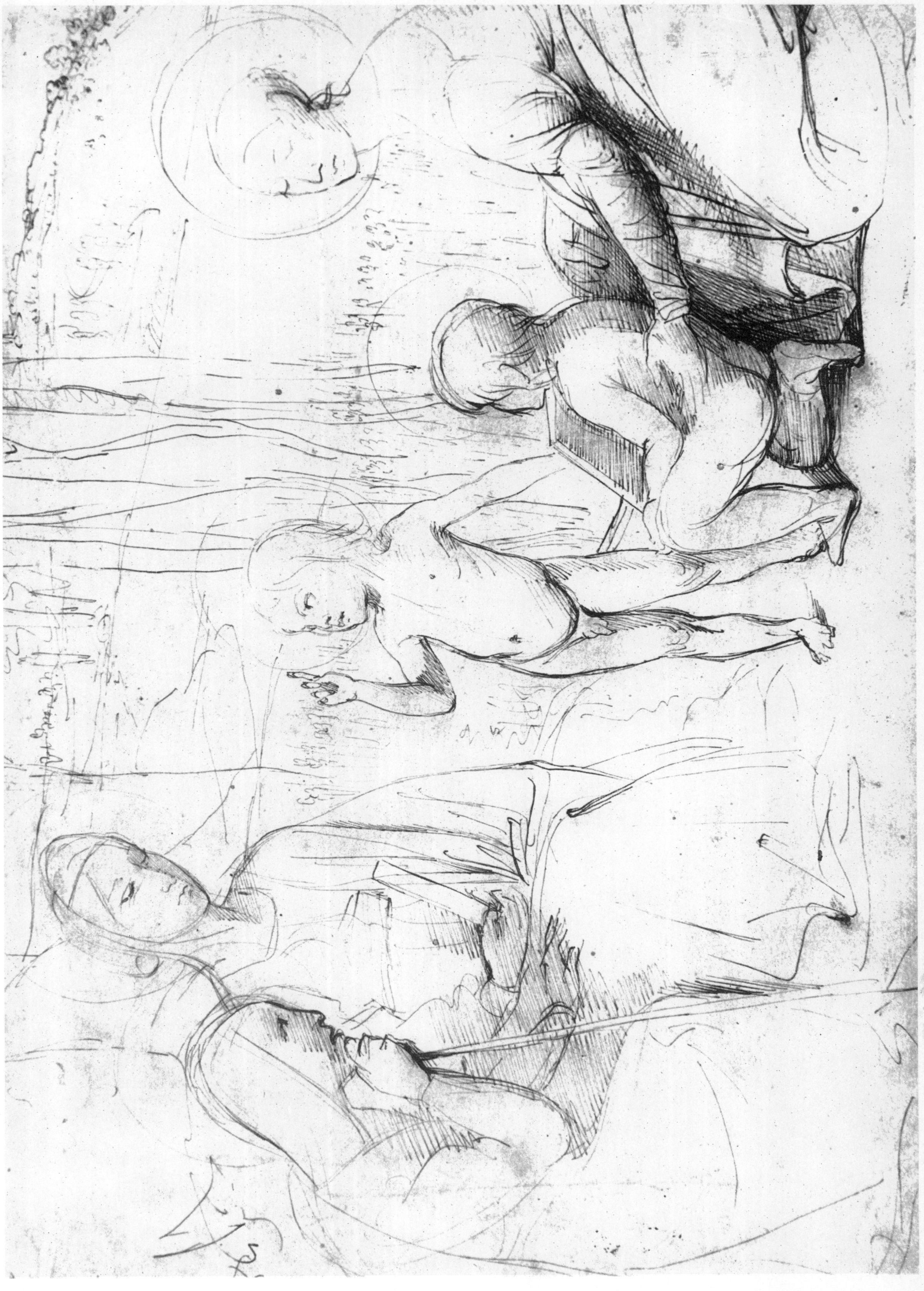

## EUGENE DELACROIX

3 CICERO ACCUSING VERRES

Pencil, 21.6×23.1 cm. (inside the surround). Marked below centre with seal of acquisition: E. D. National Gallery, Prague (K 33 624), acquired 1960, formerly Degas collection, then Georges Viau collection.

This is one of the sketches drawn by Delacroix for the murals of the senate at the Palais Bourbon, between 1838 and 1847. It represents Cicero showing the assembly the art objects stolen by the vice-consul Verres during his governorship over the conquered provinces. Intended for one of the pendentives of the library dome.

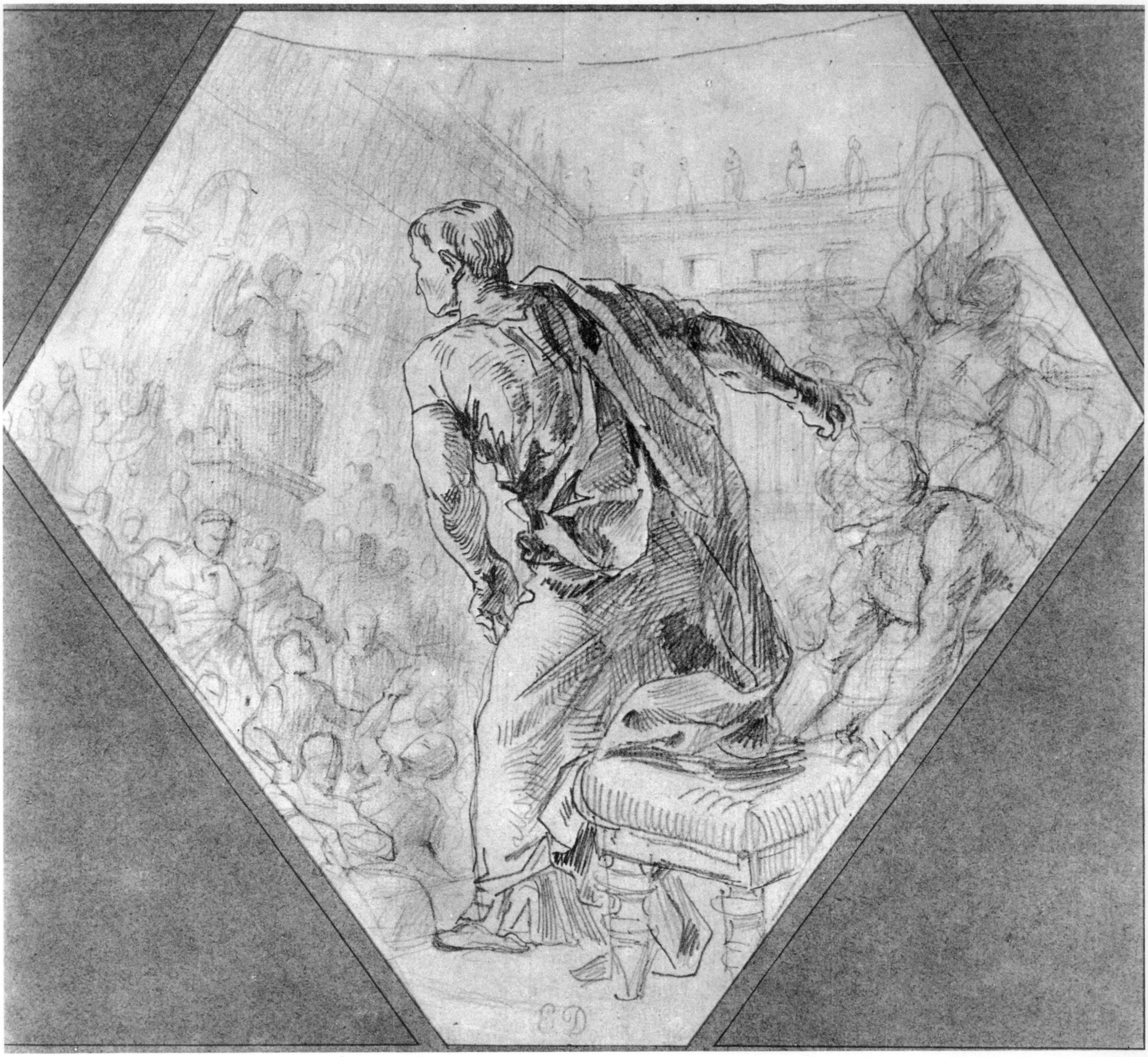
ED

THEODORE GERICAULT

4 The Slain Horse

Pencil on paper, 20×24.7 cm. Museum of Czech Literature–Karásek Gallery, Prague, formerly Galippe collection.

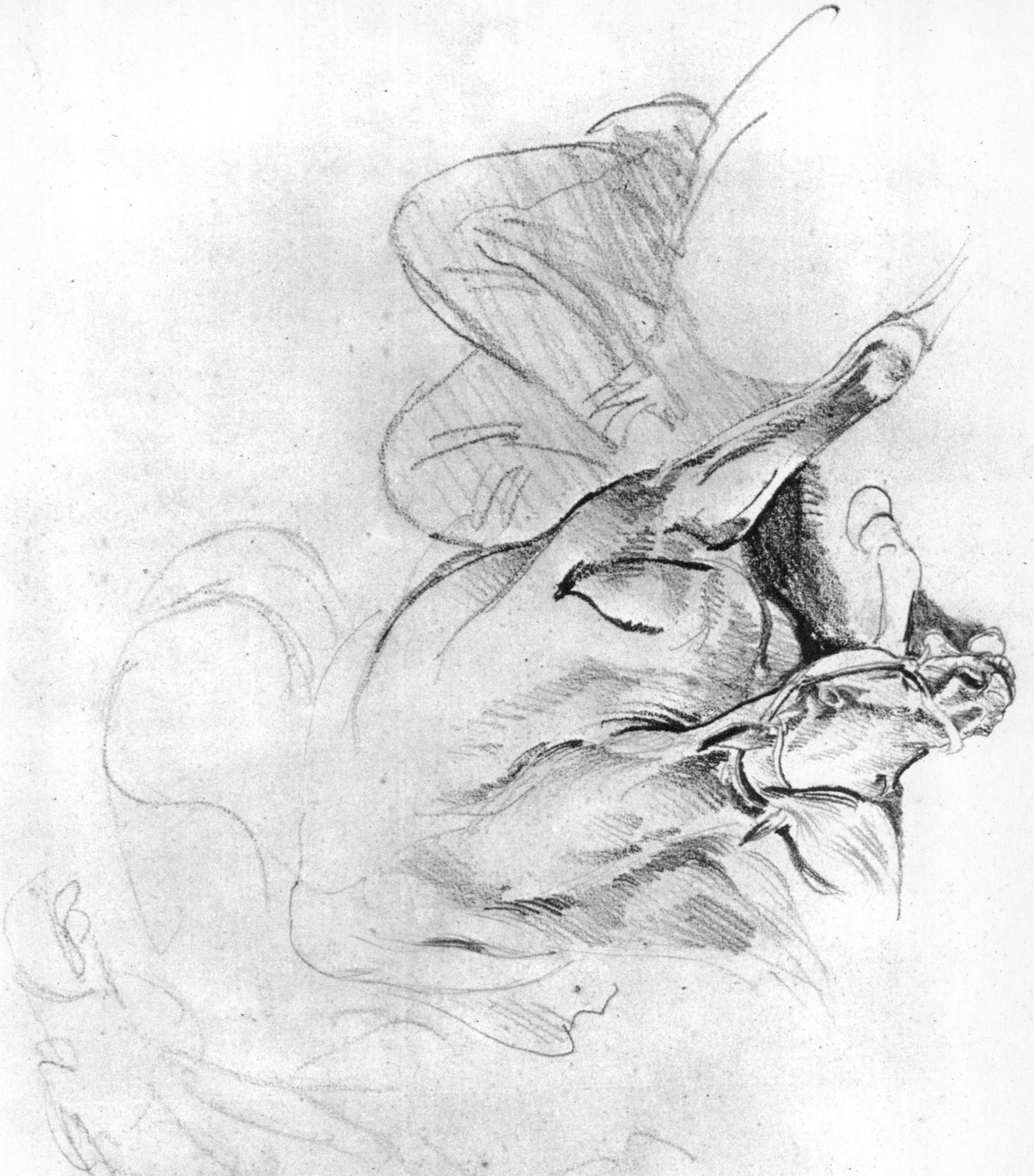

THEODORE GERICAULT

5 The Grenadier

Pencil on paper, 27.8 × 16.8 cm. Museum of Czech Literature–Karásek Gallery, Prague, formerly Galippe collection.

The theme and composition of these two drawings are nearest to Géricault's earliest drawing (1818–19).

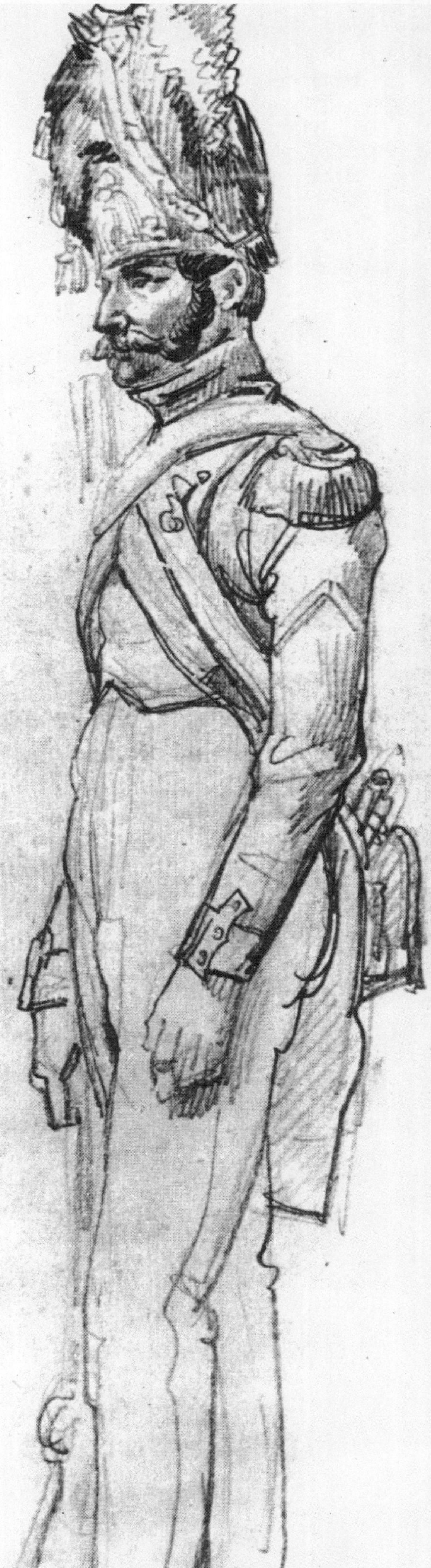

## AUGUSTE RAFFET

6 STUDIES OF SOLDIERS

Black chalk on silk paper, 32.6 × 23.4 cm. National Gallery, Prague (K 37 329), acquired 1963, formerly Vries collection, then Nedoma collection.

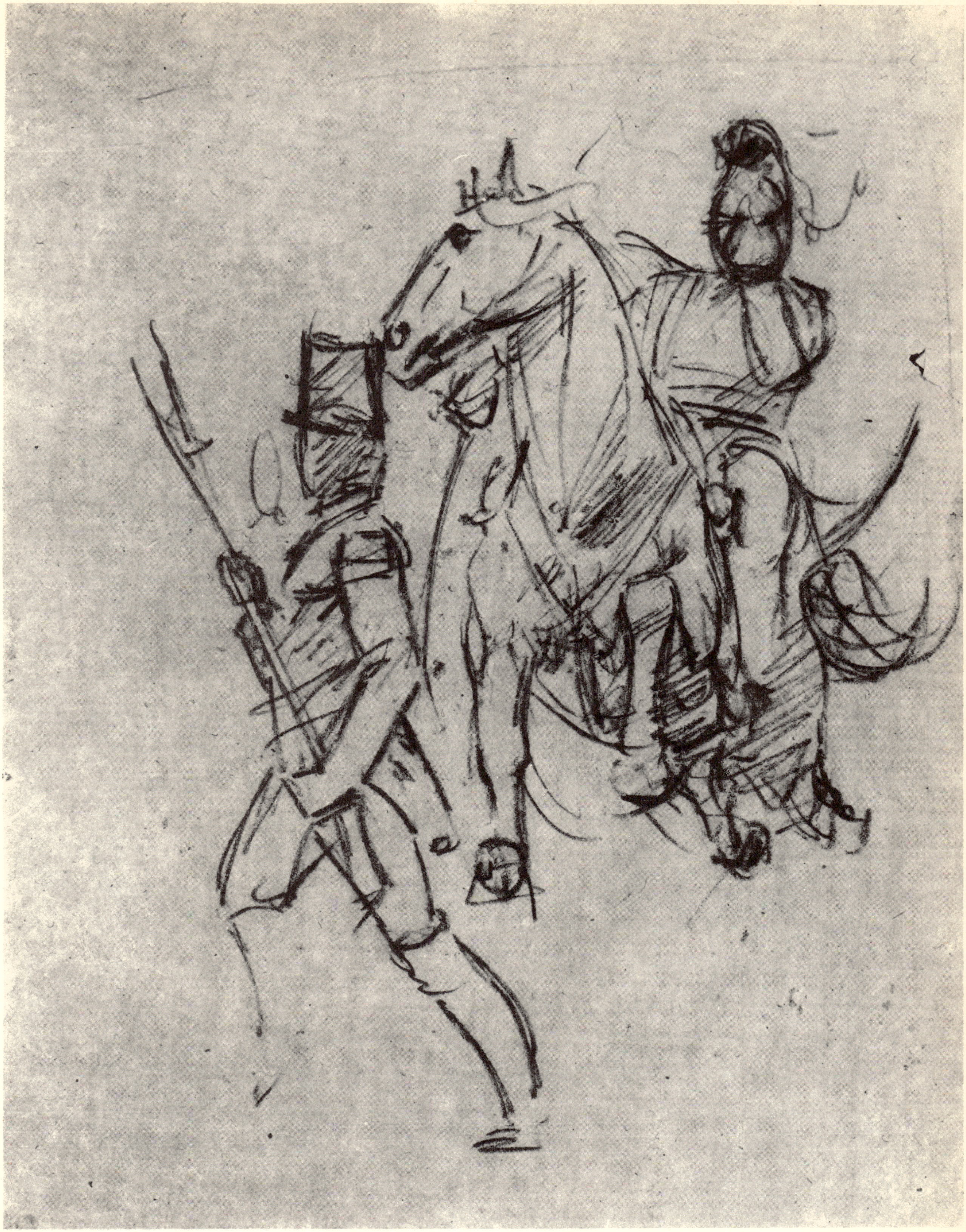

EUGENE ISABEY

7 Boats

Black and white chalks on grey paper, 19.8×31.7 cm. Marked bottom right with the seal: Vente E. Isabey. Museum of Czech Literature–Karásek Gallery, Prague.

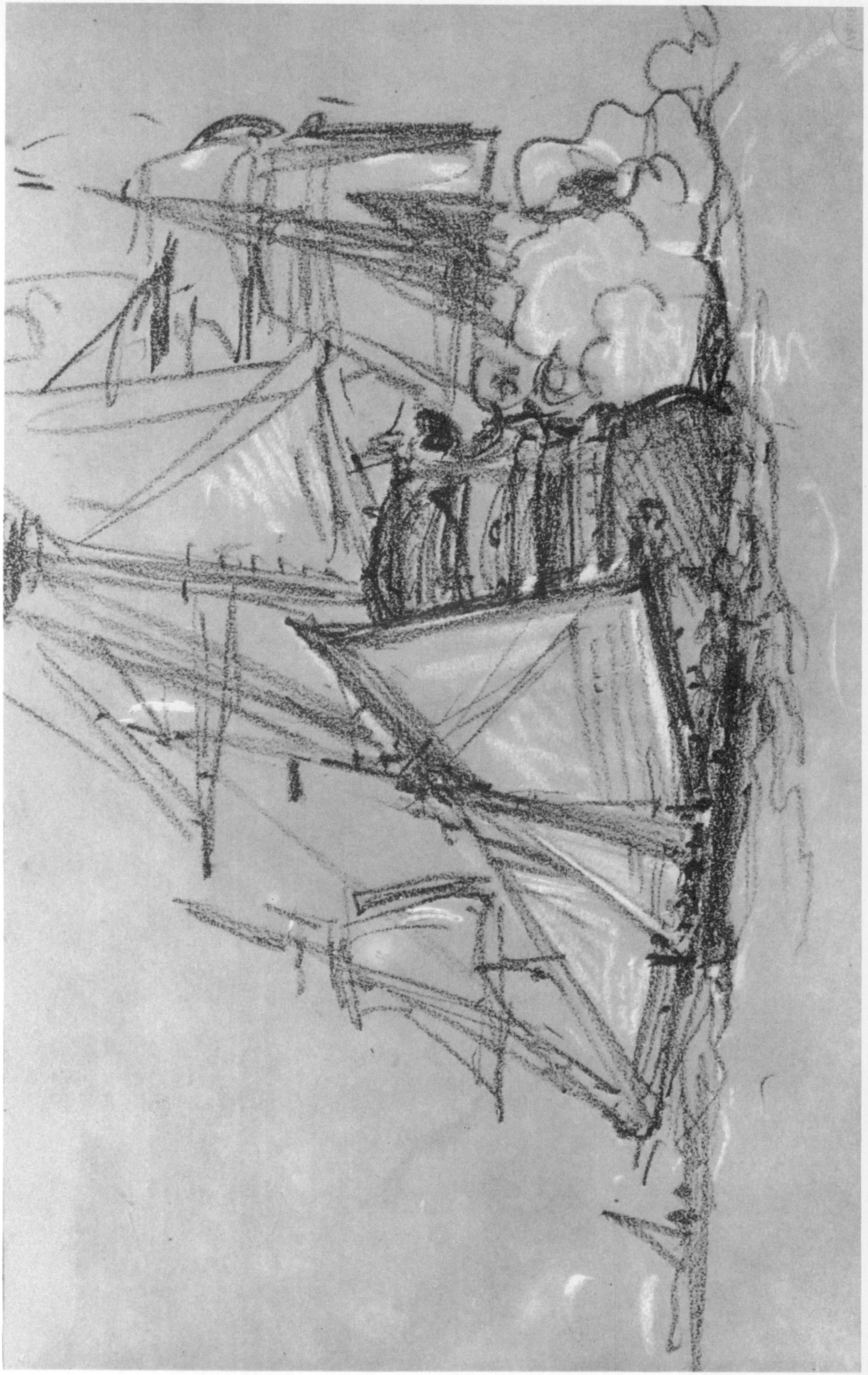

CAMILLE COROT

8 CIVITA CASTELLANA

Sepia, pen and pencil, 28.3 × 45.2 cm. Added bottom right in pencil: Civita Castellana Juin 1826. National Gallery, Prague (K 13 929), acquired 1923, formerly Fourcand collection.

This drawing is one of the series of landscape studies, most of which are now in the Louvre, made by Corot during his first stay in Italy near Cività Castellana.

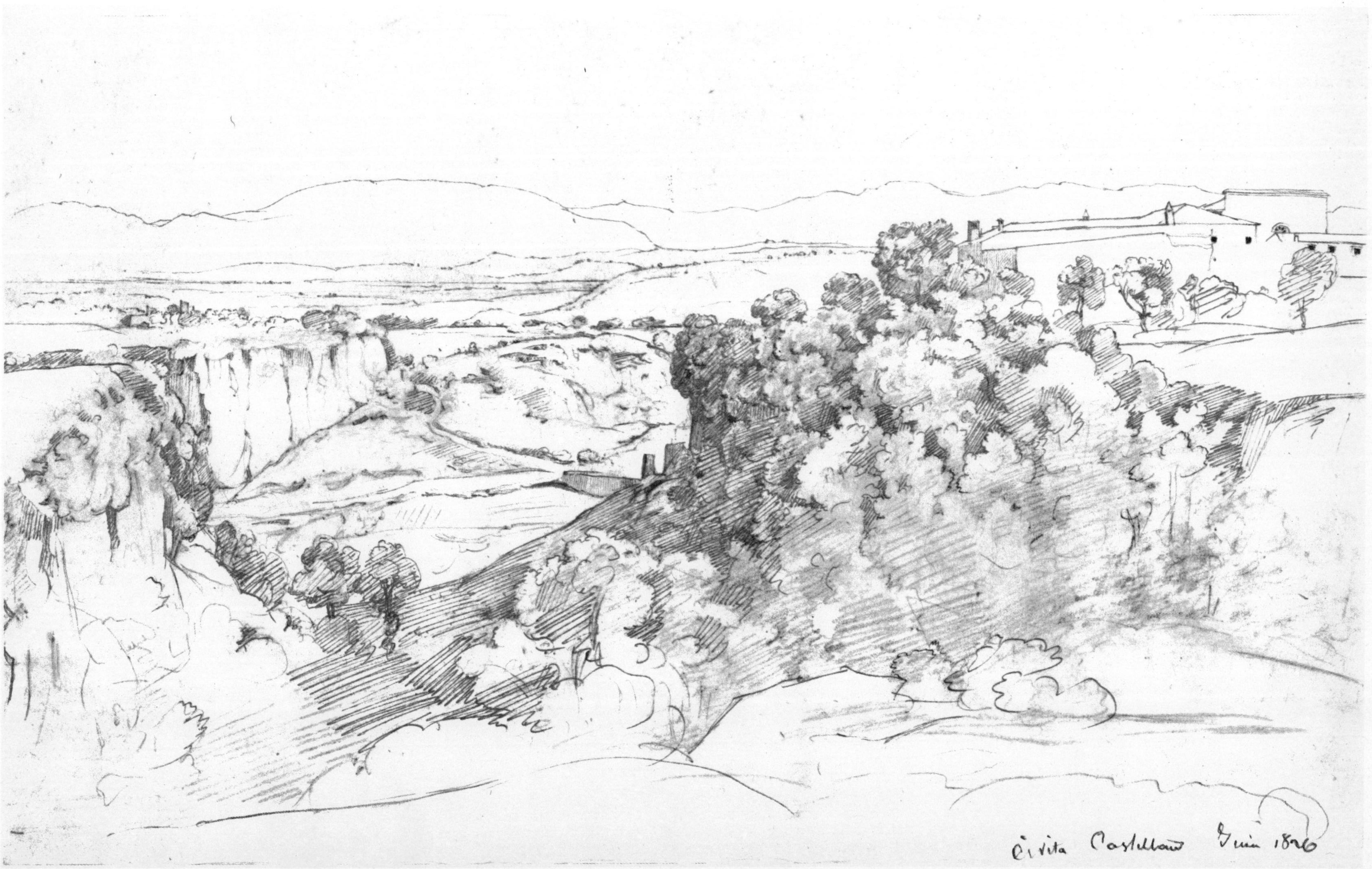
Civita Castellana Juin 1826

CAMILLE COROT

9 LANDSCAPE NEAR NAPLES

Sepia on paper, 18.2×24.4 cm. Marked bottom right in pencil: Corot; added right of centre in sepia: Napoli. National Gallery, Prague (K 16 560), acquired 1936.

This drawing also comes from Corot's stay in Italy, between 1826 and 1828. Here Corot rejoins the classical landscape of Claude Lorraine.

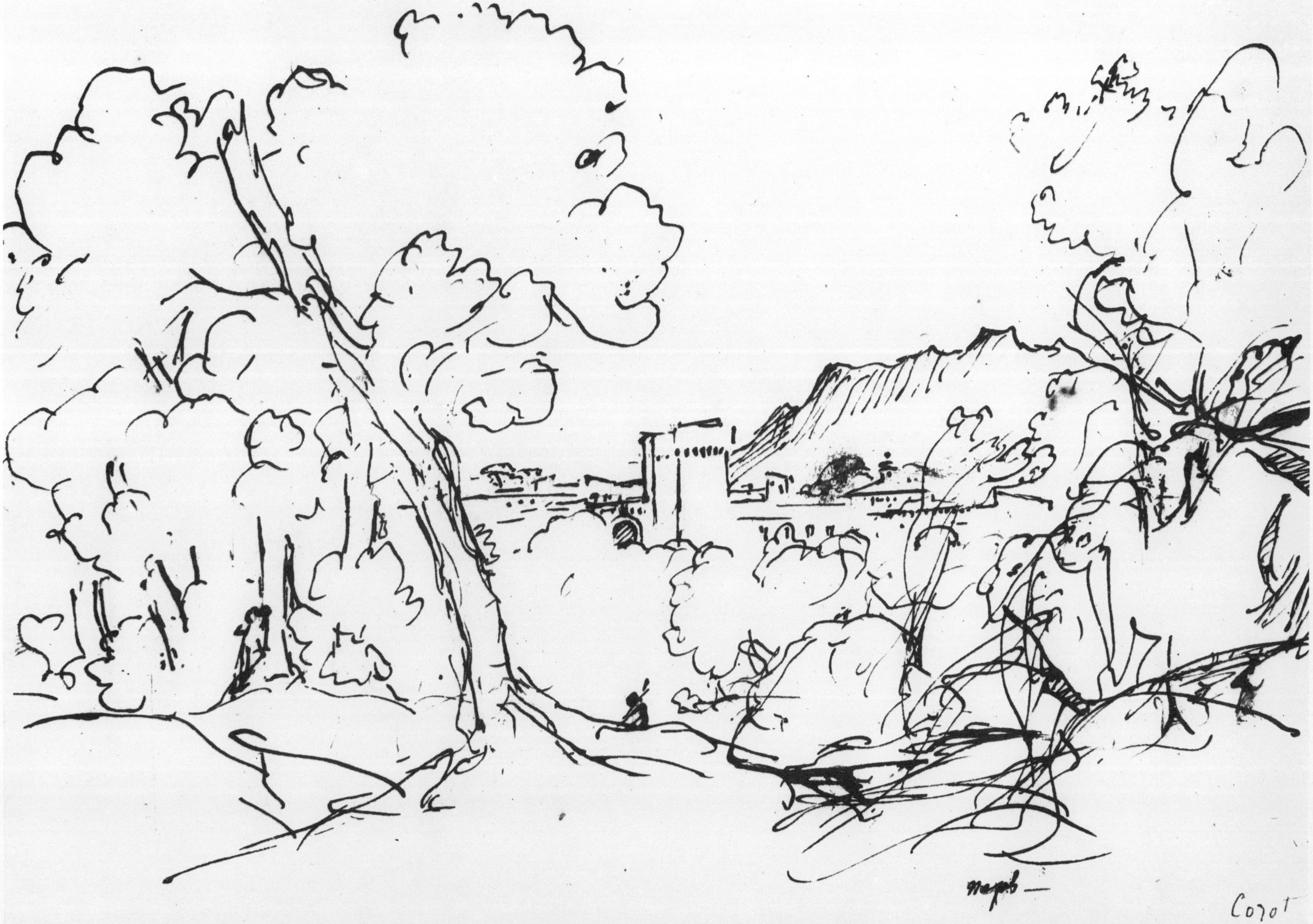
Corot

CAMILLE COROT

10 TOWN ON A RIVER

Charcoal and white chalk on grey paper, 31.3 × 48.4 cm. National Gallery, Prague (K 18 621), acquired 1950.

The concrete theme of the landscape and the pictorially conceived drawing correspond to Corot's work done in the mid-nineteenth century when he was painting river scenes at Ville d'Avray and at Douai.

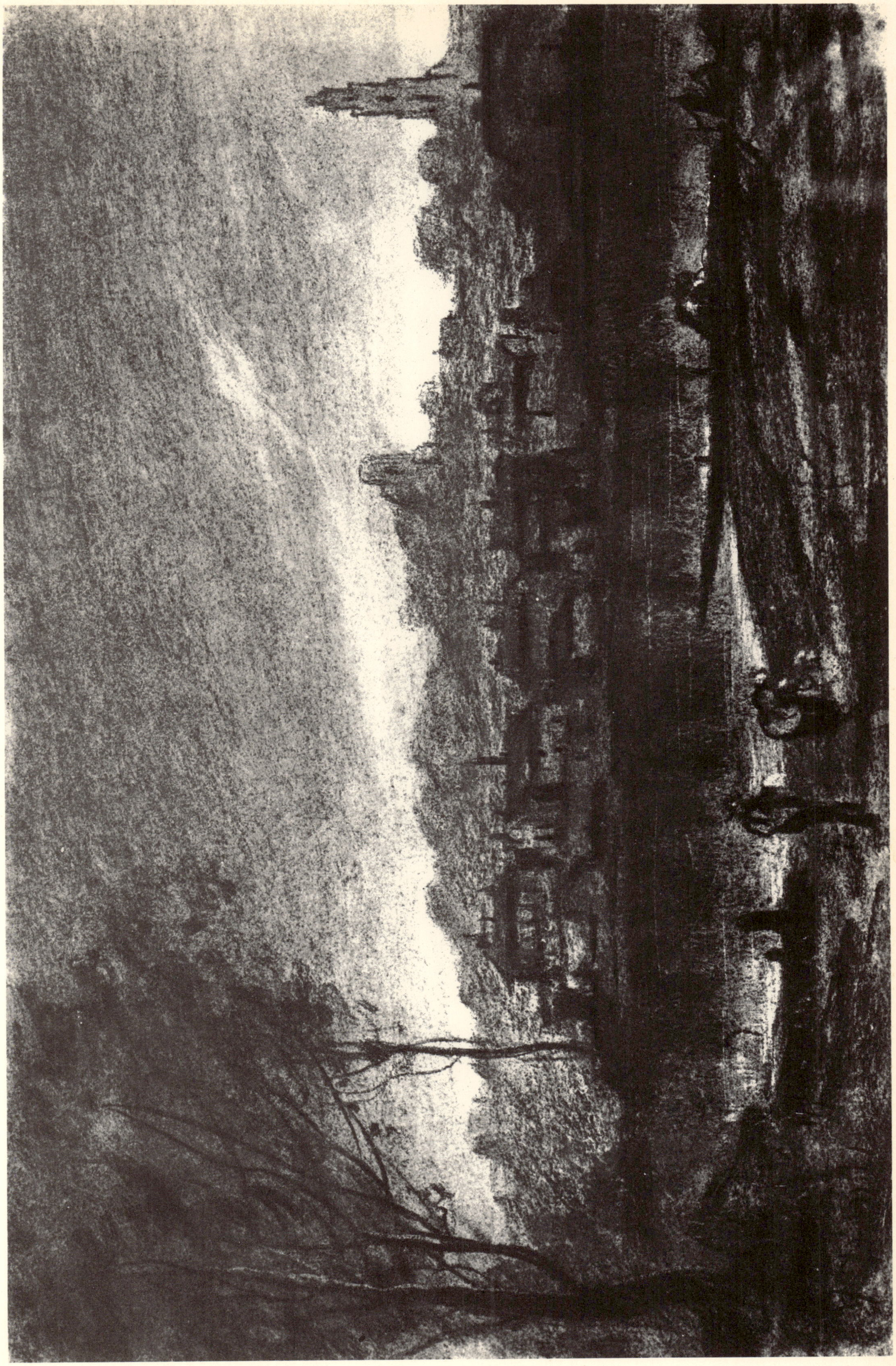

CAMILLE COROT

11 LANDSCAPE

Red chalk on paper, 41.3 × 50.3 cm. Signed bottom right: COROT. National Gallery, Prague (DK 693), acquired 1945.

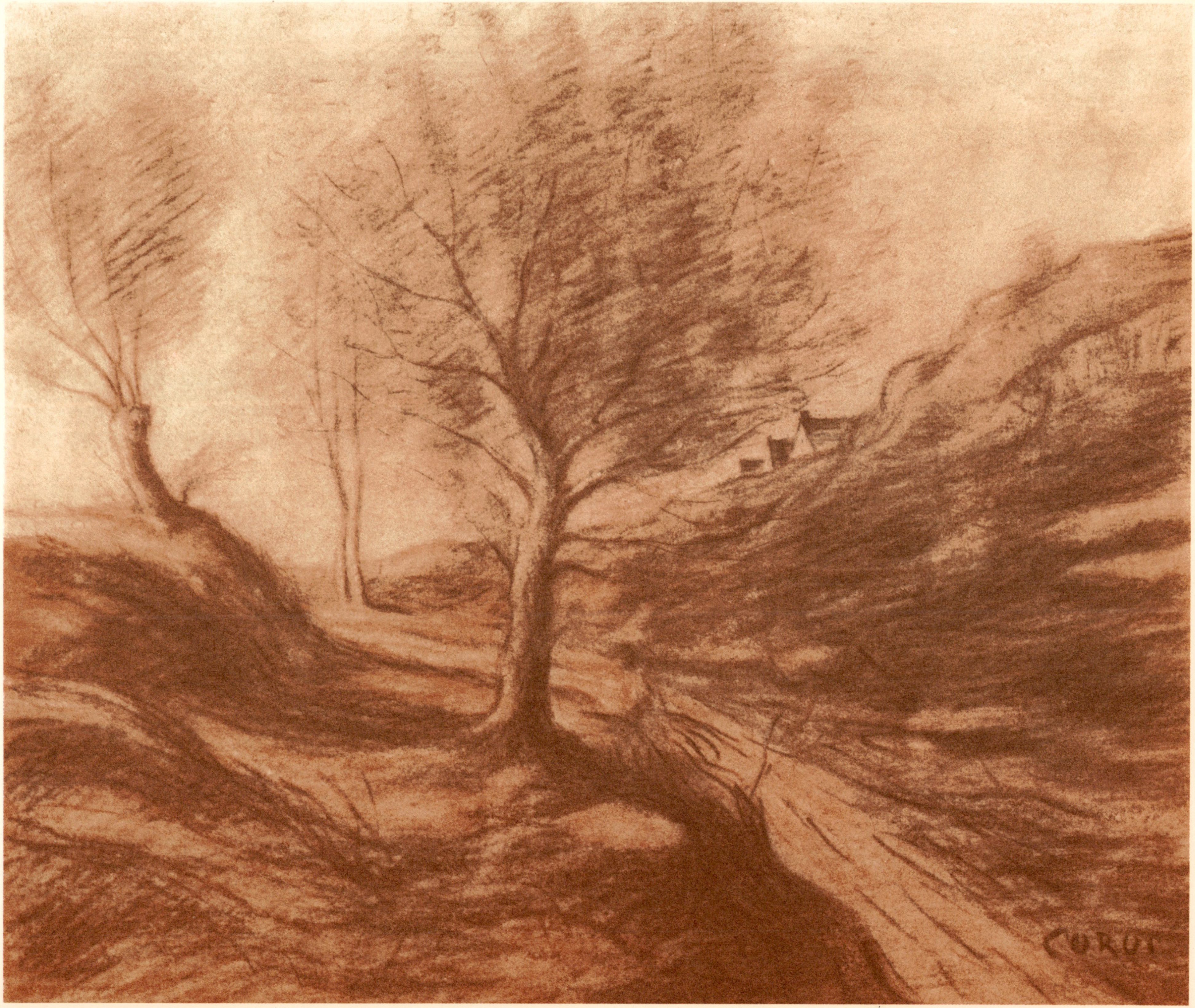
COROT

CAMILLE COROT

12 LANDSCAPE WITH TALL TREES

Charcoal and Indian ink applied with the brush on brown paper, 43.9×28.7 cm. Private collection, Prague.

The drawing is an example of the late lyrical landscapes by Corot. (To be compared, for example, with the drawing *Orpheus Hailing the Light*, of 1864; A. Roubaut and E. Moreau-Nélaton, *L'oeuvre de Corot*, 4 vols. Paris 1910. Page 224.)

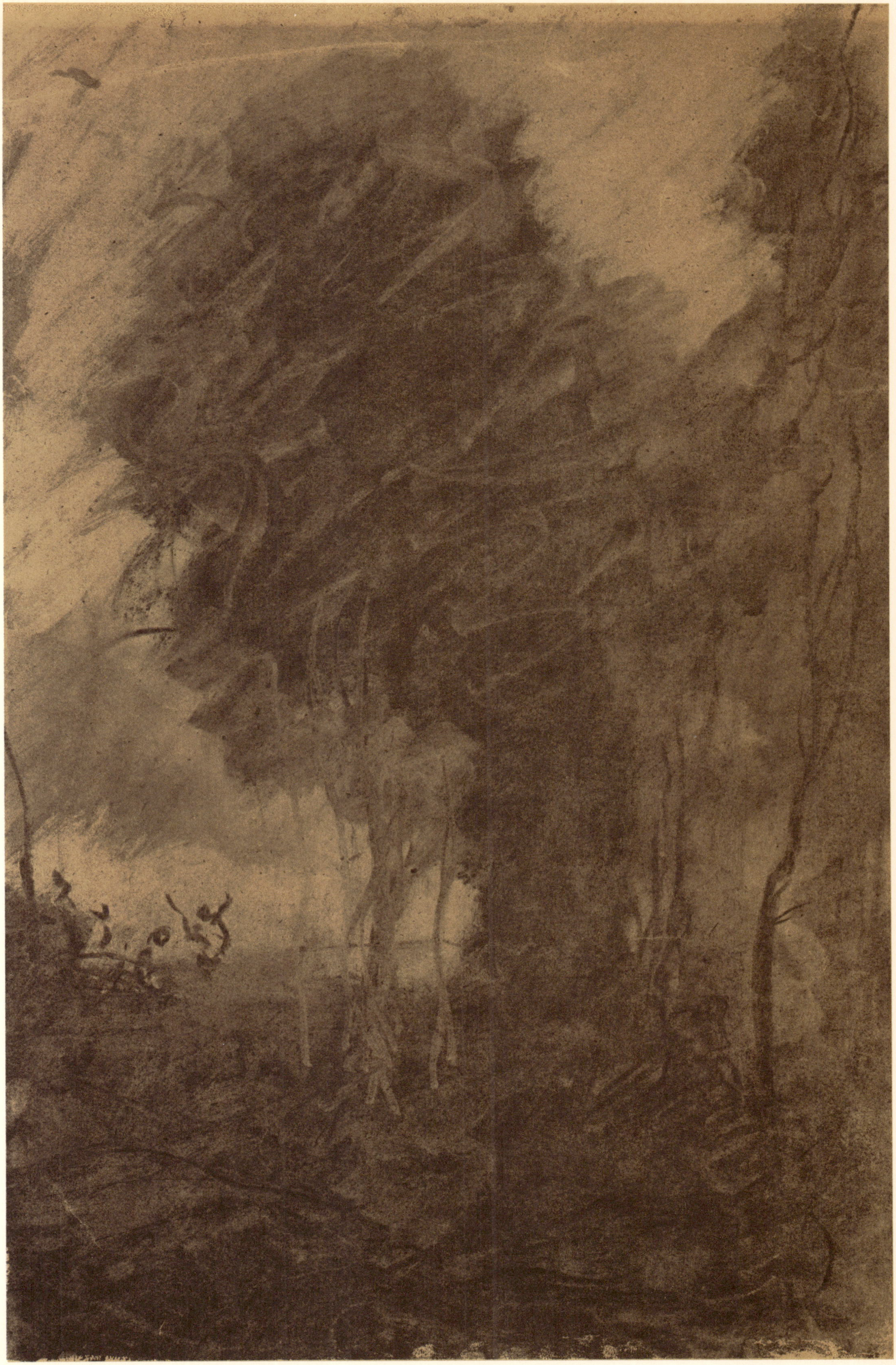

THEODORE ROUSSEAU

13 Twisted Tree

Pencil on paper, 11 × 6.3 cm. Marked with the seal: TH. R.
Museum of Czech Literature–Karásek Gallery, Prague.

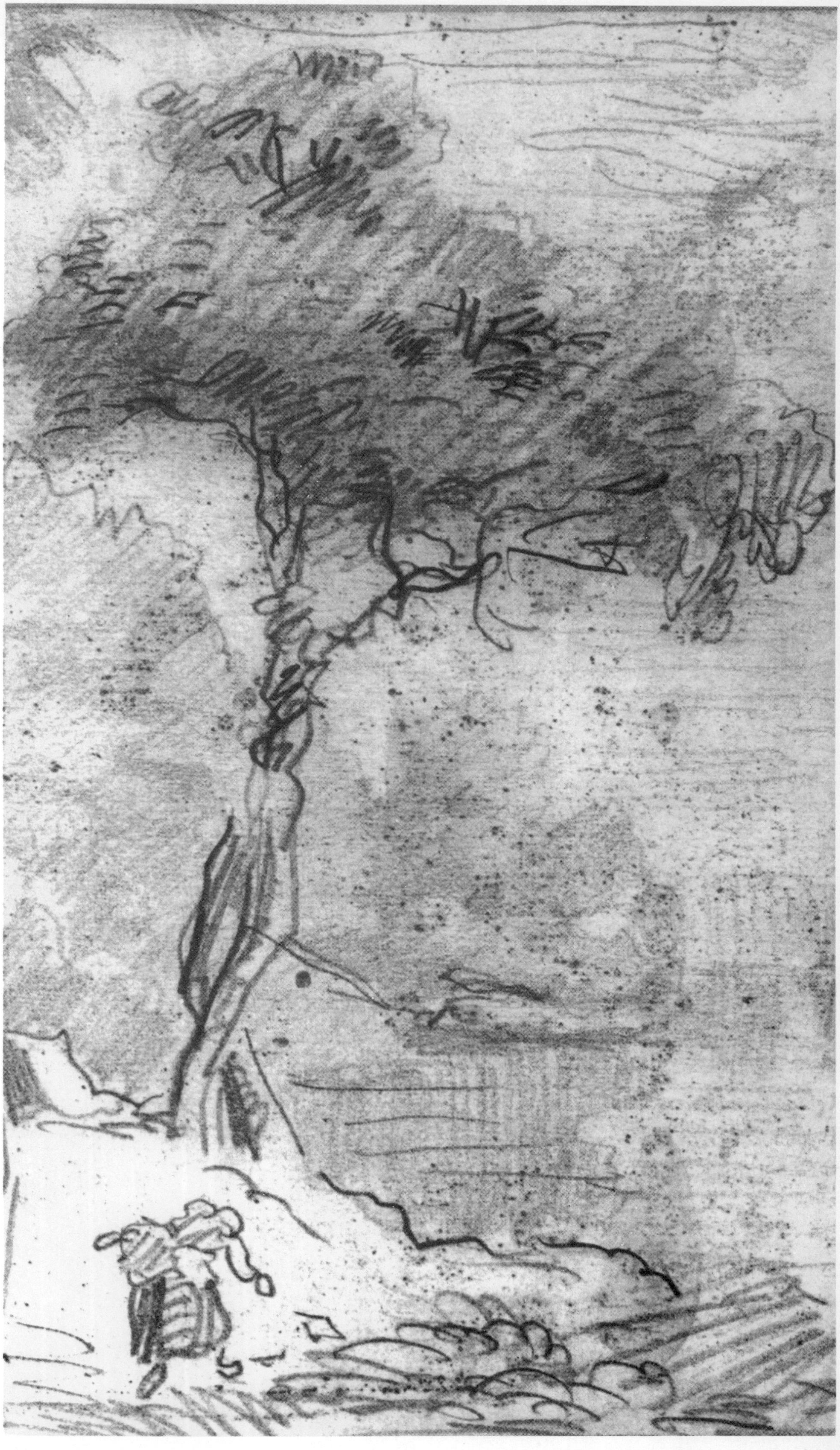

THEODORE ROUSSEAU

14 PEOPLE IN A THICKET

Pencil on paper, 24.1 × 14.2 cm. Marked with the seal: TH. R. Museum of Czech Literature–Karásek Gallery, Prague.

The two drawings are leaves from a sketch-book.

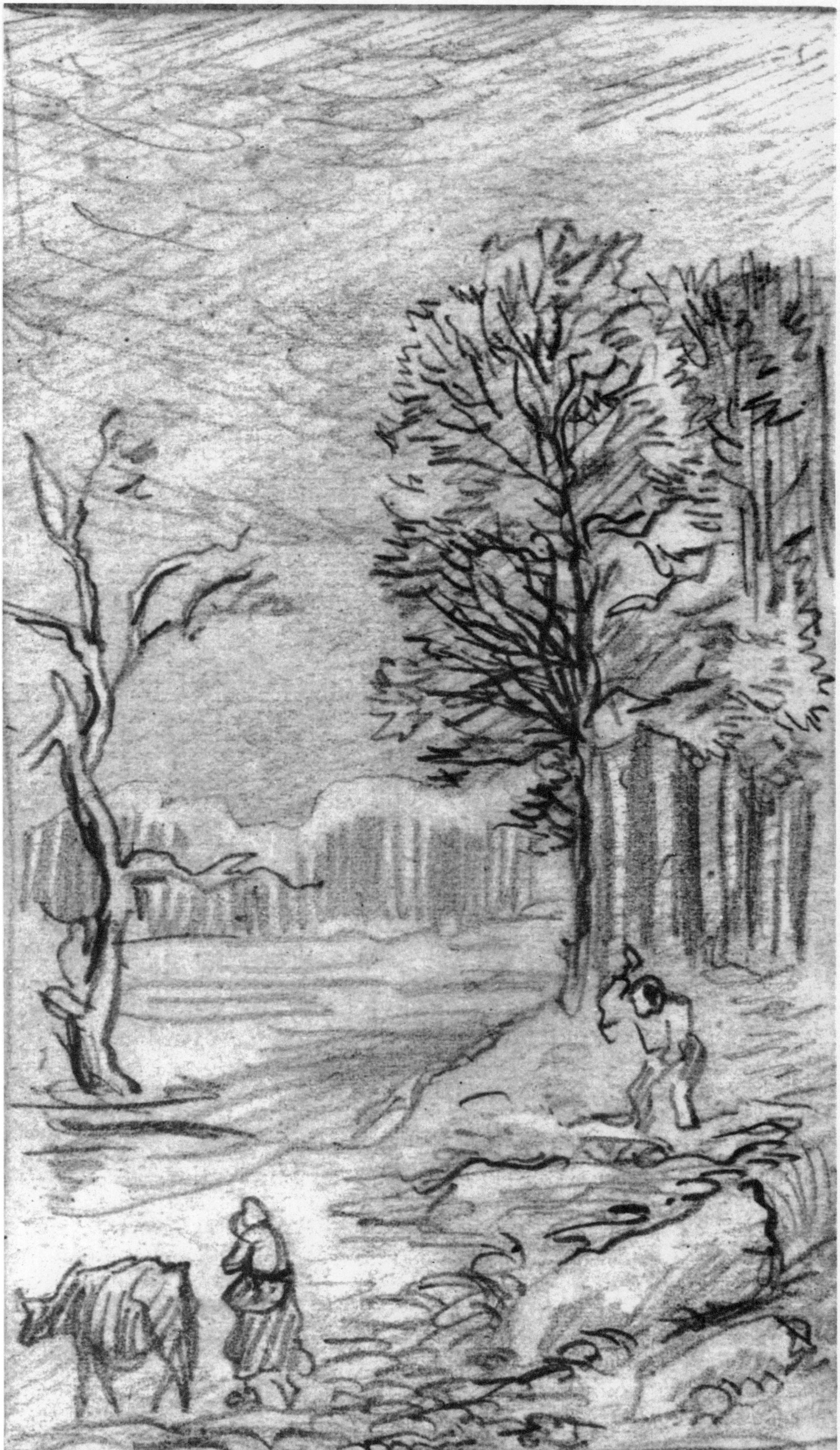

CONSTANTIN GUYS

15 THE CARRIAGE

Wash, 15×21.7 cm. Moravian Gallery, Brno (B 2 918).

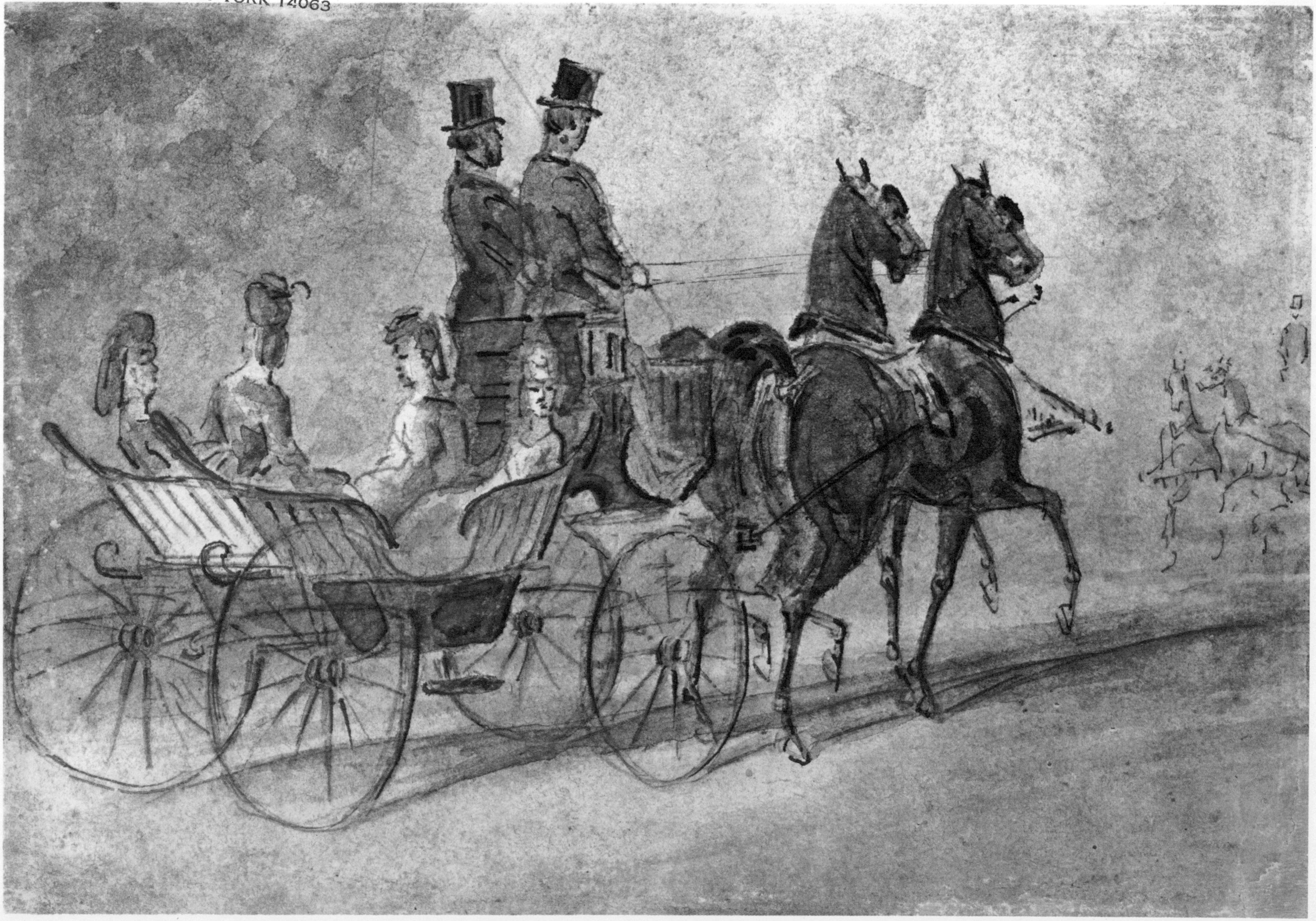

HONORE DAUMIER

16 THE WASHERWOMAN

Pencil, 20.9 × 11 cm. National Gallery, Prague (K 16 565), acquired 1936.

This sketch is a variant on the theme of Parisian washerwomen which interested Daumier in about 1860.

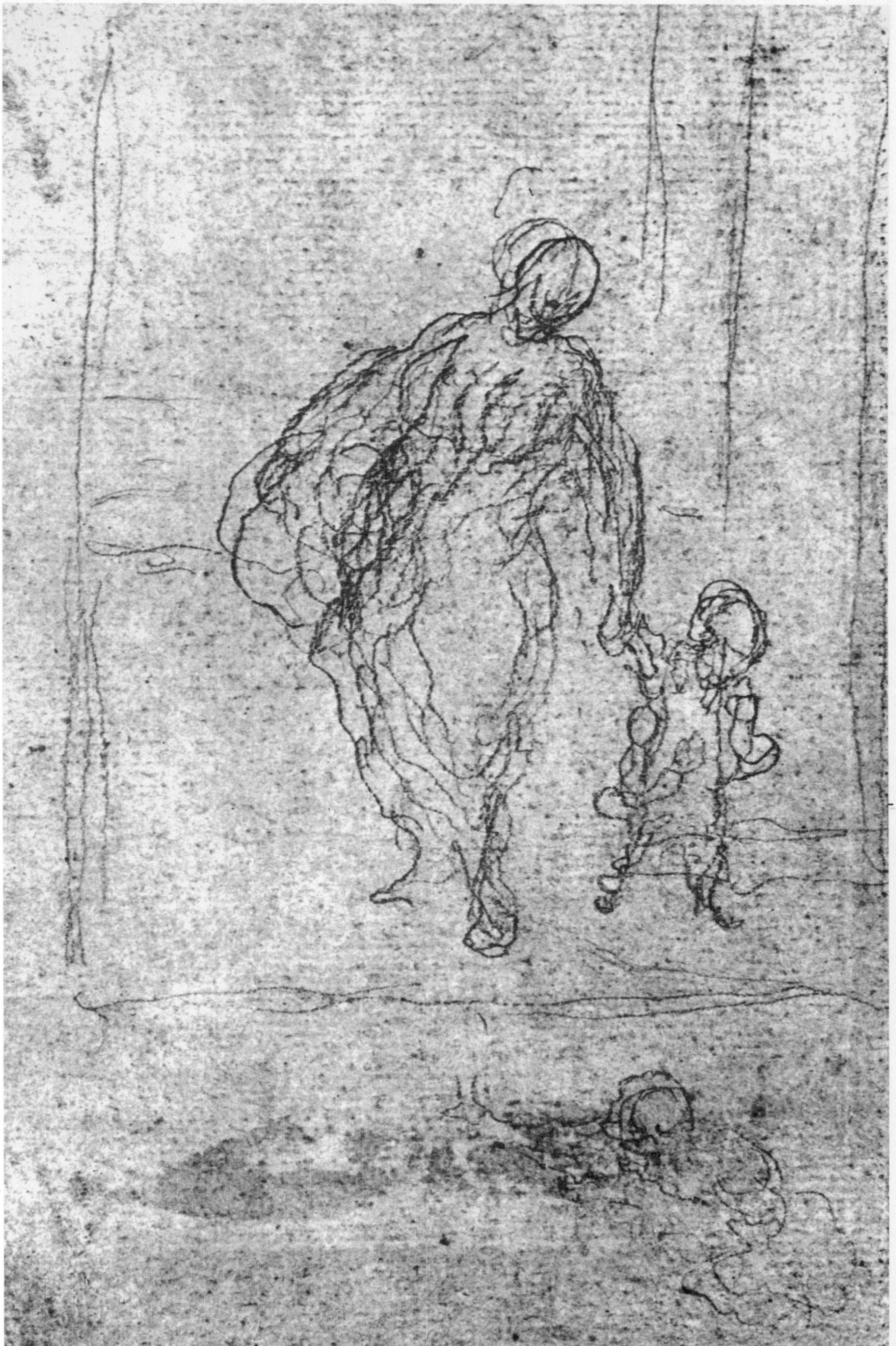

CONSTANTIN GUYS

17 THE HORSEMAN

Wash, sepia, pen and brush, 17×21.3 cm. National Gallery, Prague (18 593), acquired 1950.

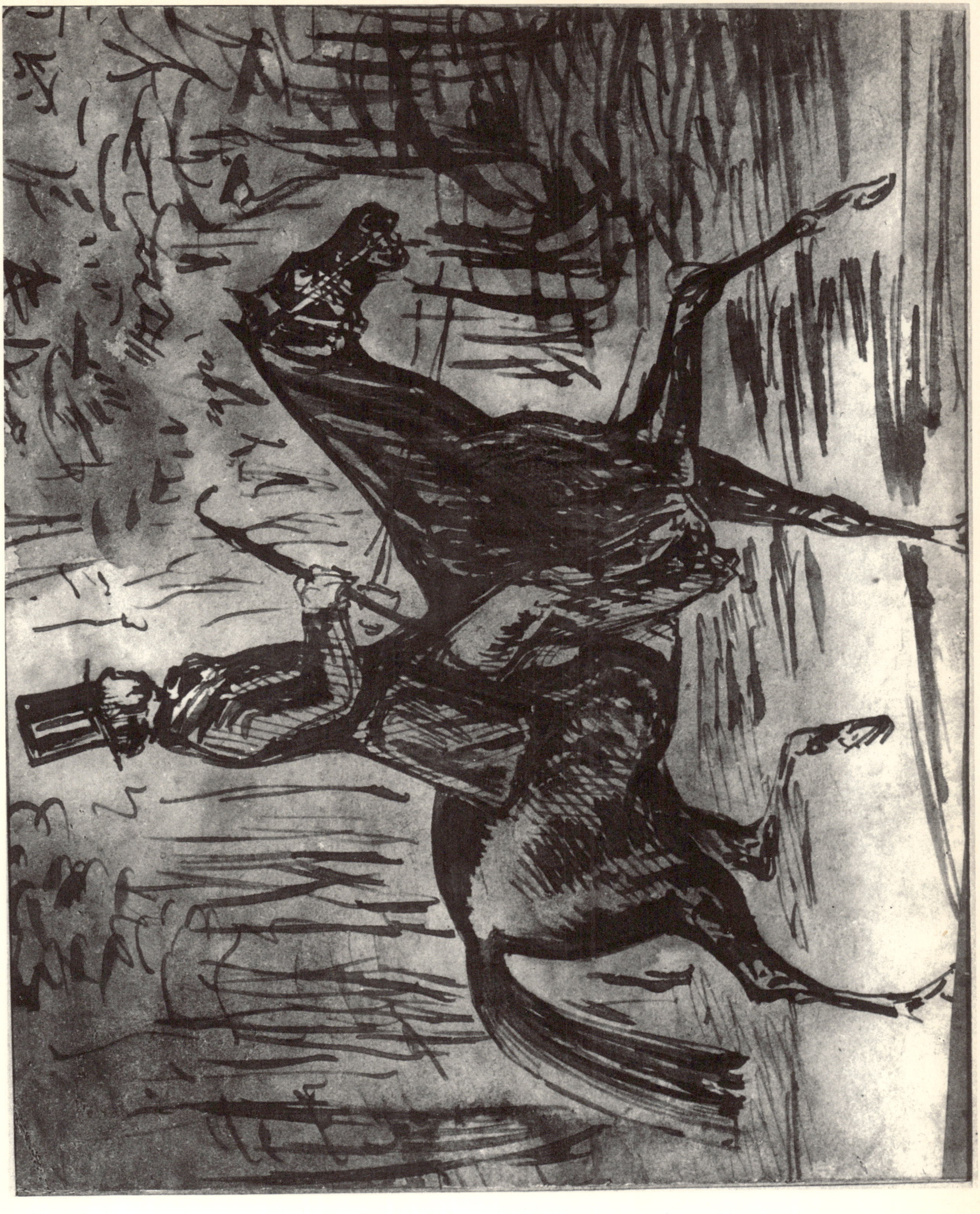

GUSTAVE DORE

18 SKETCH AFTER A PAINTING BY TITIAN

Watercolour, 33.3 × 19.1 cm. Signed bottom right: G. Doré.
Private collection, Prague.

Sketch after a painting by Titian in the Doges' palace in Venice.

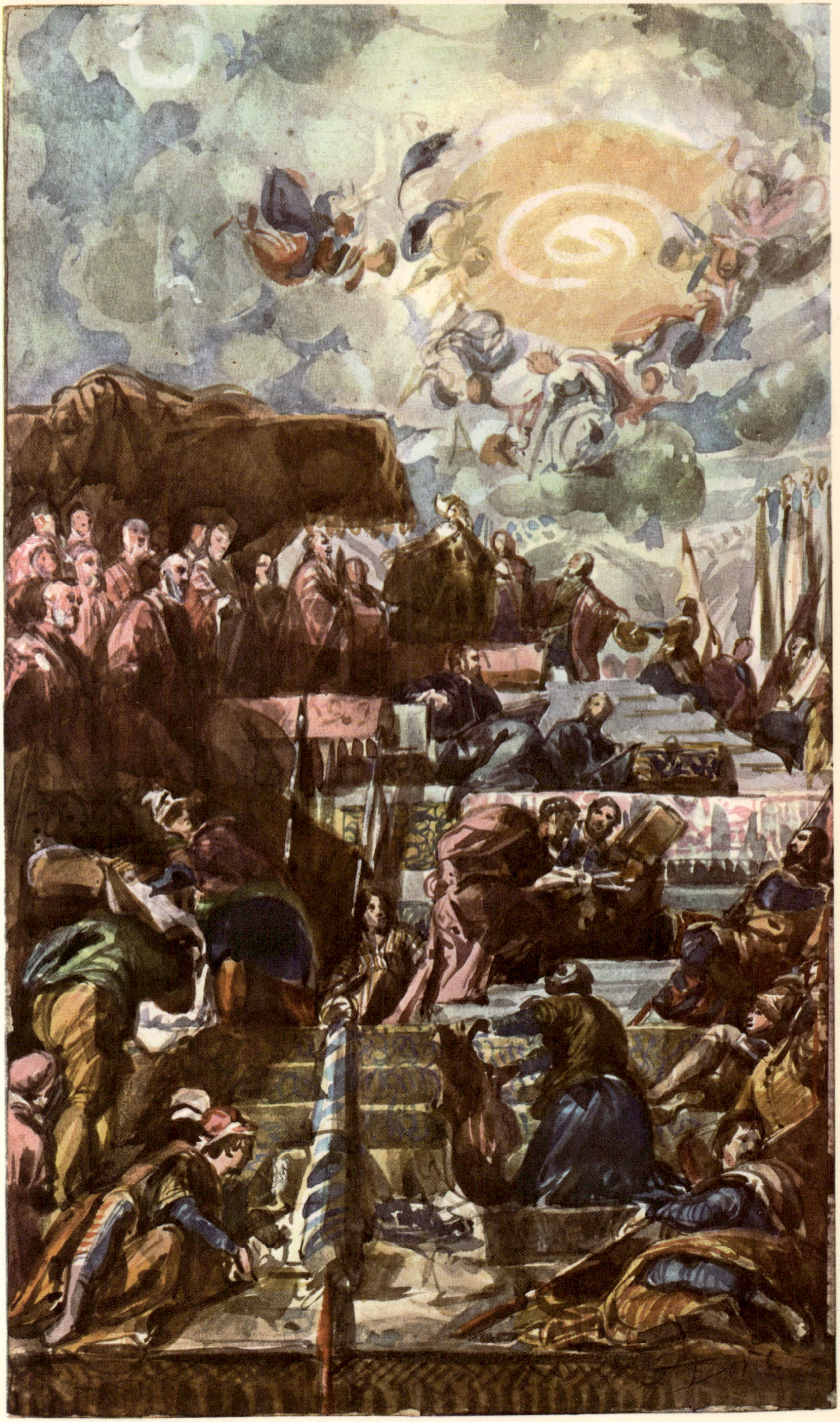

CONSTANTIN GUYS

19 The Horseman

Wash, Indian ink with brush on grey paper, 16.3 × 15.3 cm. National Gallery, Prague (K 37 372), acquired 1963, formerly Emil Orlik collection.

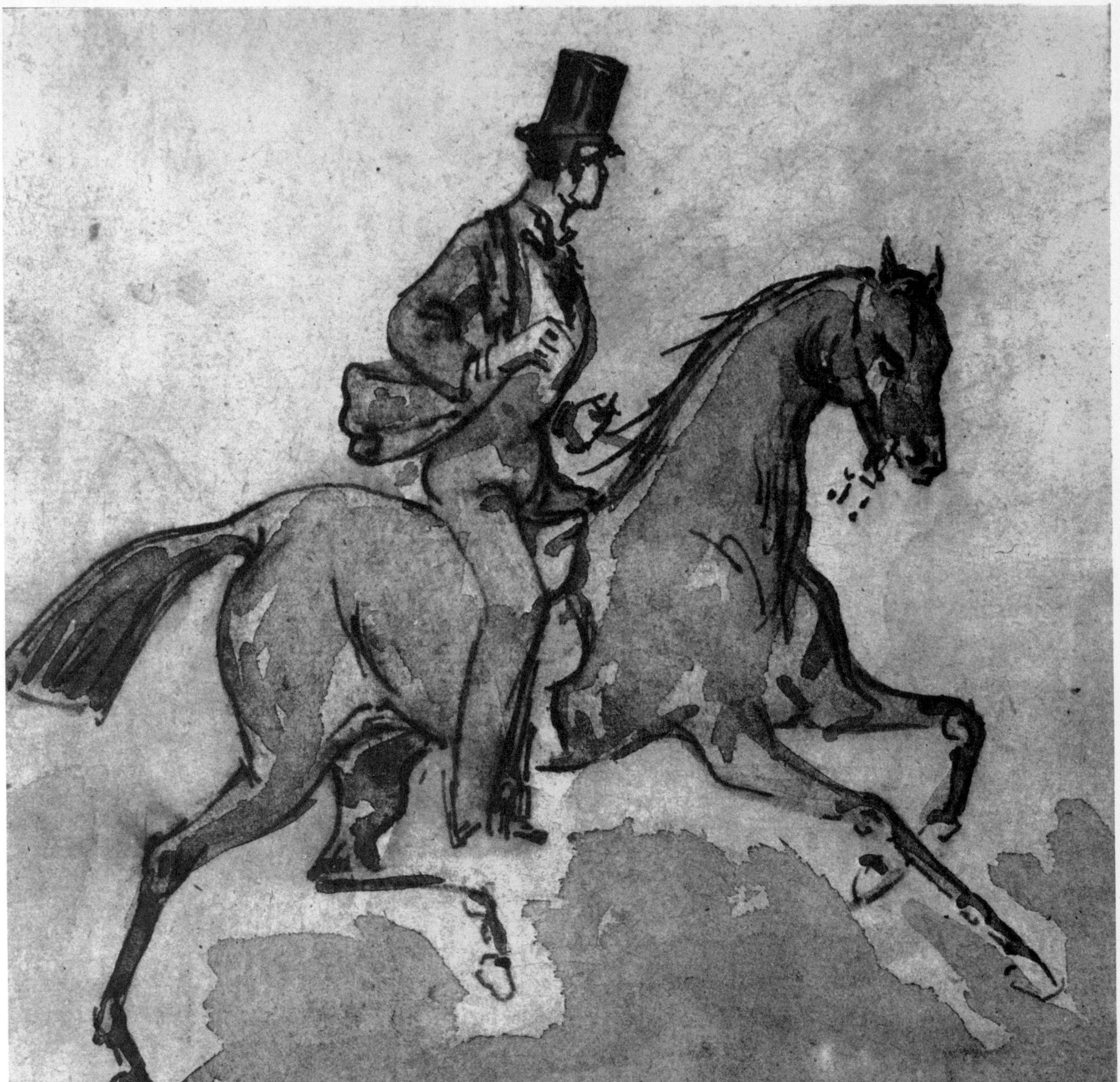

## GUSTAVE DORE

20 DON QUIXOTE

Pencil, 23 × 18.7 cm. Marked bottom left: G. D. National Gallery, Prague (K 37 331), acquired 1963, formerly de Vries collection, subsequently the Nedoma collection.

This drawing, done in about 1862, is a variation of the composition of the illustration at the end of the eighth chapter of Cervantes' *Don Quixote*. The figure is from the head of the ninth chapter.

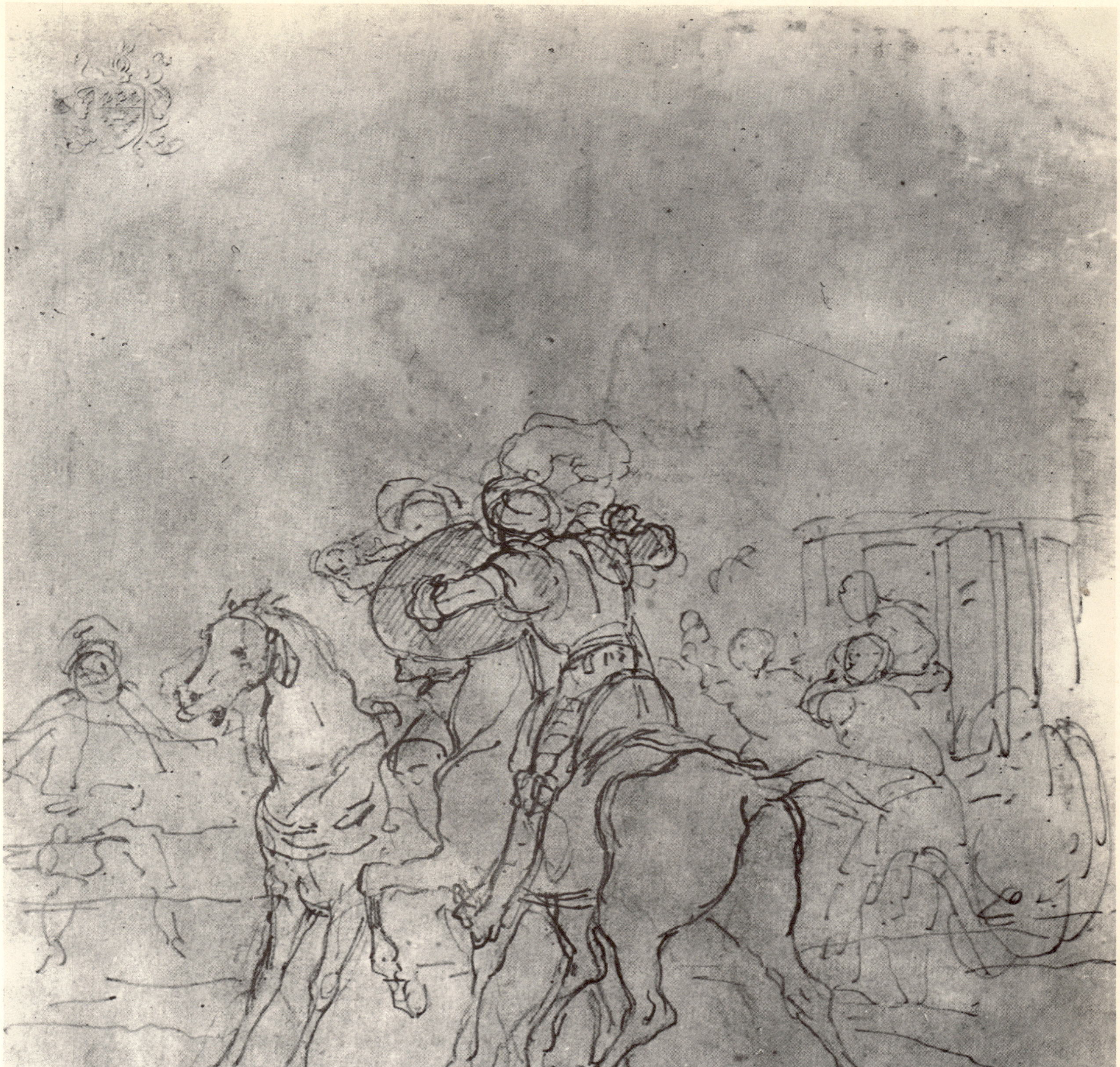
G. D.

GUSTAVE DORE

21 ILLUSTRATION

Pencil, pen, sepia and charcoal, 17.2 × 26.5 cm. Marked bottom right: G. D. 1873. Private collection, Prague.

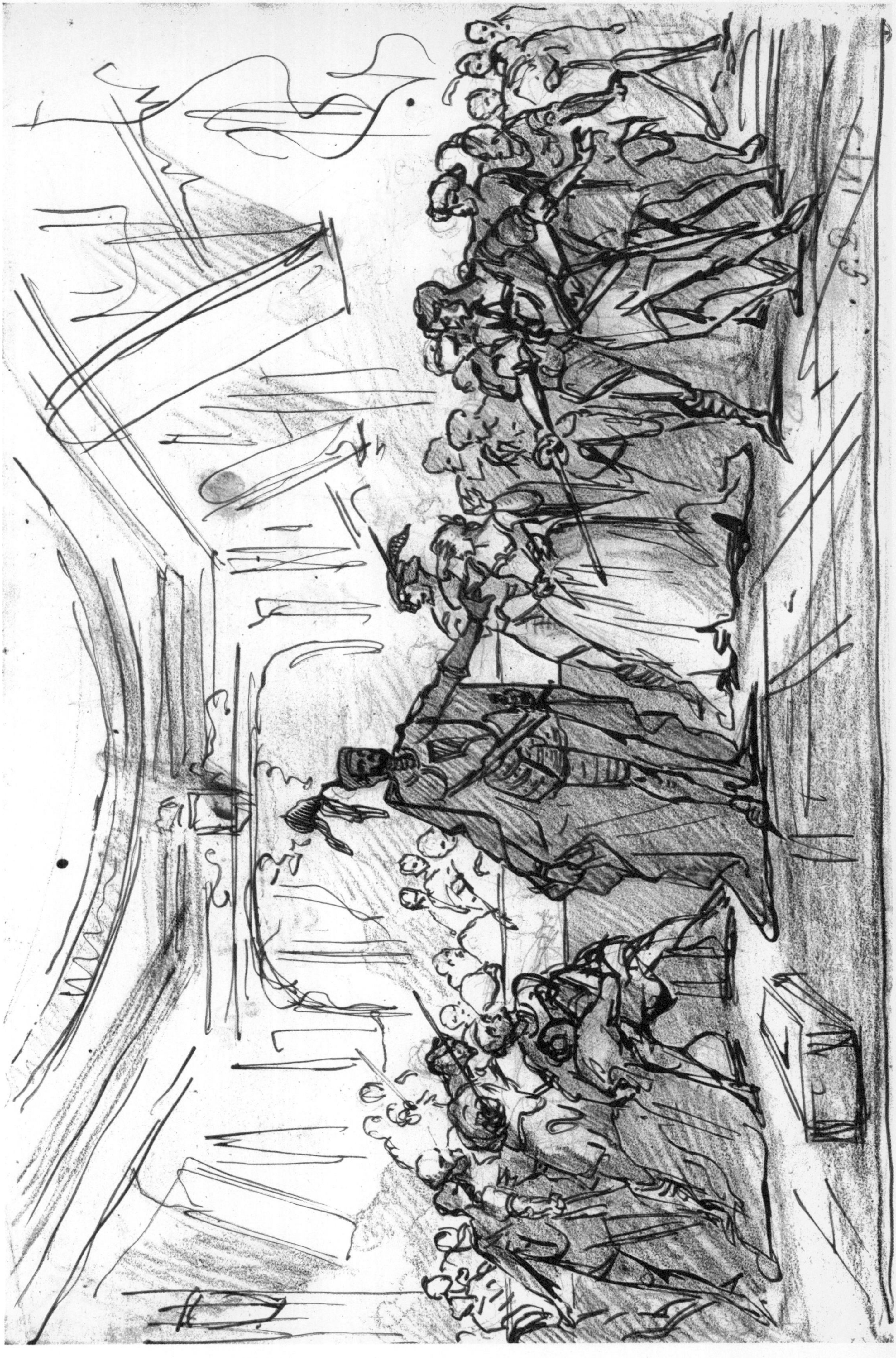

ALFRED SISLEY

22 The Ferryman

Coloured chalks, 29.8 × 47.3 cm. Marked bottom right: Sisley. National Gallery, Prague, acquired 1945.

This drawing comes from the period between 1870 and 1875 when the painter's style developed. In subject-matter it most closely resembles *The Seine at Port-Marly* of 1873.

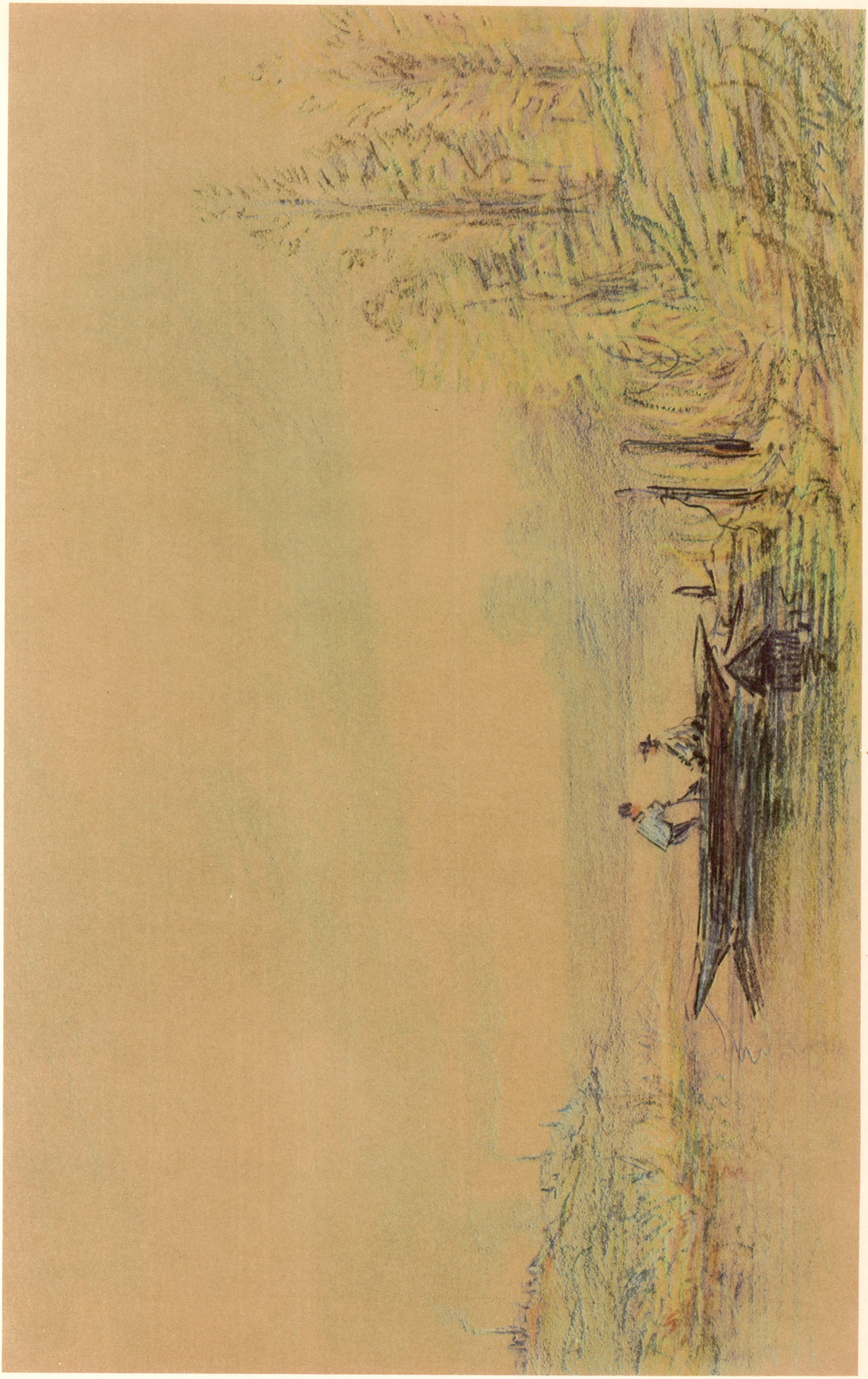

AUGUSTE RENOIR

23 Study of Young Girls

Pencil, 46.5 × 65.3 cm. Marked bottom right: Renoir. National Gallery, Prague (K 13 928), acquired 1923.

One of the studies for the picture *Young Girls Playing at Battledore and Shuttlecock* of 1887 (Institute of Arts, Minneapolis).

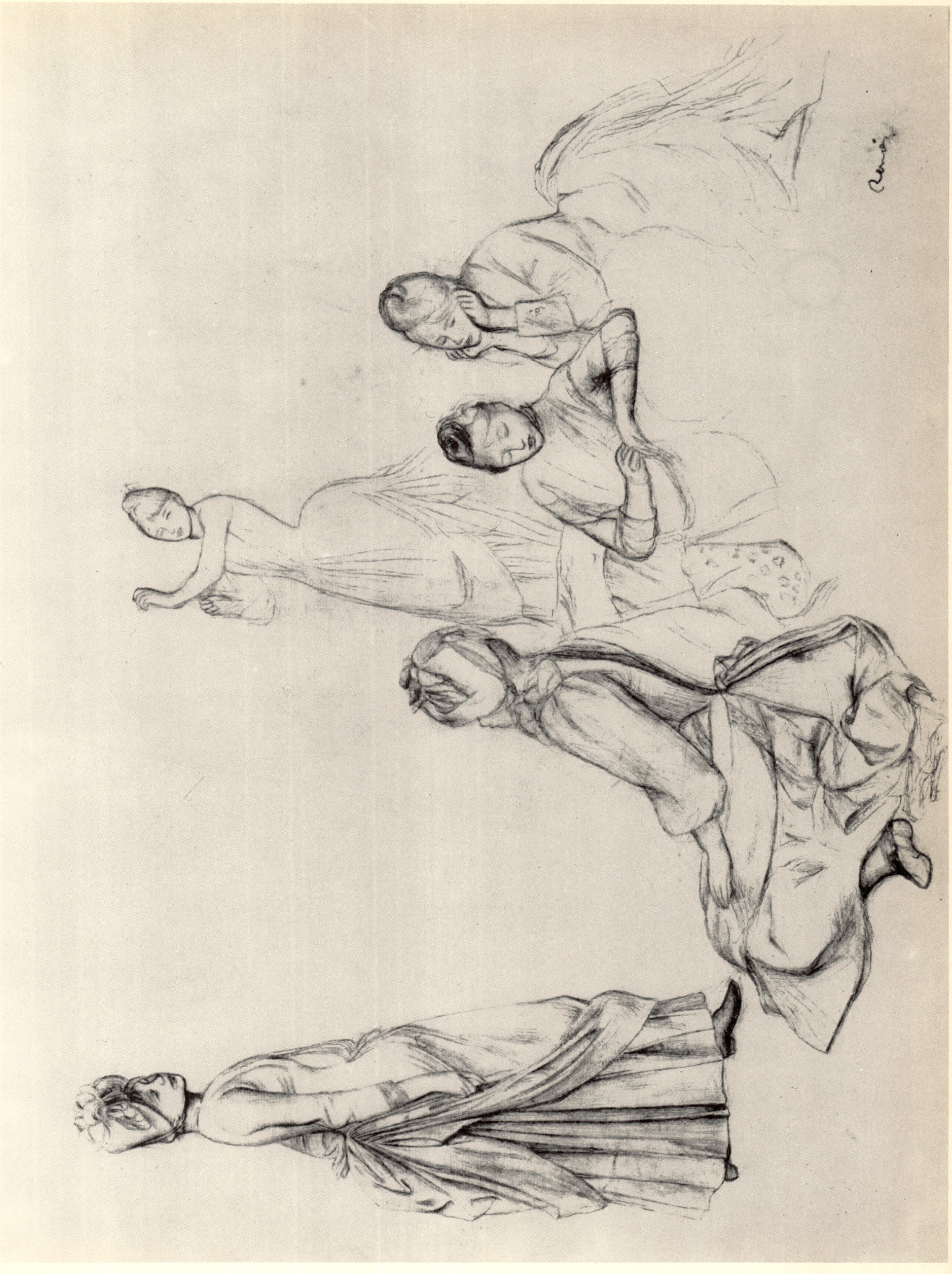
Renoir

## PIERRE PUVIS DE CHAVANNES

24 SKETCH FOR *SUMMER*

Charcoal, 31.3 × 39.7 cm. National Gallery, Prague (K 13 936), acquired 1923.

One of the sketches of about 1889–93 for the mural composition *Summer*, intended for the decoration of the town hall in Paris.

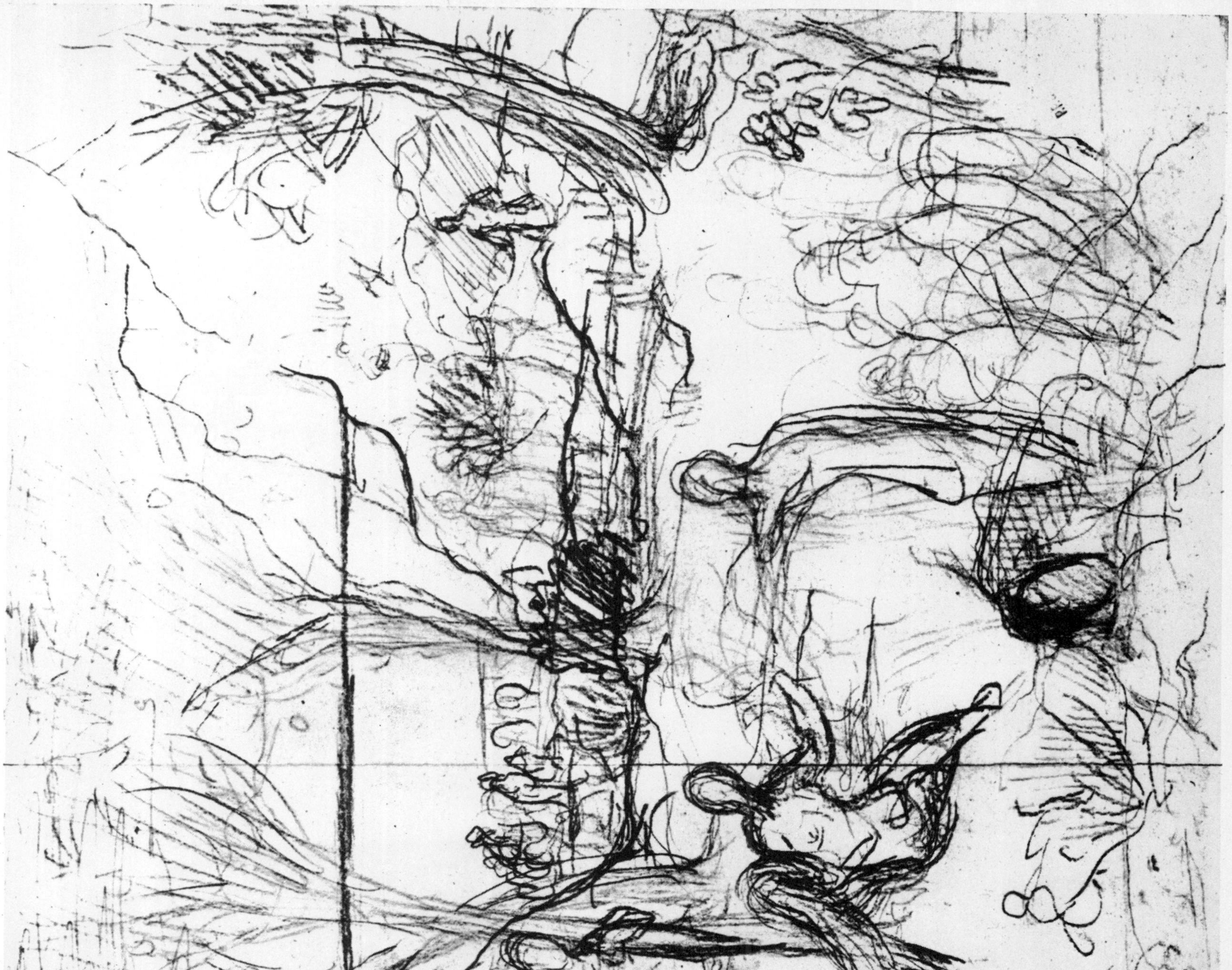

## PIERRE PUVIS DE CHAVANNES

25 INTER ARTES ET NATURAM

Blue chalk and diluted Indian ink, 20.5 × 30.8 cm. Marked bottom right with seal: P. P. C. National Gallery, Prague (K 13 939), acquired 1923.

Study of left-hand side group of three figures of women for the mural picture, *Inter artes et naturam*, for Rouen Museum (between 1890 and 1892).

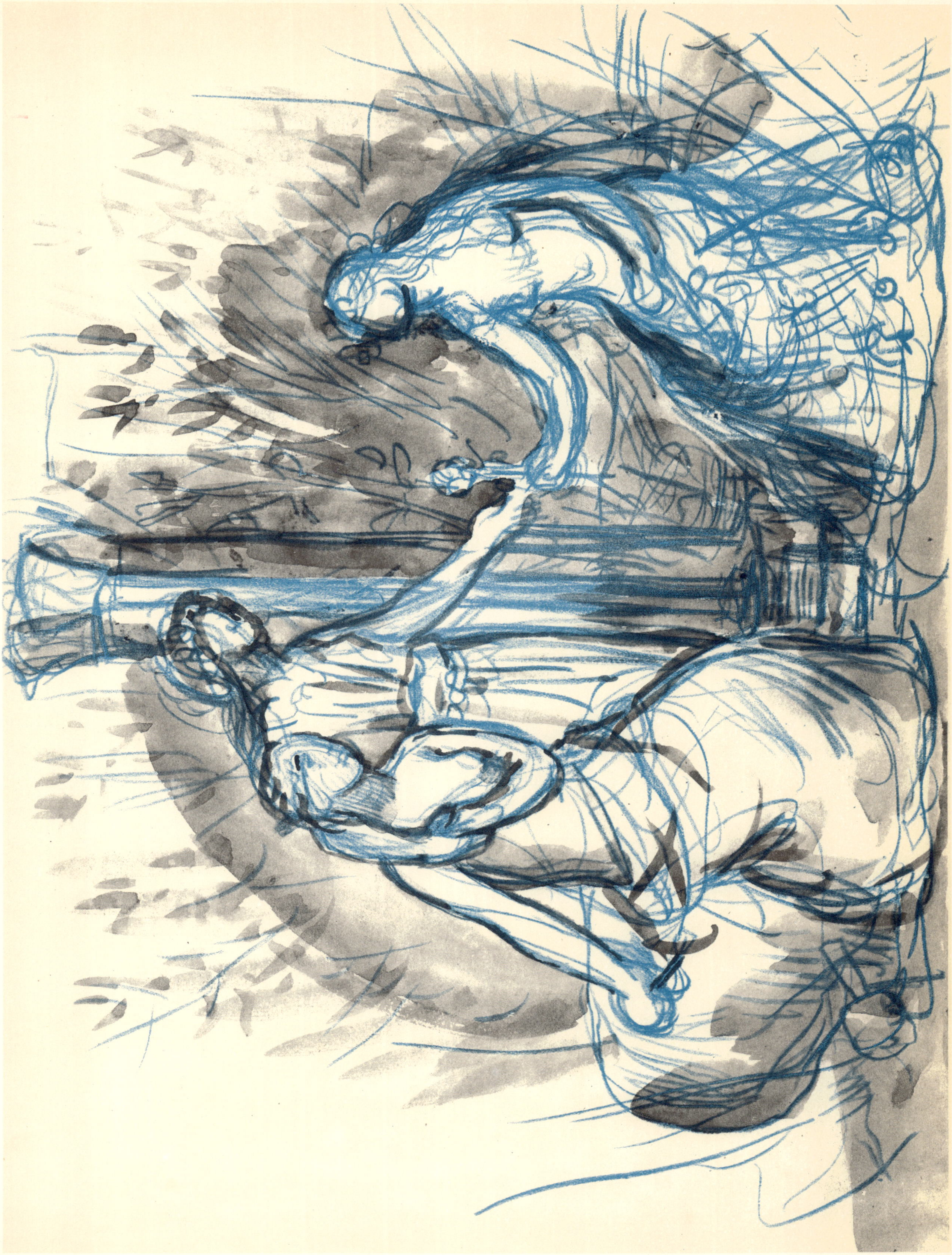

PAUL SIGNAC

26 THE BOSPHORUS

Watercolour, 11.8 × 17.2 cm. Marked bottom left: P. Signac. Museum of Czech Literature–Karásek Gallery, Prague.

From between 1907 and 1910.

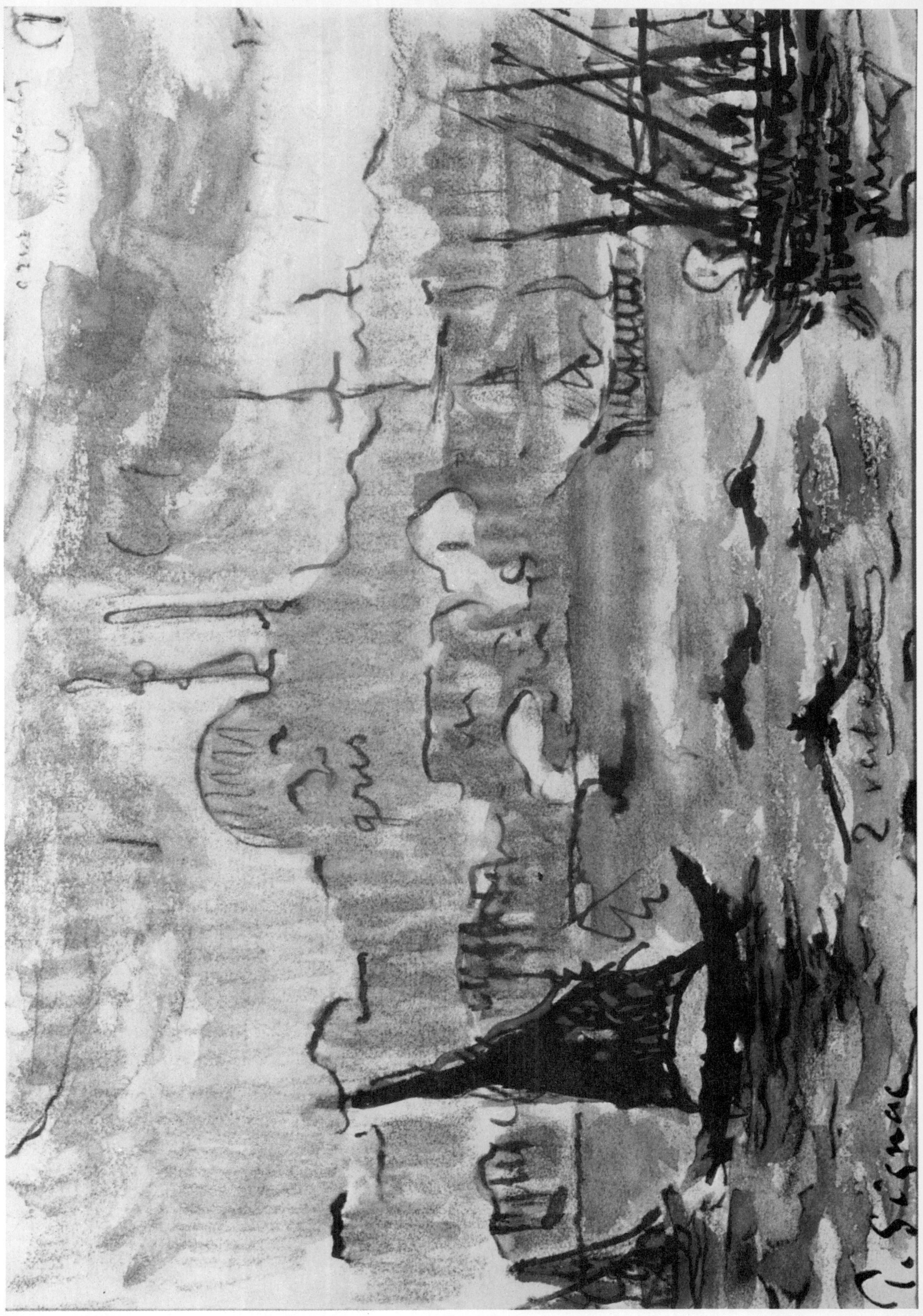

PAUL SIGNAC

27 ROUEN

Watercolour and charcoal, 27.5×44 cm. Marked bottom right: P. Signac – Rouen. National Gallery, Prague (K 18 262), acquired 1924.

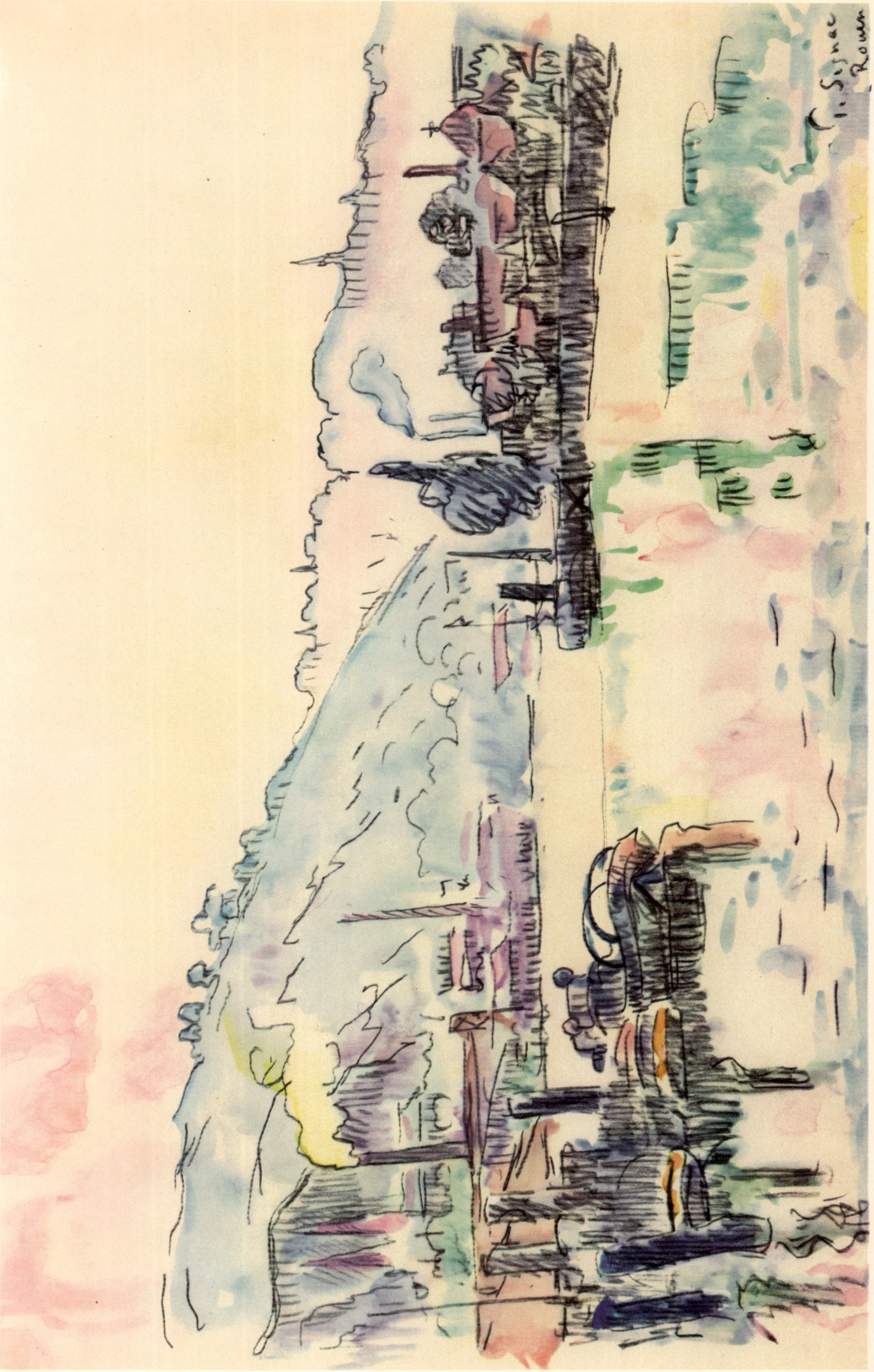
P. Signac
Rouen

PAUL SIGNAC

28 LORNALO

Watercolour and charcoal, 27.5 × 42.7 cm. Marked bottom left: P. Signac Lornalo. National Gallery, Prague (K 18 261), acquired 1924.

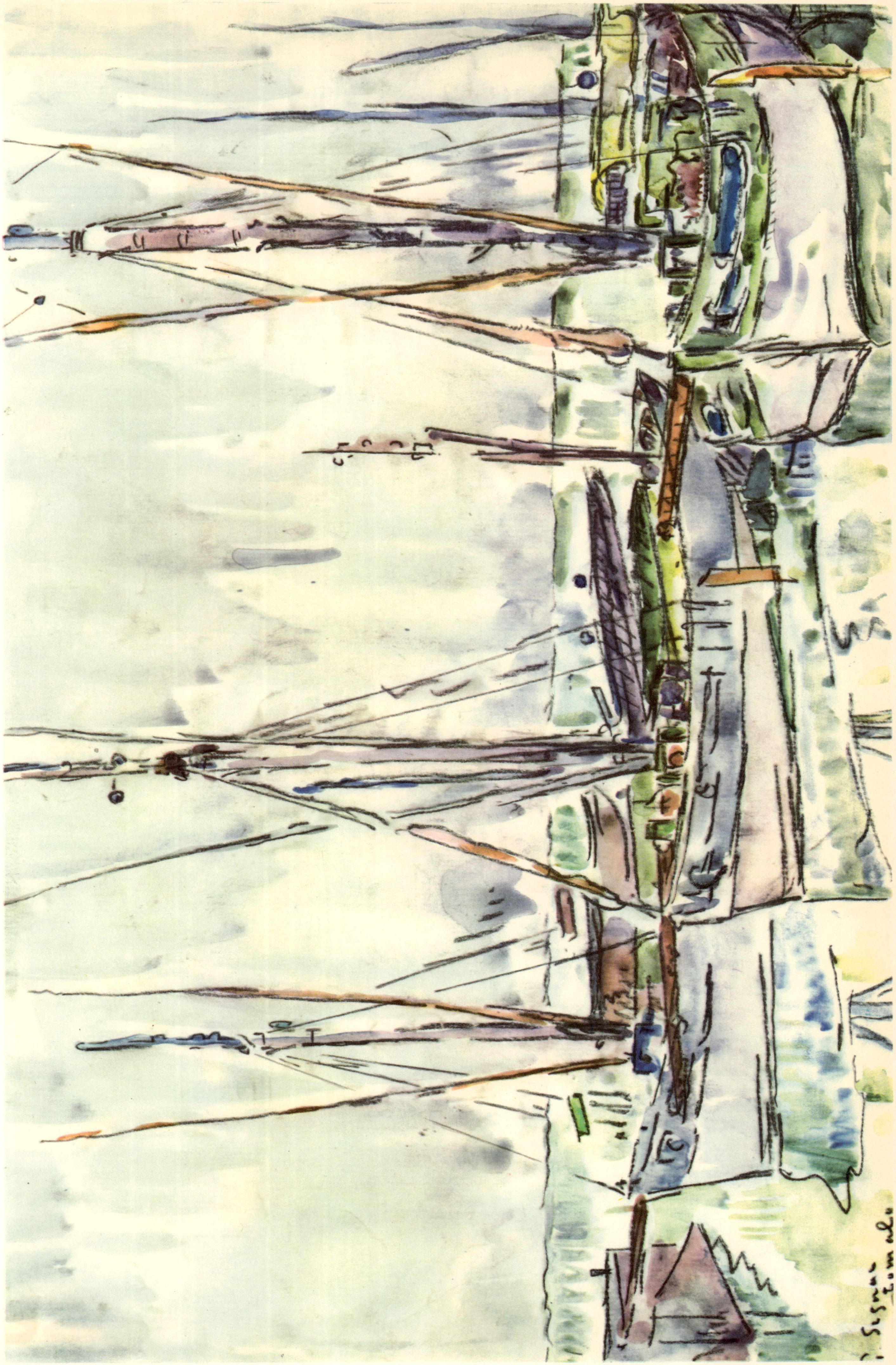

## PAUL SIGNAC

29 PETIT-ANDELY

Watercolour and charcoal, 30×44.4 cm. Marked bottom right: P. Signac 1923 Petit Andely. National Gallery, Prague (K 18 264), acquired 1924.

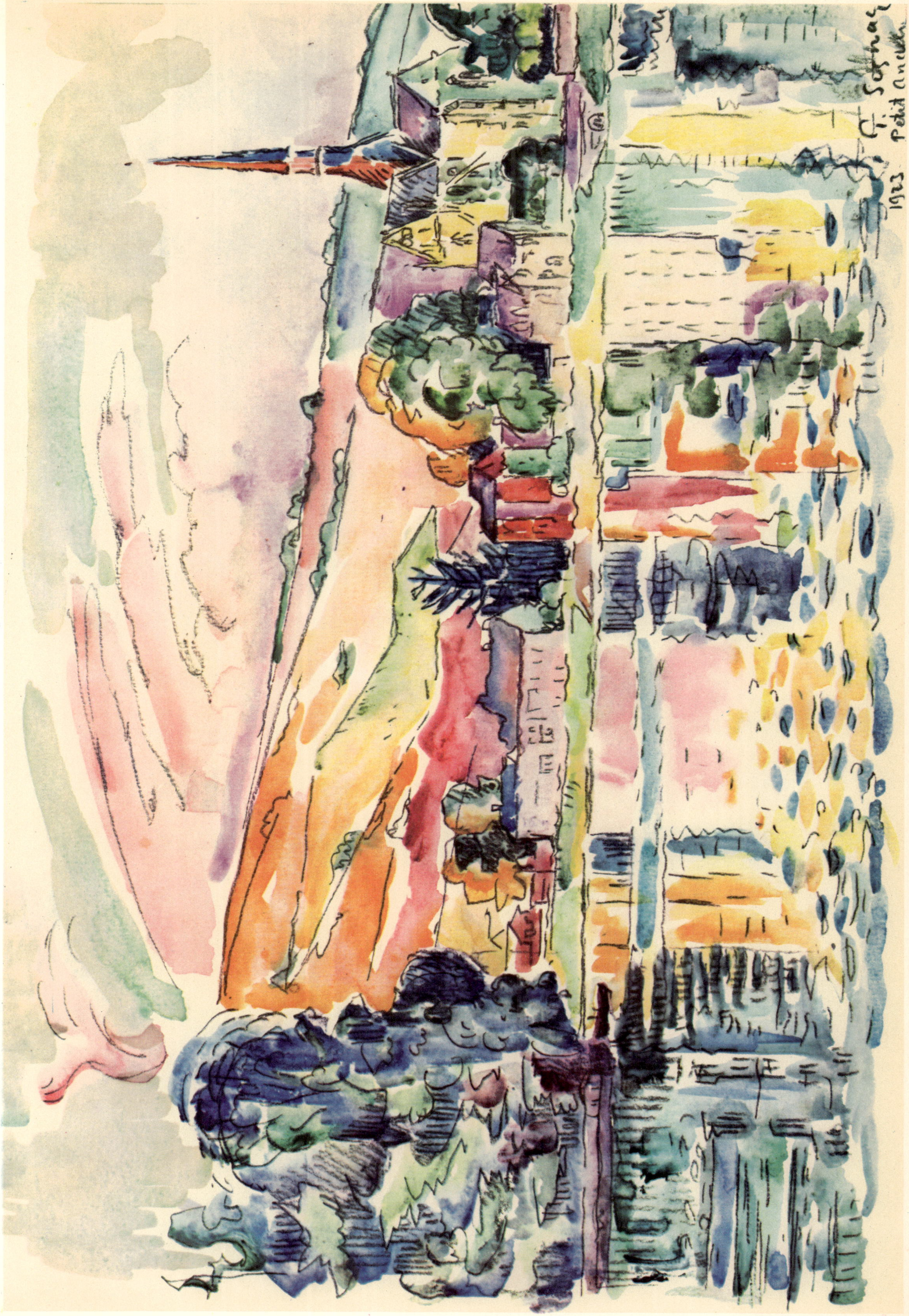
P. Signac
1923 Petit

PAUL SIGNAC

30 CROIX-DE-VIE

Watercolour and charcoal, 27.3 × 42.4 cm. Marked bottom left: P. Signac Croix-de-Vie. National Gallery, Prague (K 18 262), acquired 1924.

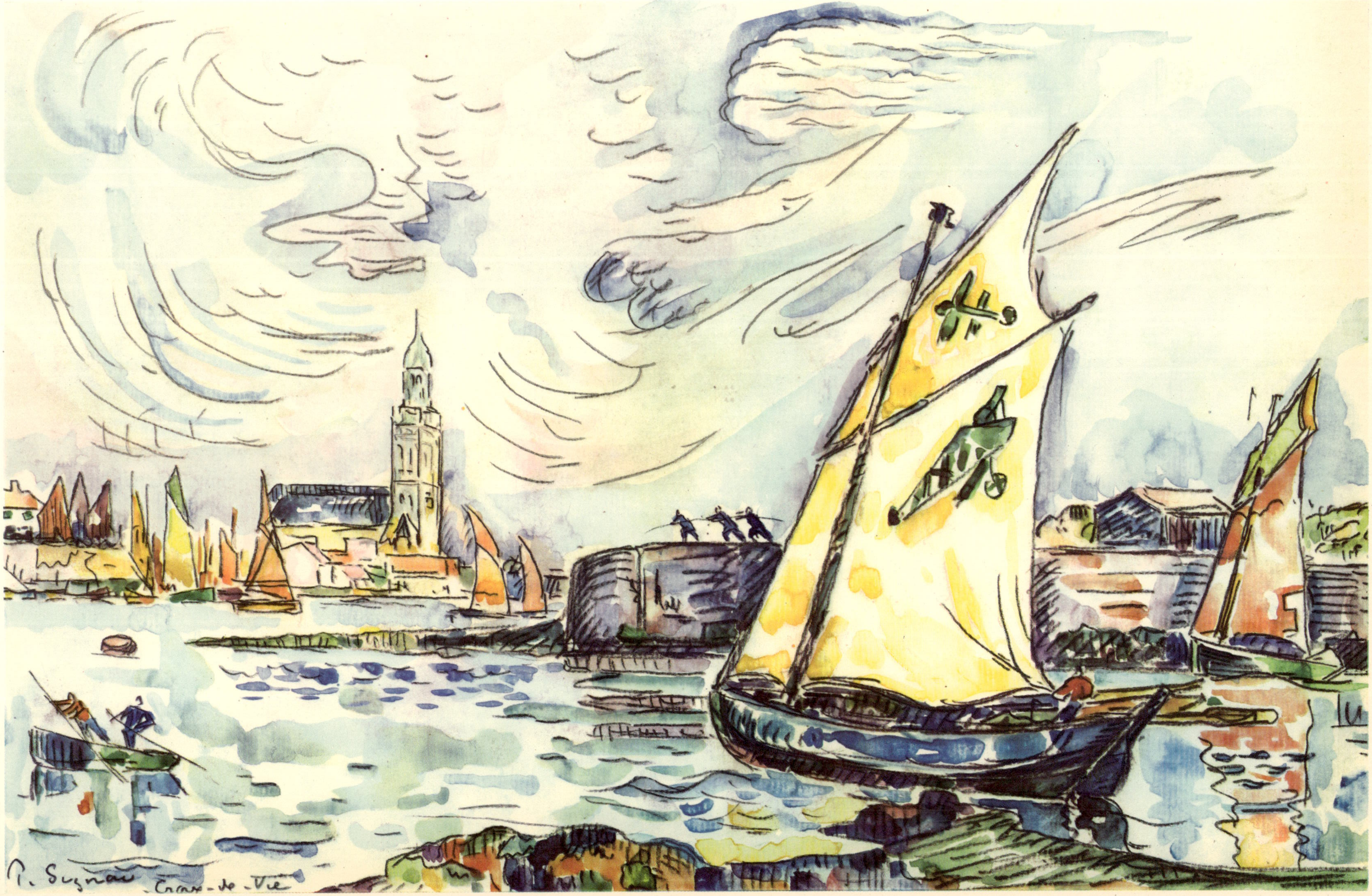

## PAUL SIGNAC

31 Still-life with Jug

Indian ink with brush on charcoal ground, yellow paper, 46.3 × 63.3 cm. Marked bottom right: P. Signac. National Gallery, Prague (K 18 265), acquired 1924.

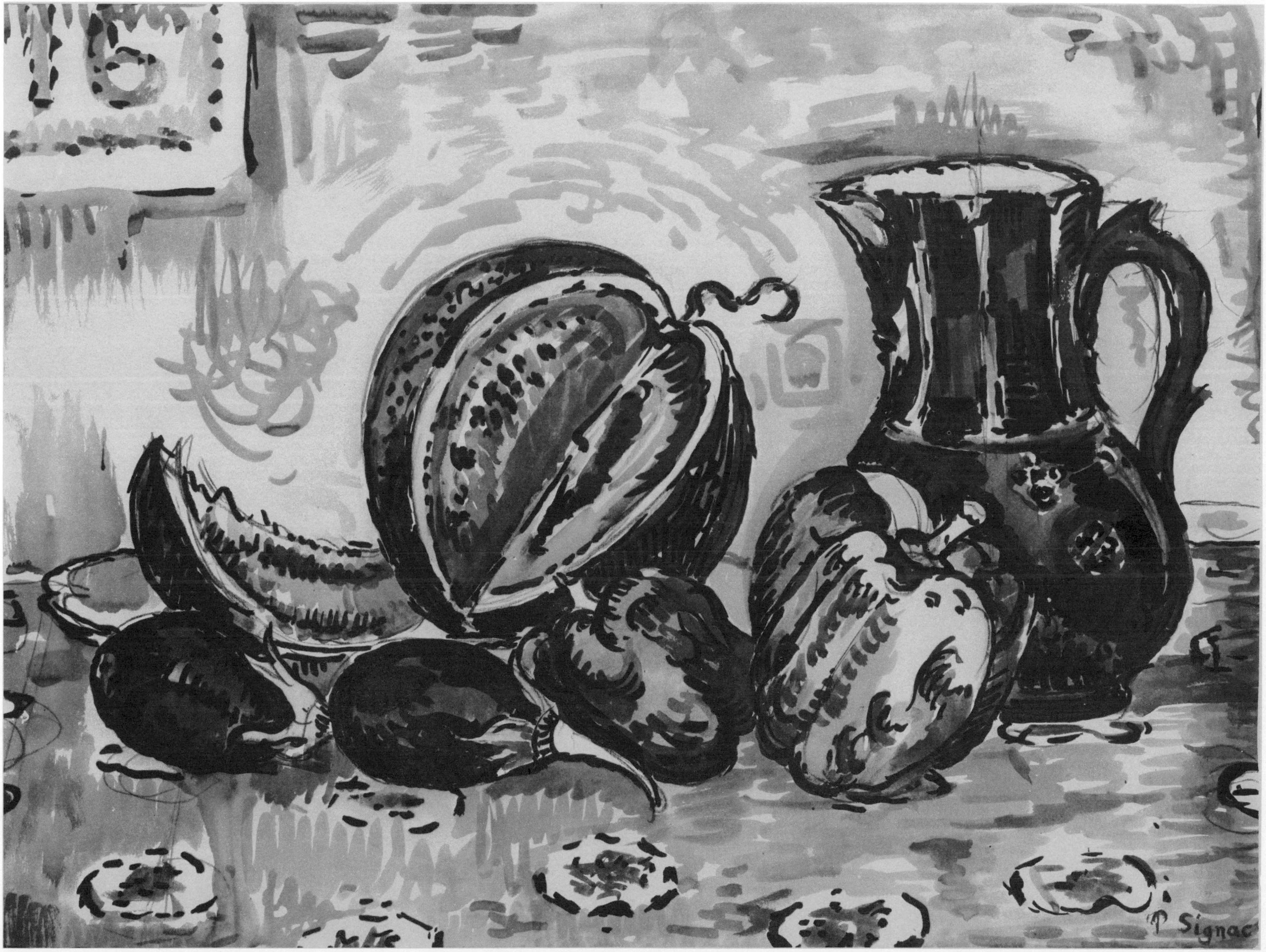
P. Signac

JEAN-LOUIS FORAIN

32 FIGURE STUDIES

Pen and watercolour, 31 × 19.9 cm. Marked bottom left: L. Forain. National Gallery, Prague (K 20 538), acquired 1951.

This drawing from the period between 1870 and 1880 is linked with Forain's work as an illustrator for a Paris review.

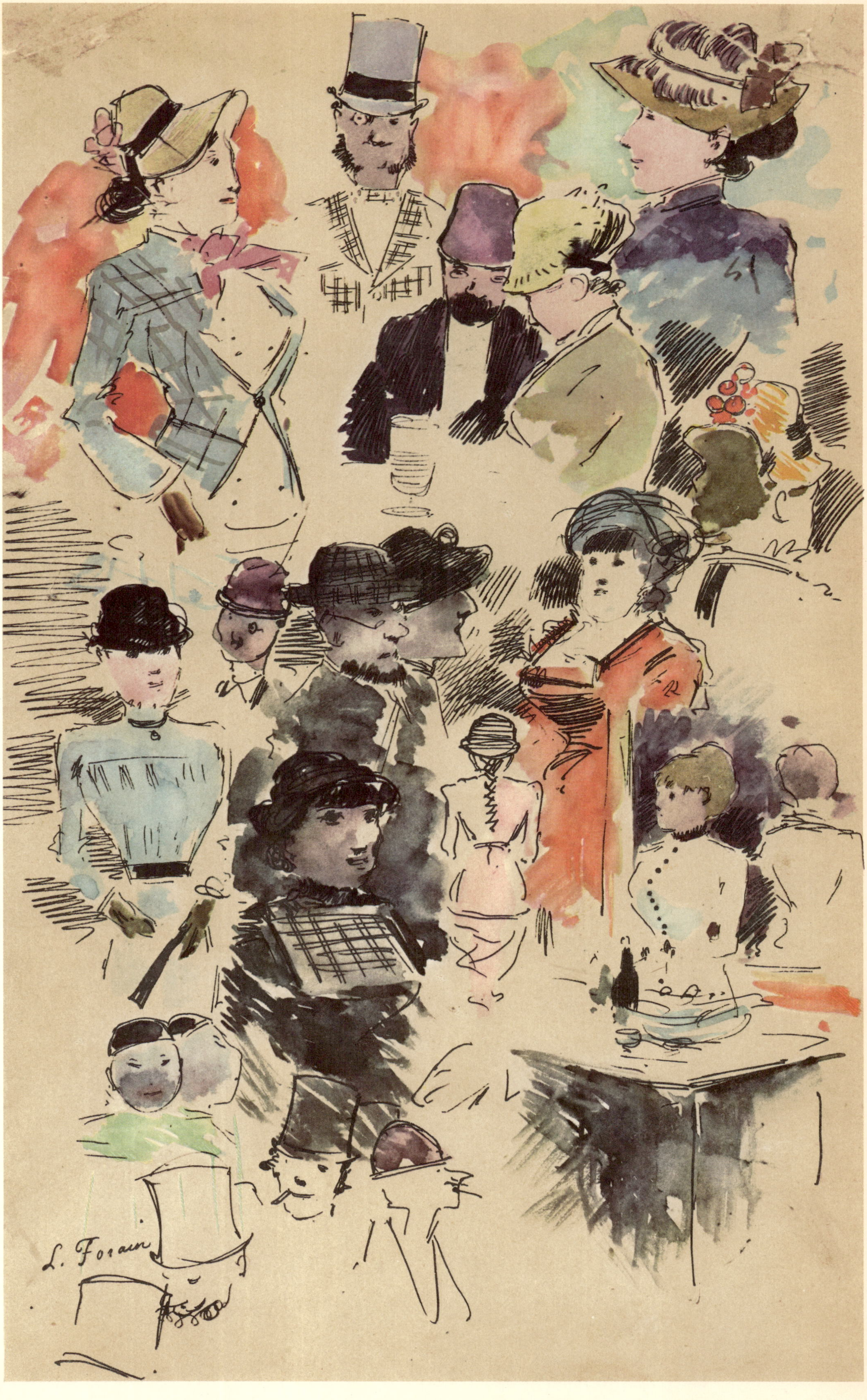
L. Forain

## JEAN-LOUIS FORAIN

33 THE ORATOR

Coloured chalks, 20.6×21.5 cm. Marked bottom left: Forain. National Gallery, Prague (K 33 819), acquired 1961.

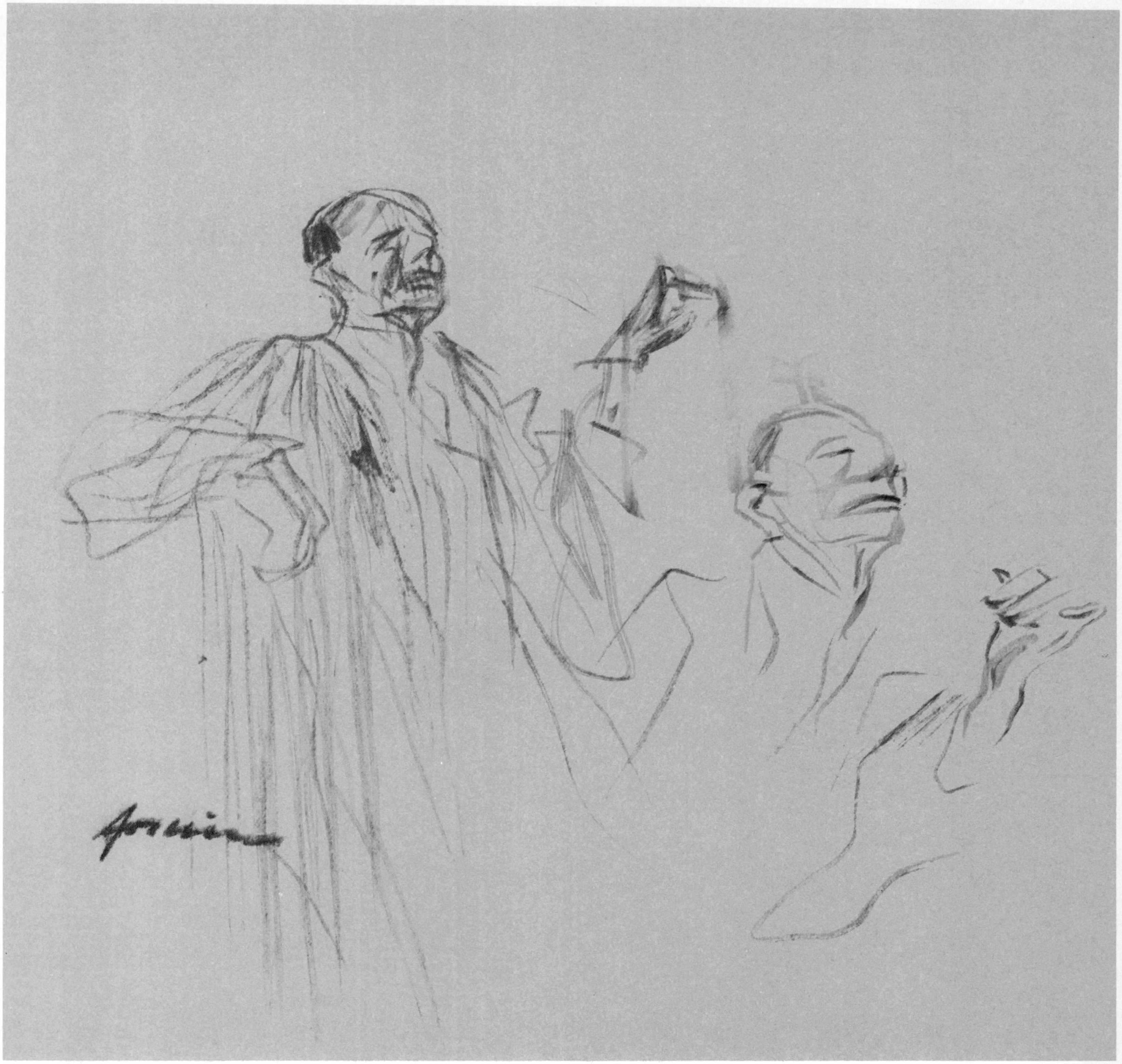

FELICIEN ROPS

34 IN A PARISIAN CAFE

Indian ink with brush on writing paper. Museum of Czech Literature–Karásek Gallery, Prague.

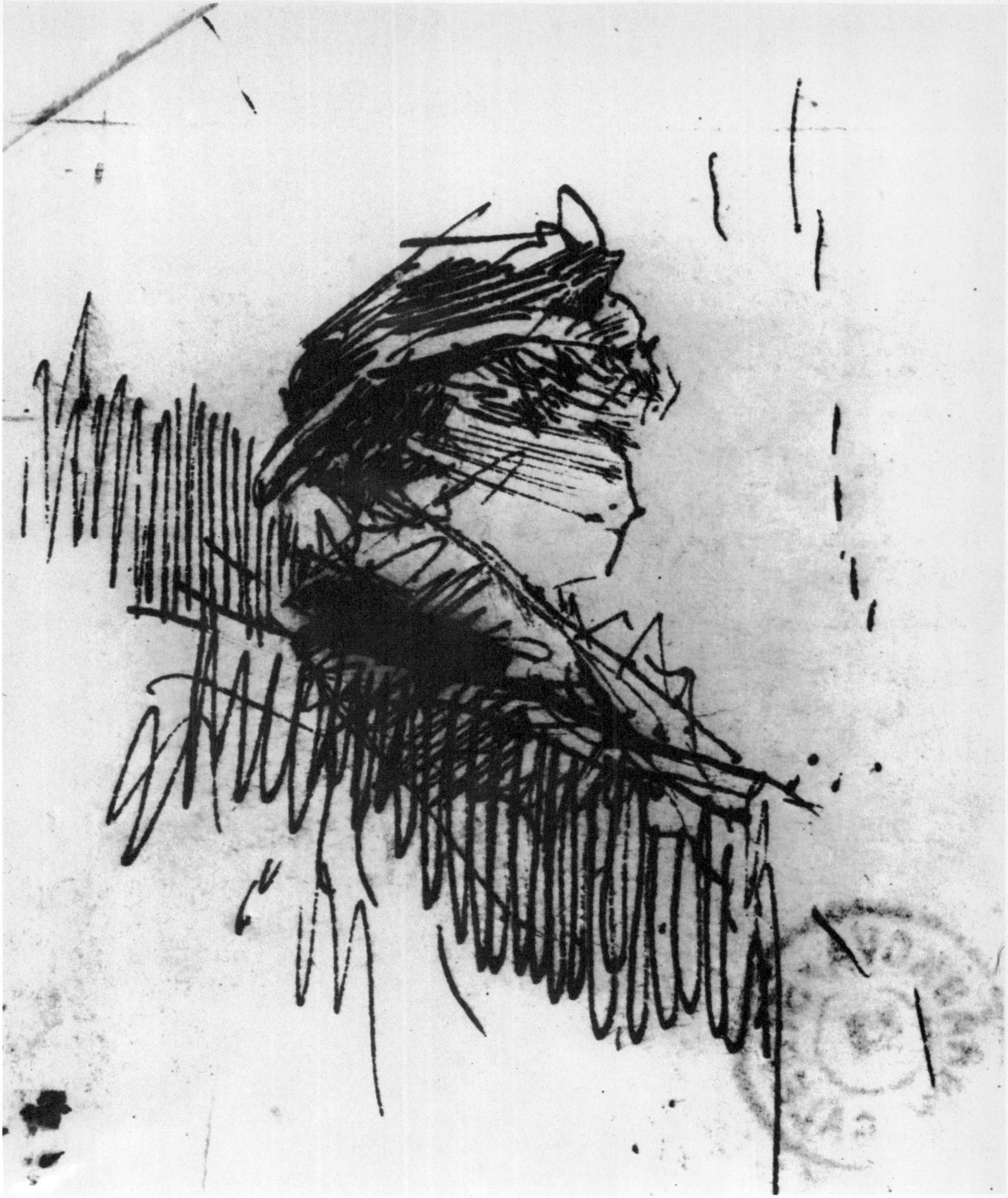

FELICIEN ROPS

35 IN A PARISIAN CAFE

Indian ink with brush. Museum of Czech Literature–Karásek Gallery, Prague.

This sketch and the preceding one are probably from the period between 1875 and 1880 when Rops had settled in Paris.

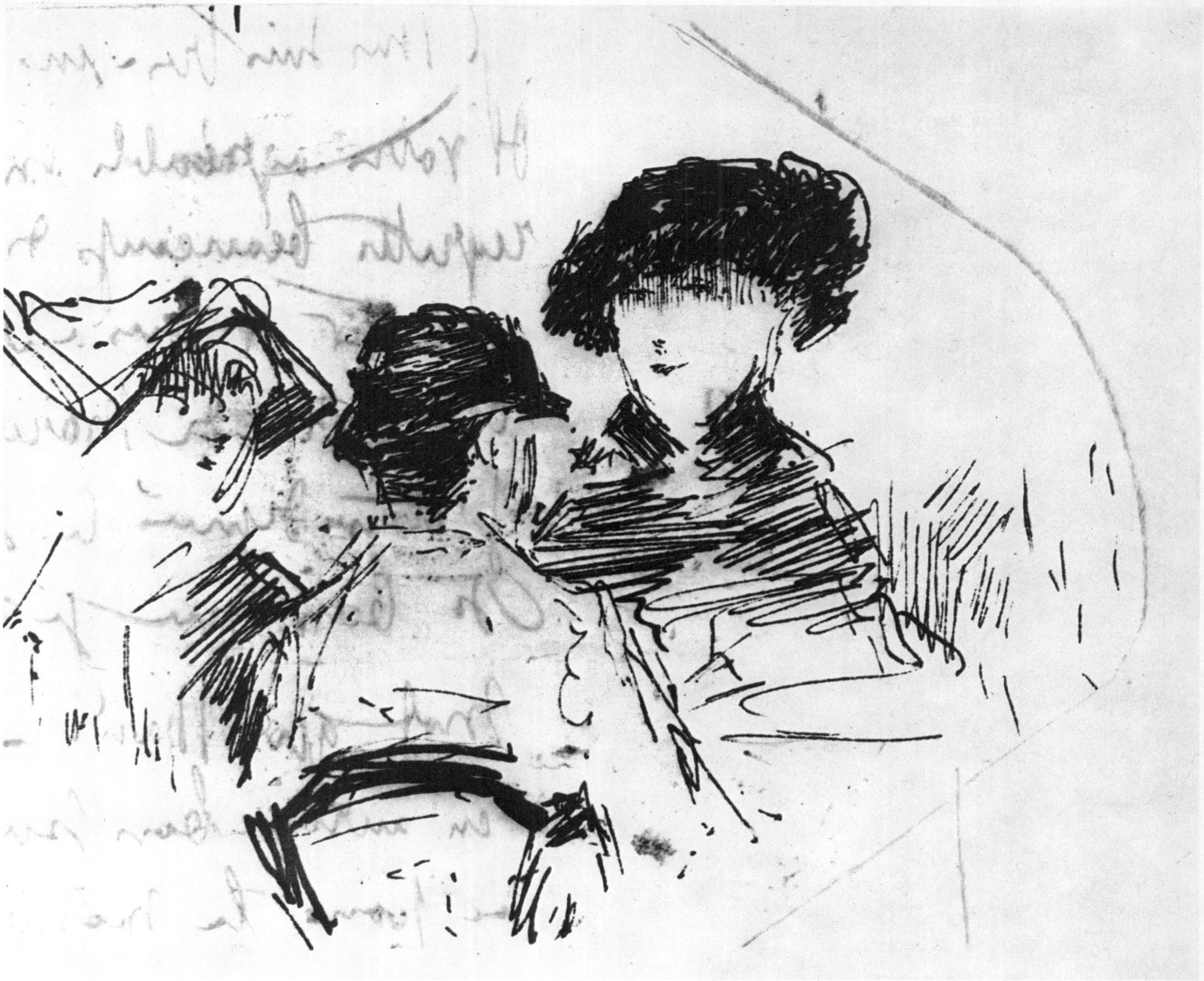

THEOPHILE ALEXANDRE STEINLEN

36 NUDE

Charcoal, 20.5 × 21 cm. Marked bottom left with the seal: St. Private collection, Prague.

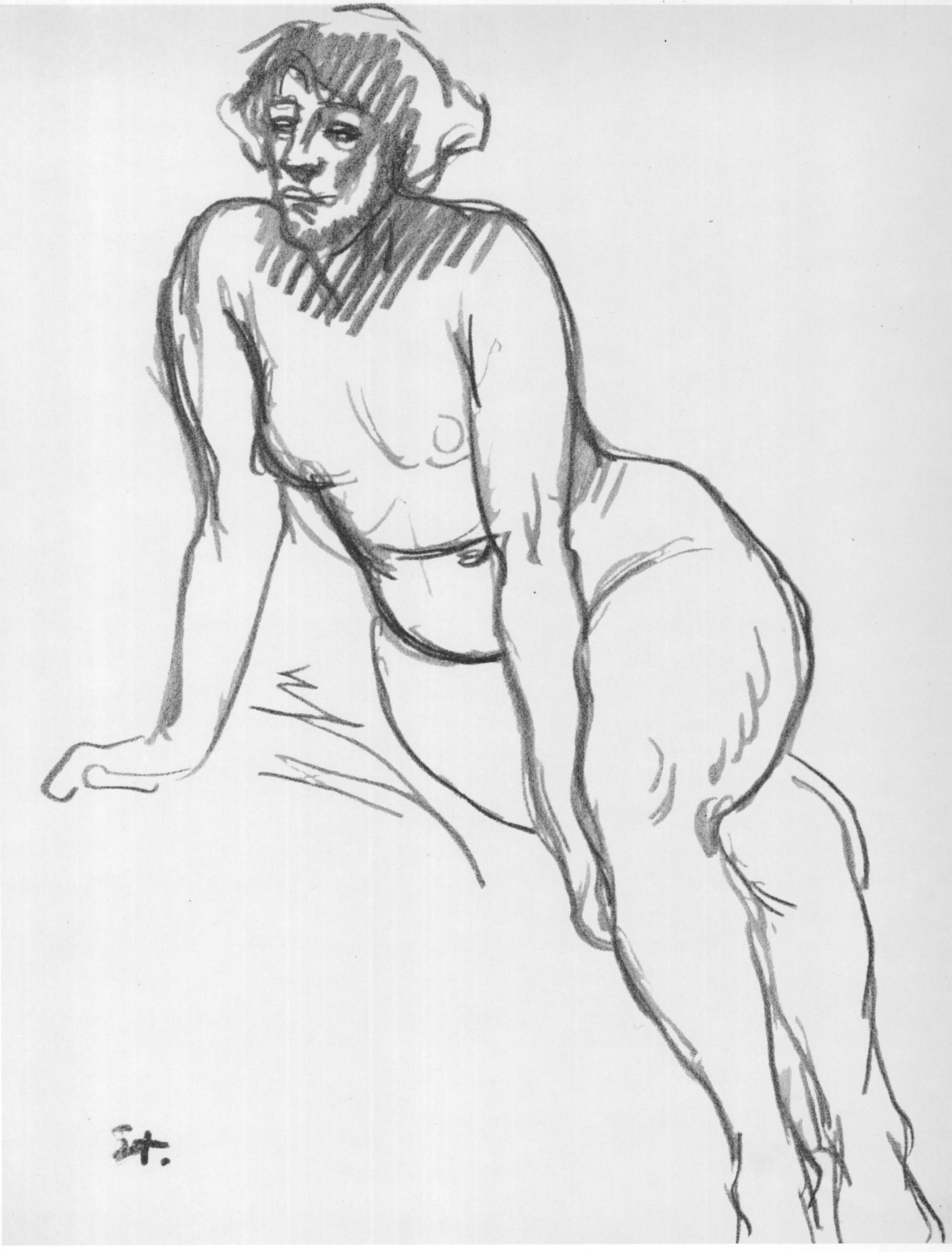

HENRI DE TOULOUSE-LAUTREC

37 SKETCH OF A REARING HORSE

Pencil, 11.5 × 14.5 cm. Museum of Czech Literature–Karásek Gallery, Prague.

From about 1880.

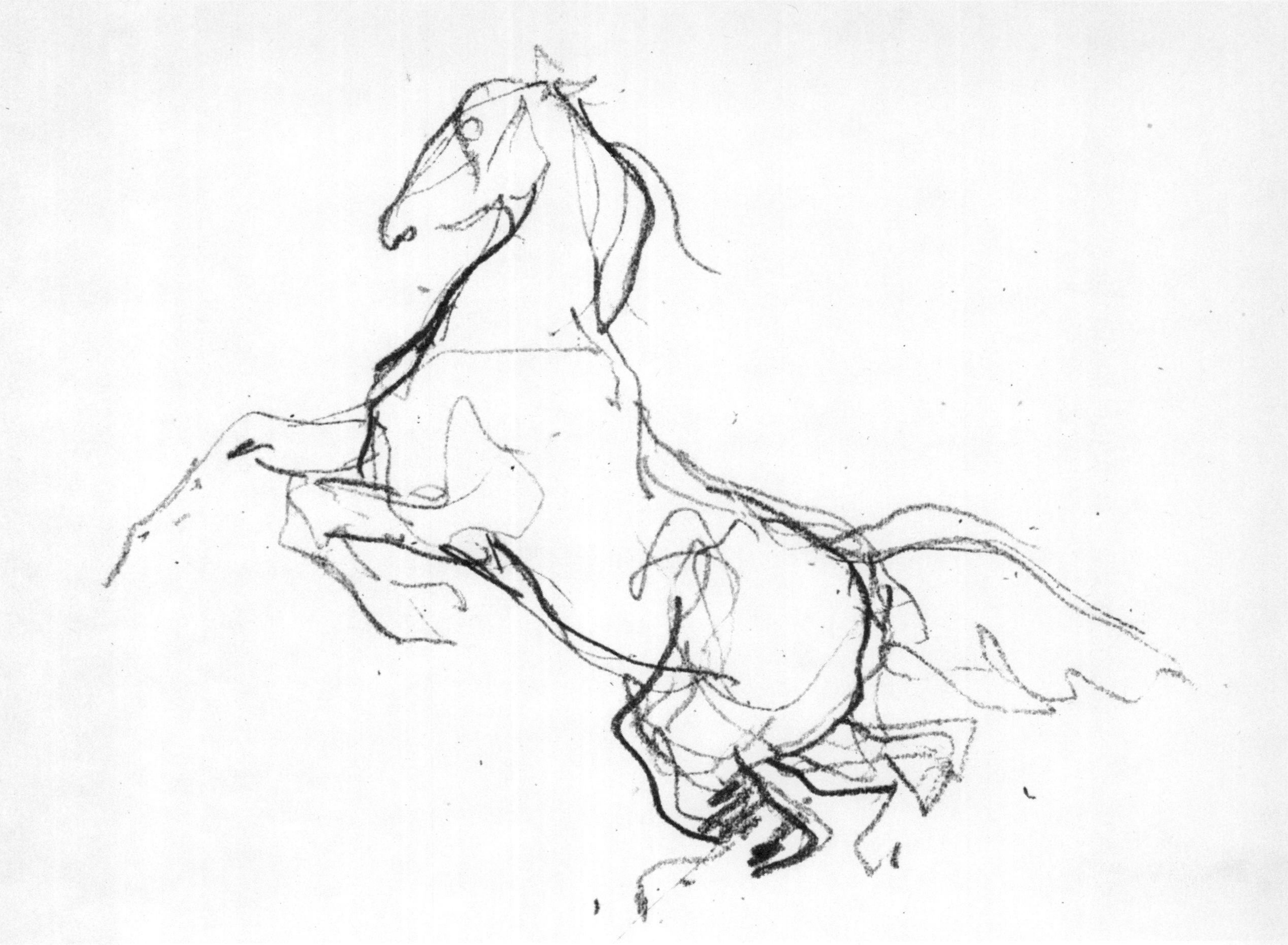

AUGUSTE RODIN

38 STUDY OF A STANDING NUDE

Pencil, 23.8 × 16.7 cm. National Gallery, Prague (K 31 655), acquired 1957.

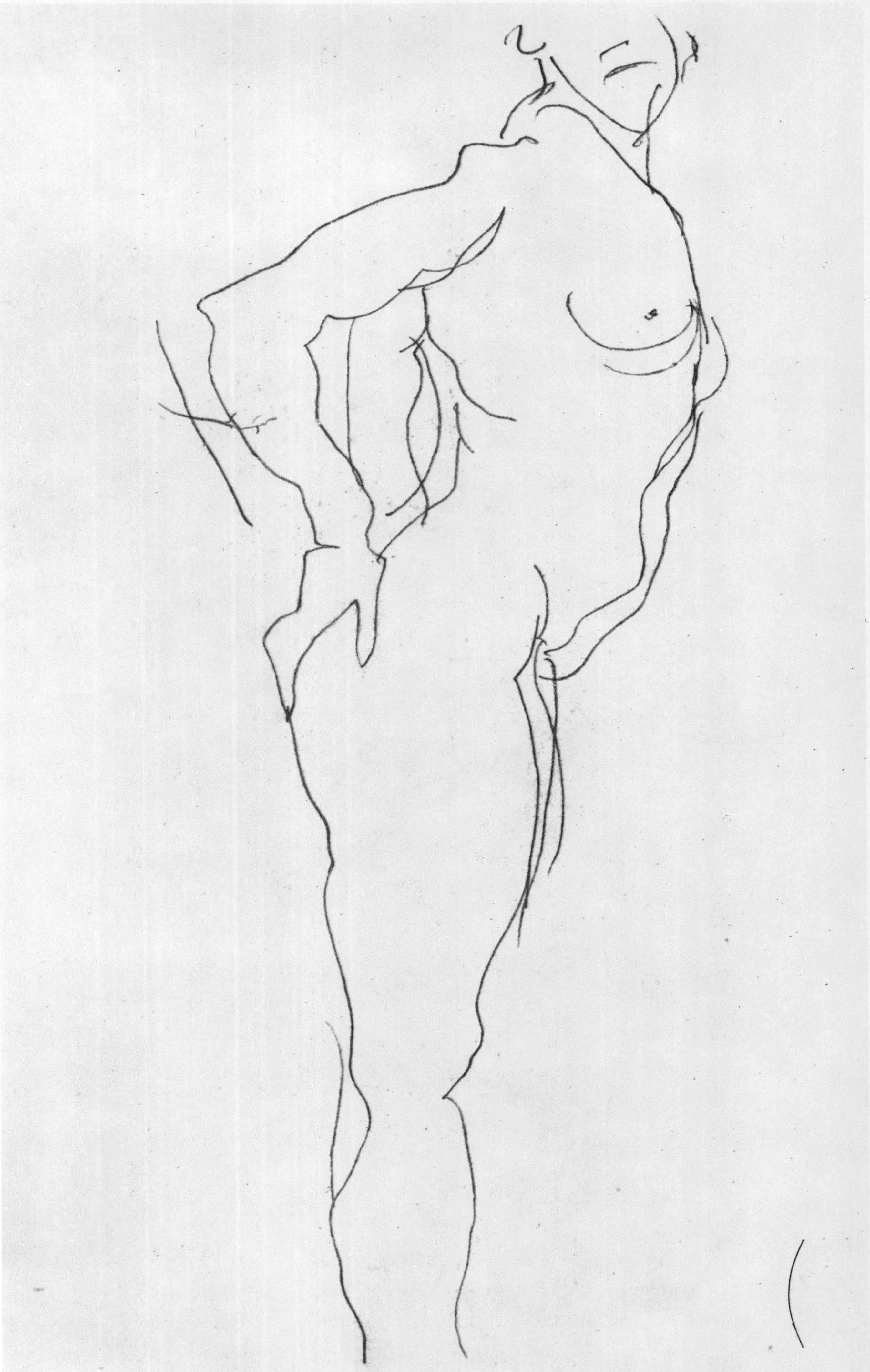

AUGUSTE RODIN

39 NUDE KNEELING WOMAN

Watercolour and pencil, 27.7×23 cm. Marked bottom right: Aug. Rodin. National Gallery, Prague (K 16 589), acquired 1936.

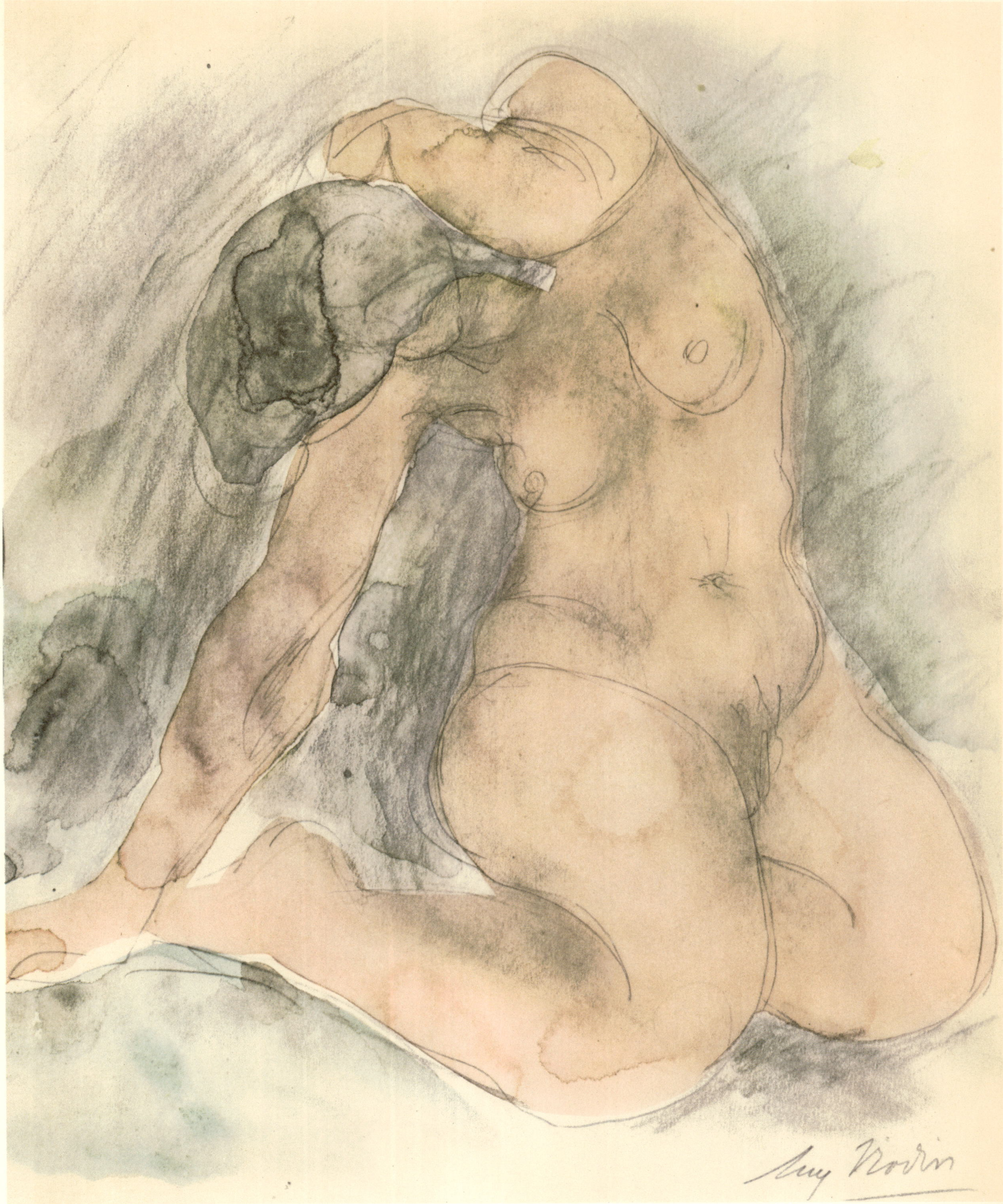
Aug Rodin

AUGUSTE RODIN

40 STUDY OF A CROUCHING NUDE

Pencil, 17.7×24.2 cm. National Gallery, Prague (K 31 656), acquired 1957.

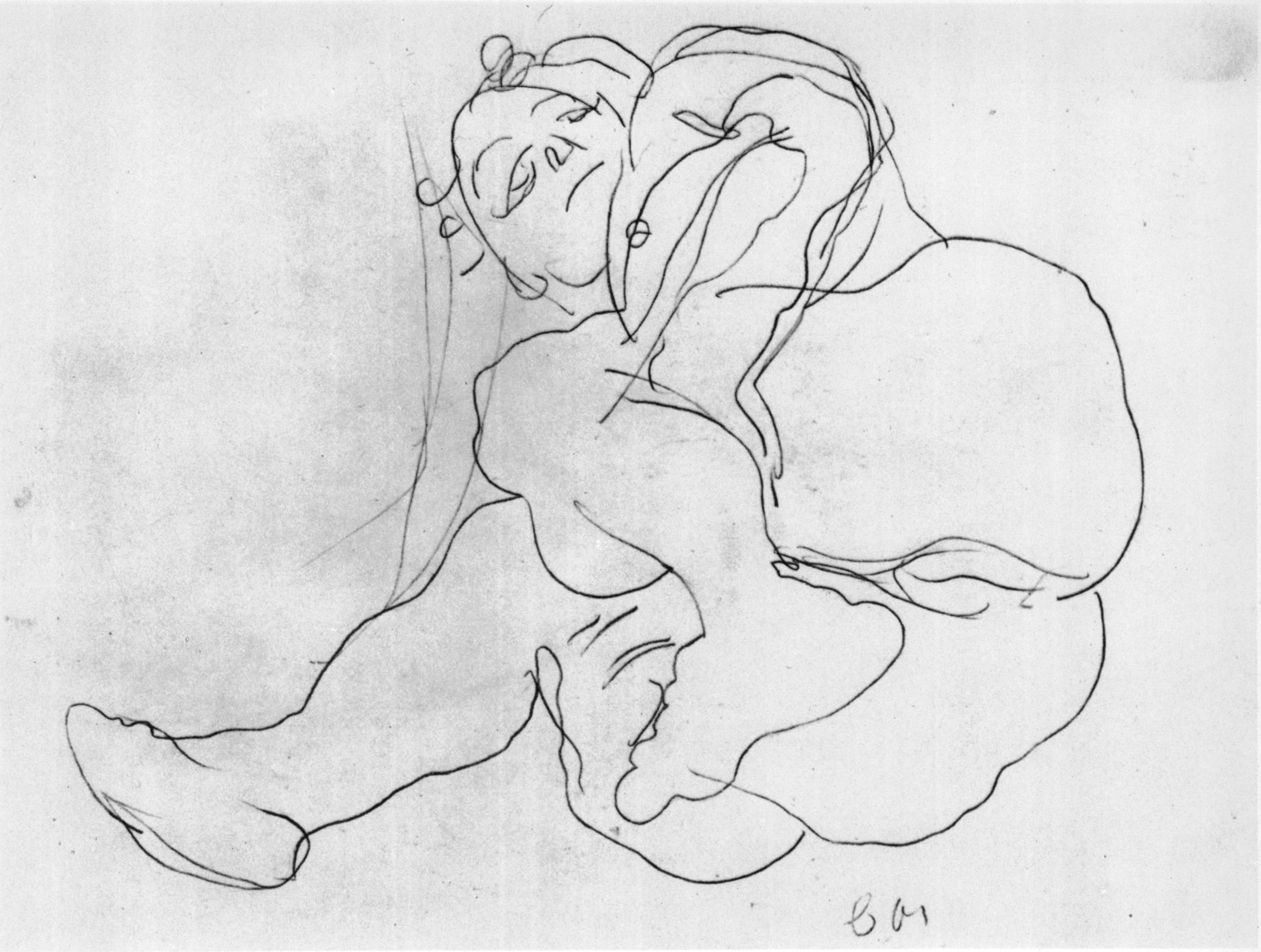

PAUL CEZANNE

41 SKETCH OF A TREE

Pencil, 47.5 × 31.3 cm. National Gallery, Prague (K 13 925), acquired 1923.

The collection of drawings by Cézanne in the gallery comes from the last period of his work when he was painting landscapes in the vicinity of Montagne Ste-Victoire and the Bibémus Quarry. These landscapes display the results of his ideas on volume and space in terms of colour which inspired the Cubists. It was at this time that he did a series of watercolours and drawings in which he was concerned with resolving these problems.

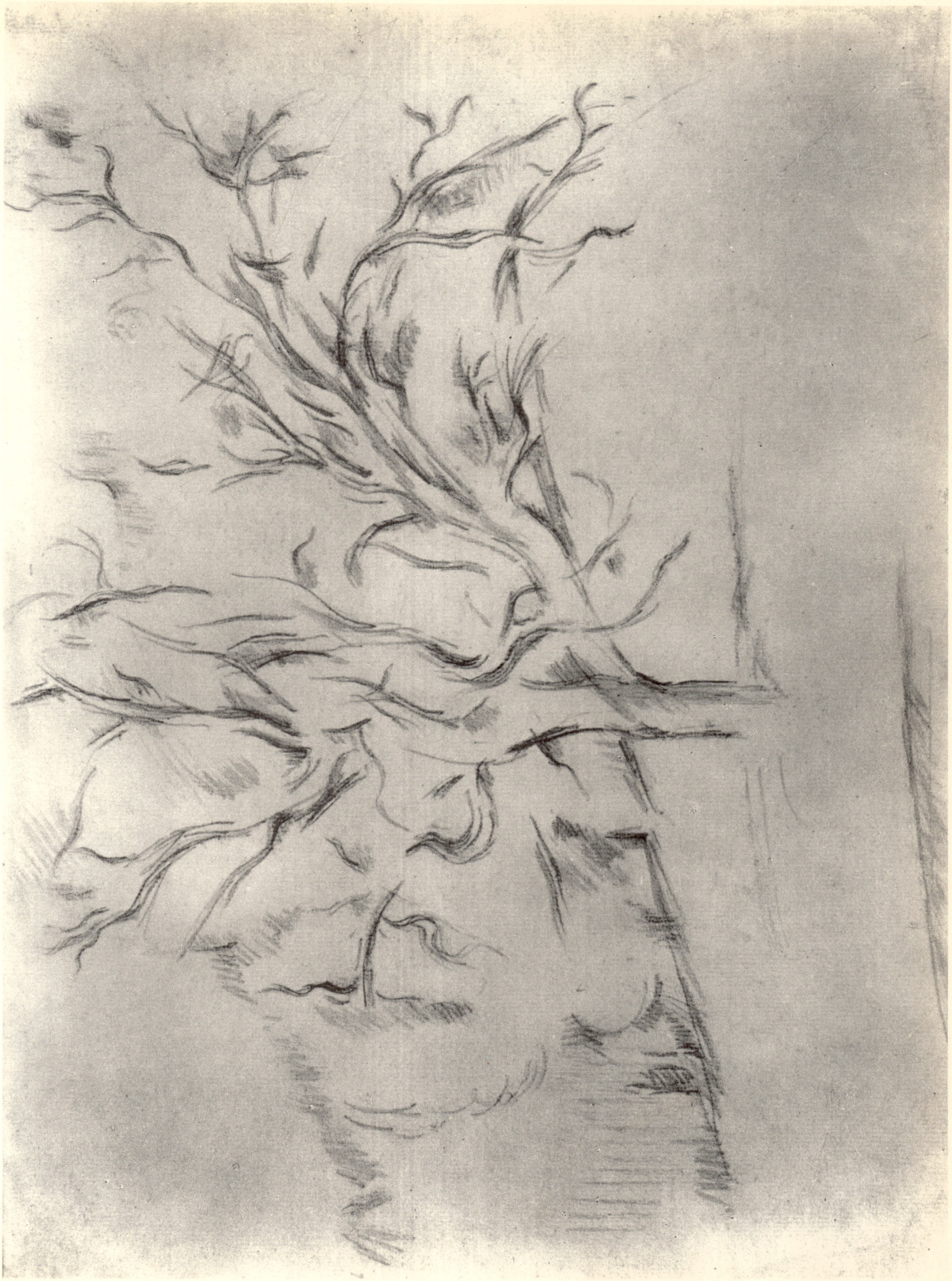

PAUL CEZANNE

42 Sketch of a Landscape

Pencil, 32.3 × 52 cm. National Gallery, Prague (K 13 923), acquired 1923.

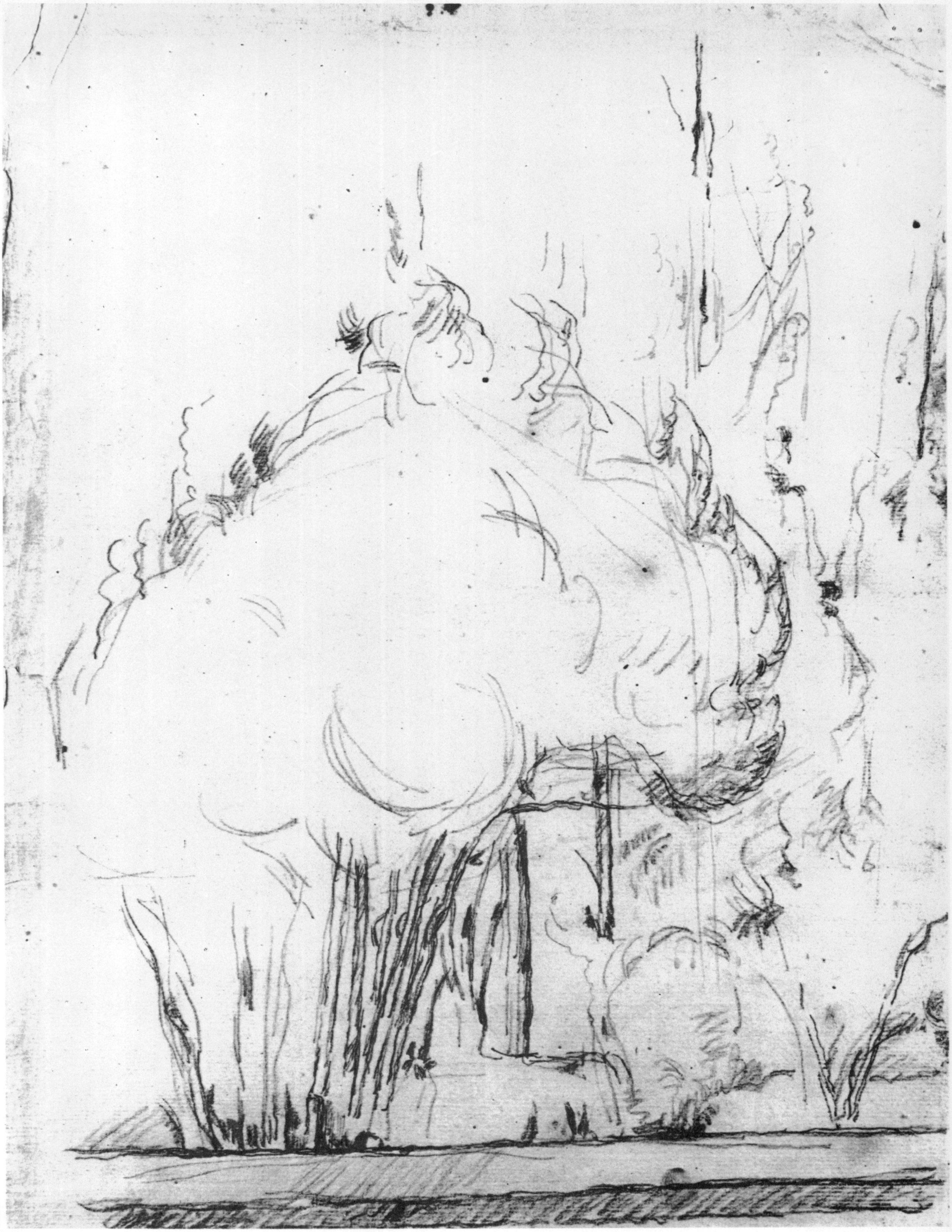

PAUL CEZANNE

43 SKETCH OF A LANDSCAPE

Pencil, 31.6 × 54.2 cm. National Gallery, Prague (K 13 924), acquired 1923.

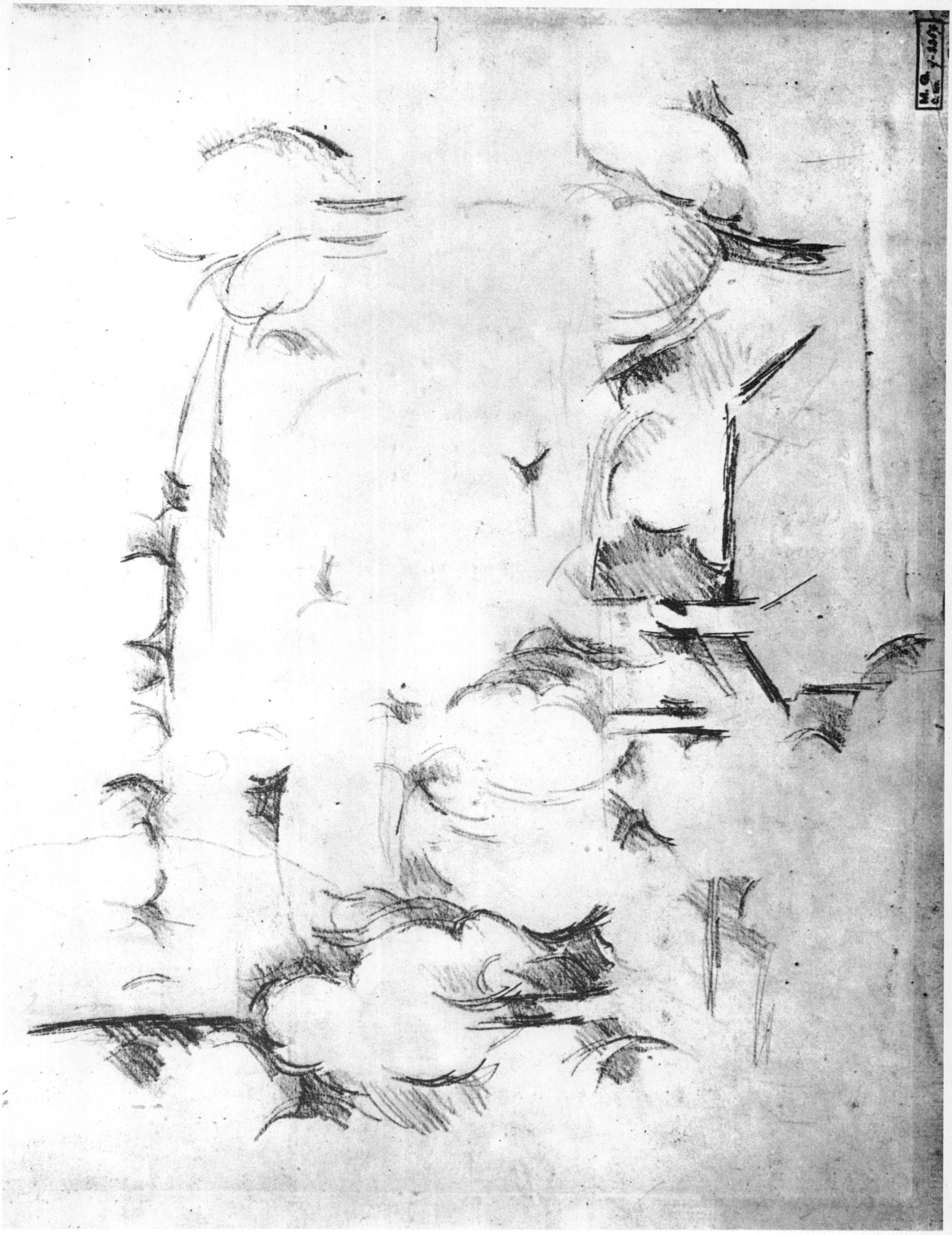

## ANDRE DERAIN

44 LANDSCAPE

Pencil and watercolour, 23 × 30 cm. Marked bottom right: a.d. National Gallery, Prague (K 37 039), acquired 1963, formerly Dr. A. Starý collection, gift of Dr. V. Nebeský.

The drawing dates from about 1910 at Cagnes when Derain was just beginning to work and was under the influence of Cézanne.

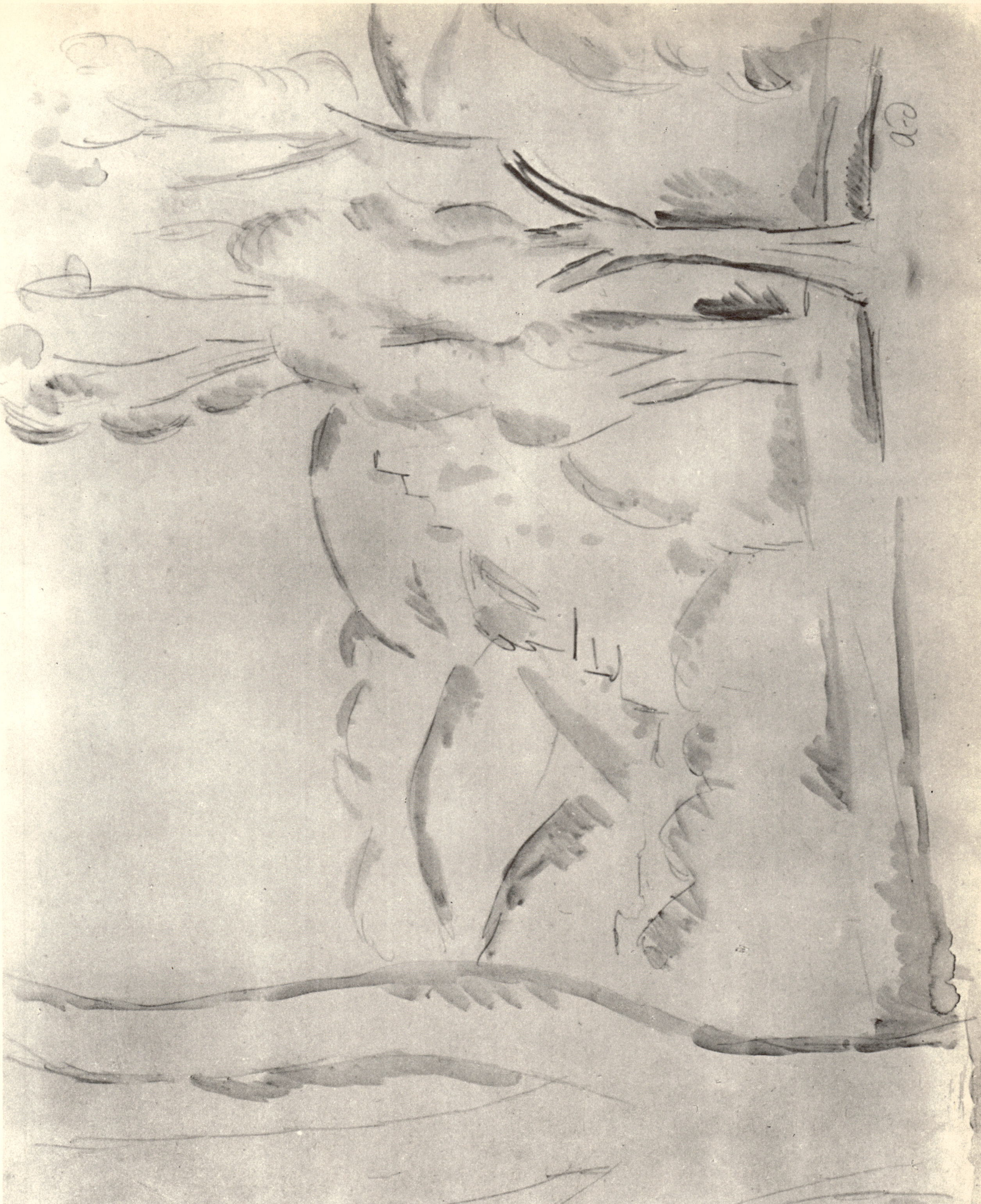

ANDRE DERAIN

45 STILL-LIFE WITH A GREEN JUG

Pencil, 22.9×26 cm. Marked bottom right: a derain. Fine Arts Gallery, Ostrava (Gr. 1453).

This drawing of 1910 anticipates the painting of the same subject.

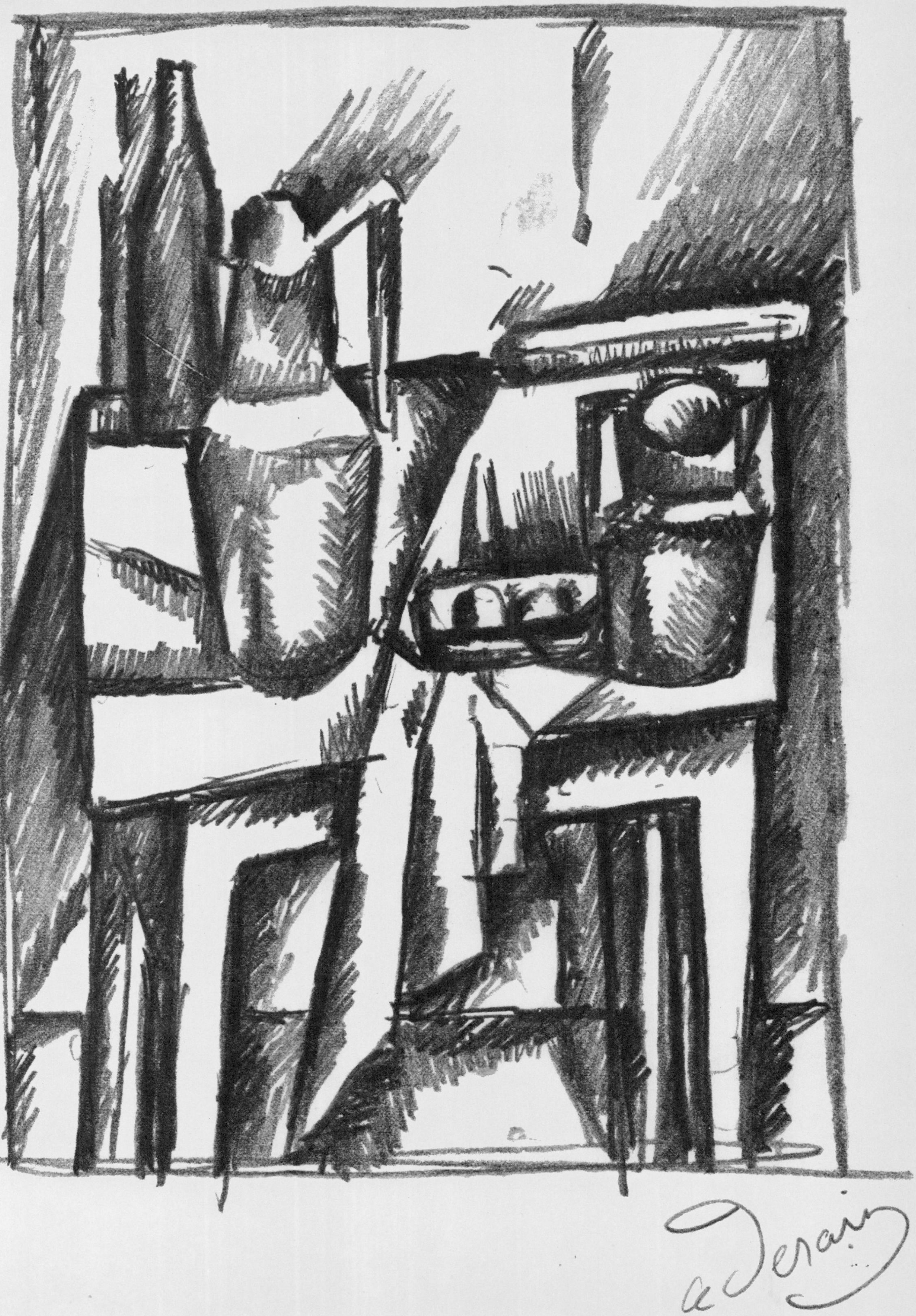
a Derain

ANDRE DERAIN

46 CAGNES LANDSCAPE

Pencil and watercolour, 45.3 × 58 cm. (inside the border). On the back a label inscribed in the artist's hand (?): derain, cagnes 1910. Private collection, Prague. The labels are those of the Kahnweiler and Vildrac Galleries, Paris, and the Emil Richter Salon, Dresden.

The drawing comes from the same period as Plate 44.

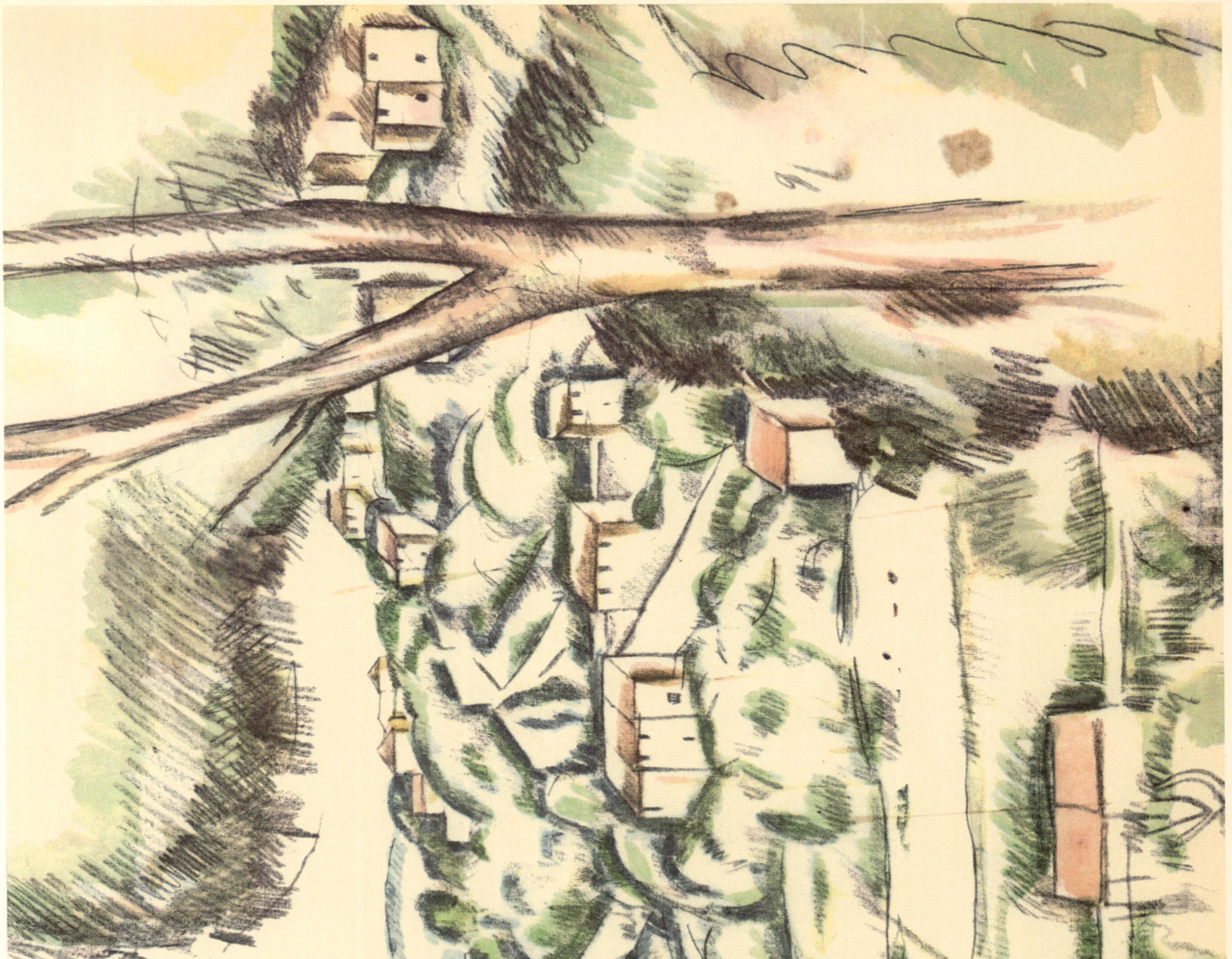

PABLO PICASSO

47 STILL-LIFE WITH A BOTTLE

Pencil on cream paper, 49.5 × 39 cm. Marked on the back above left: Picasso. Private collection, Prague.

This drawing dates from 1913–14.

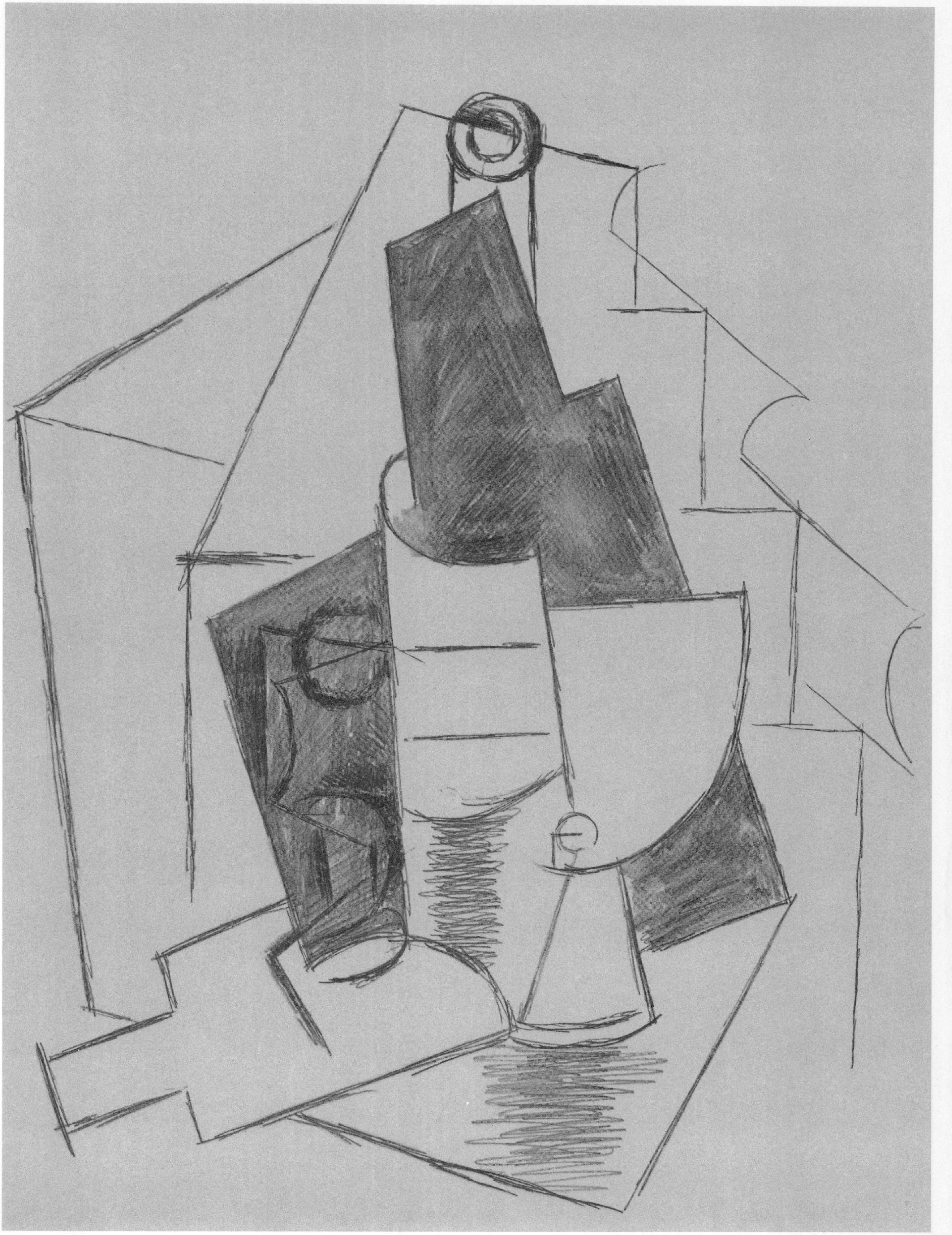

PABLO PICASSO

48 PORTRAIT OF A MAN AND A WOMAN

Black and coloured chalks, 12.6 × 17.9 cm. Marked bottom right: Picasso; above the signature, added in pen with Indian ink: A Mme Bernard. Fine Arts Gallery, Ostrava (Gr. 1445), formerly V. Kramář collection, previously Modern Gallery of H. Tannhauser, Munich.

The drawing is a classical work from the period when Picasso, on his arrival in Paris in 1900, was influenced by Toulouse-Lautrec.

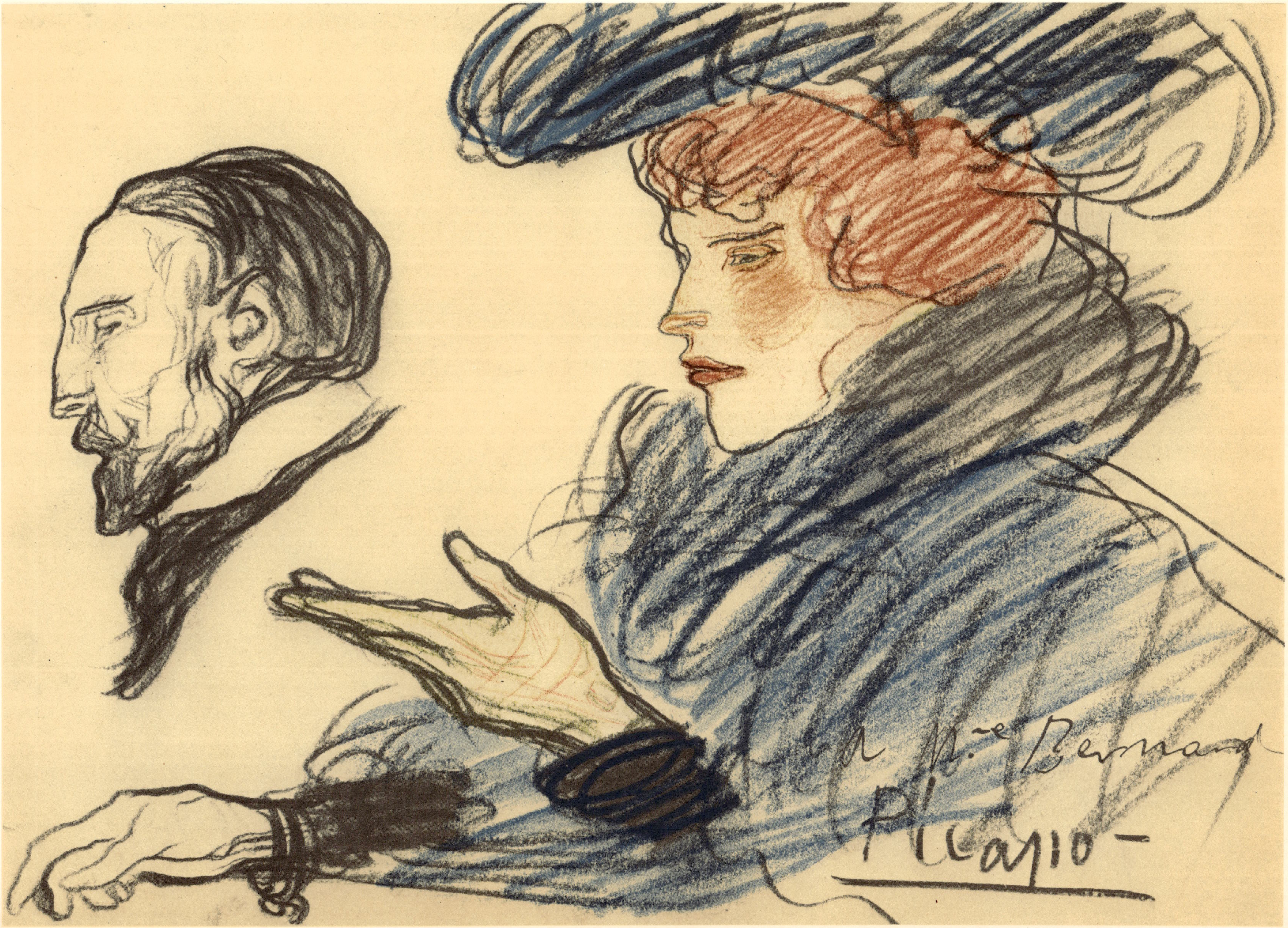
a Mme Bernard
Picasso

PABLO PICASSO

49 PROFILE OF A FEMALE NUDE

Coloured pencil, watercolour and gouache on lined paper, 20.9 × 12.1 cm. Marked on the back, bottom right: Picasso. Private collection, Prague, formerly V. Kramář collection.

This nude dates from 1905–6.

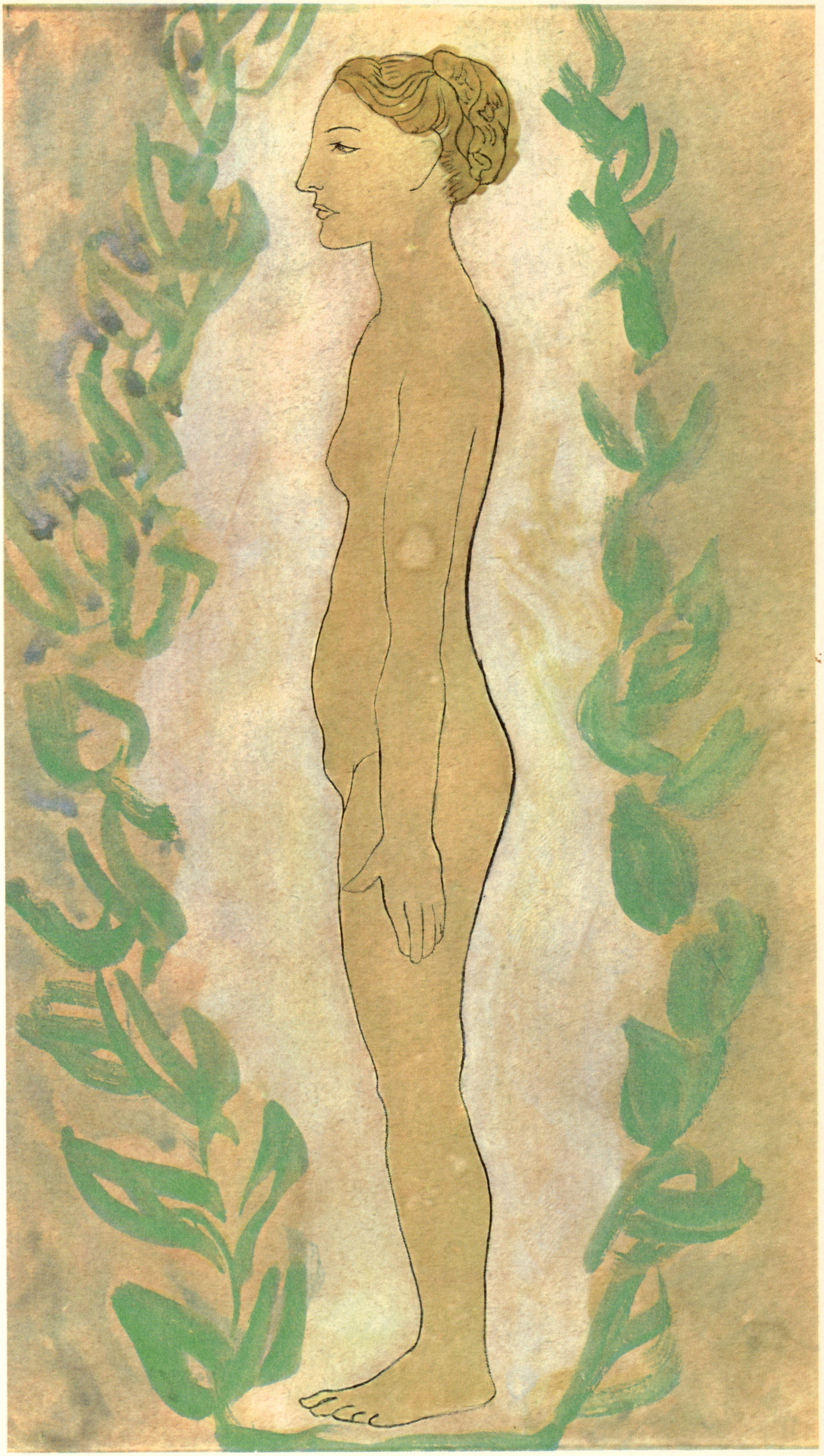

PABLO PICASSO

50 FEMALE NUDE

Pencil and watercolour, 62×46 cm. (inside the border). Marked bottom left: Picasso. National Gallery, Prague (K 34 809), acquired 1962, formerly Čeřovský collection, earlier Pierre Gallery, Paris.

This drawing is related to the studies of about 1907 for the picture *Les Demoiselles d'Avignon* (Museum of Art, New York) which bear traces of the influence of Negro sculpture.

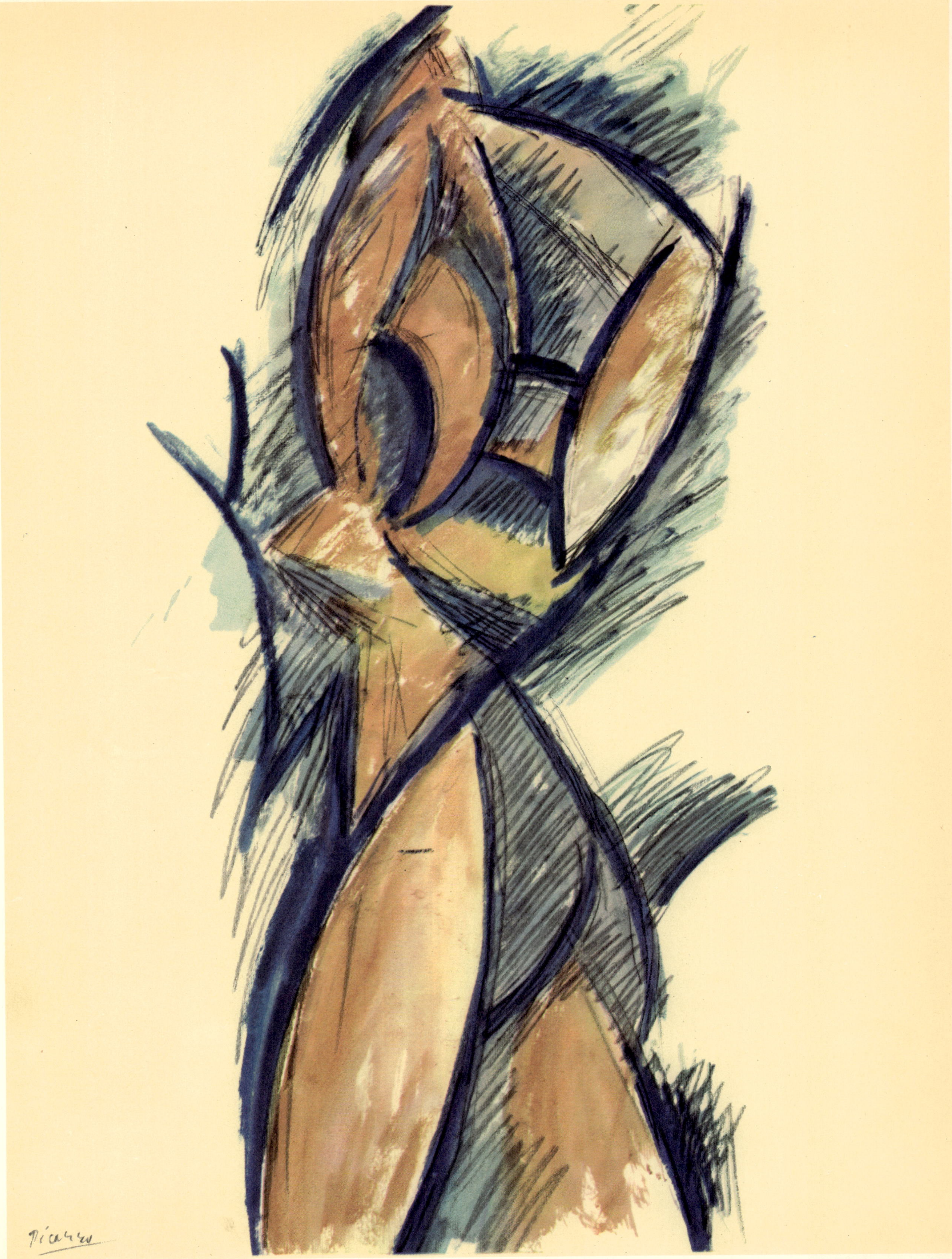
Picasso

PABLO PICASSO

51 THE GUITAR

Pencil and gouache, 62×46.5 cm. Private collection, Prague, earlier V. Kramář collection.

This drawing was executed about 1913–14. The painter has used paper imitating marble, as an optical trick; such experiments led to assemblages with glued paper.

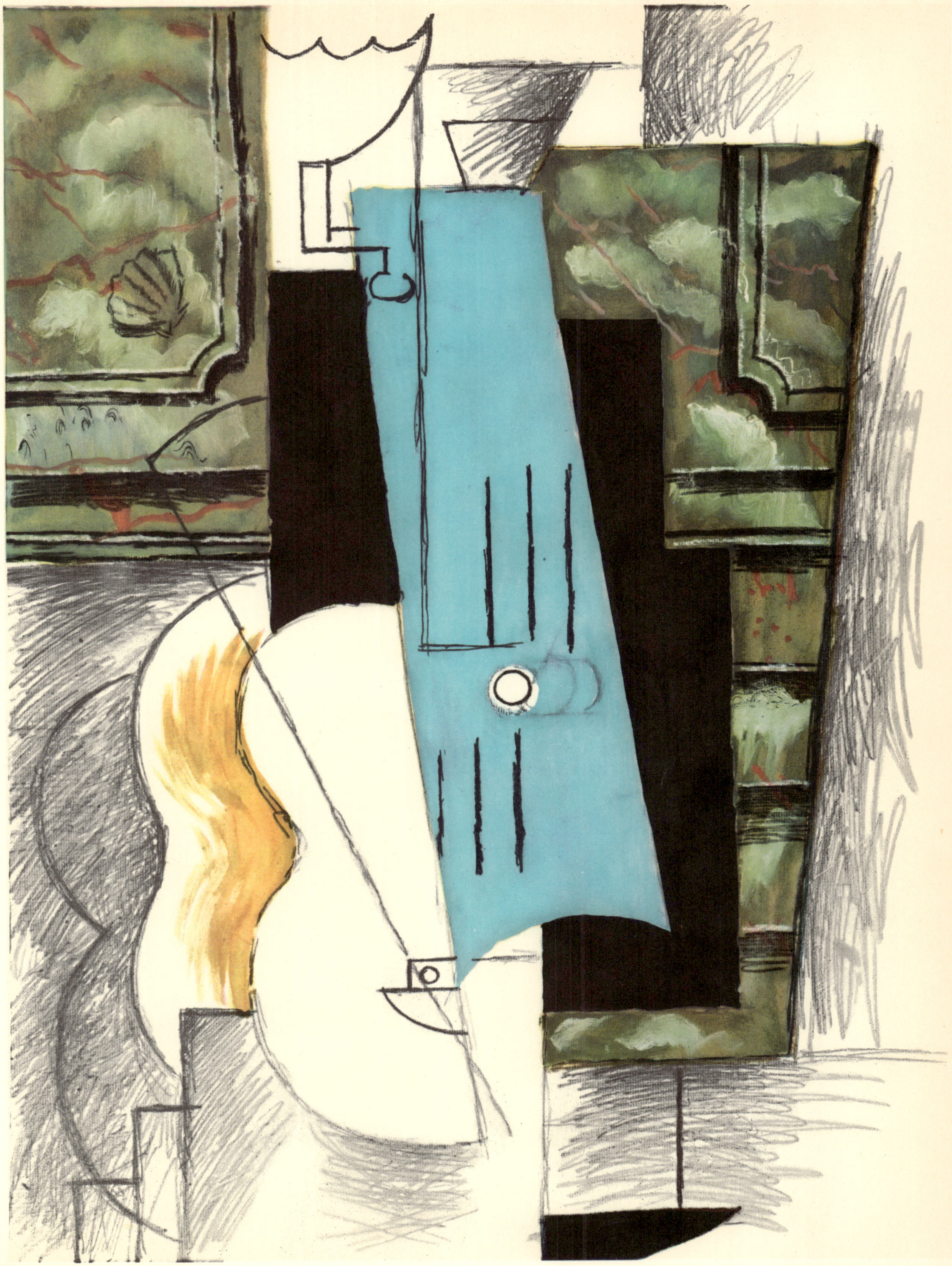

## PABLO PICASSO

52 The Sculptor's Studio

Indian ink, pen, watercolour, and silver-white. 39.5 × 50 cm. (cut out from a border). Marked bottom right: Picasso Cannes 18 Julliettes XXXIII. Private collection, Brno.

This drawing dates from a holiday in 1933 when Picasso stayed in the south of France, as does a series of other drawings on the same theme.

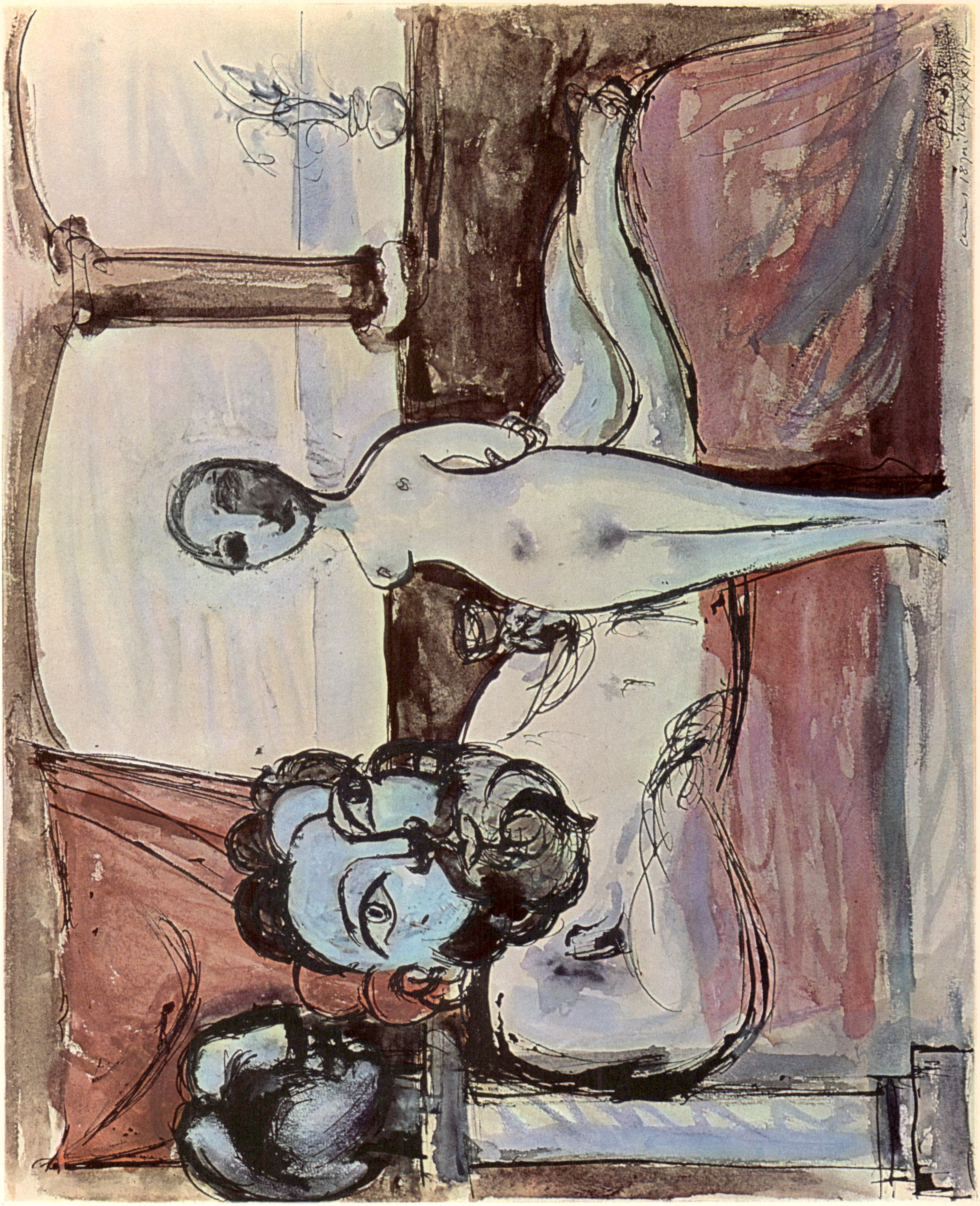

## GEORGES BRAQUE

53 STILL-LIFE WITH APPLES AND A KNIFE

Pencil, 19.7×46.3 cm. Marked bottom left: G. Braque. National Gallery, Prague (K 13 926), acquired 1923.

This drawing is linked with several still-lifes with apples painted in the early 1920s.

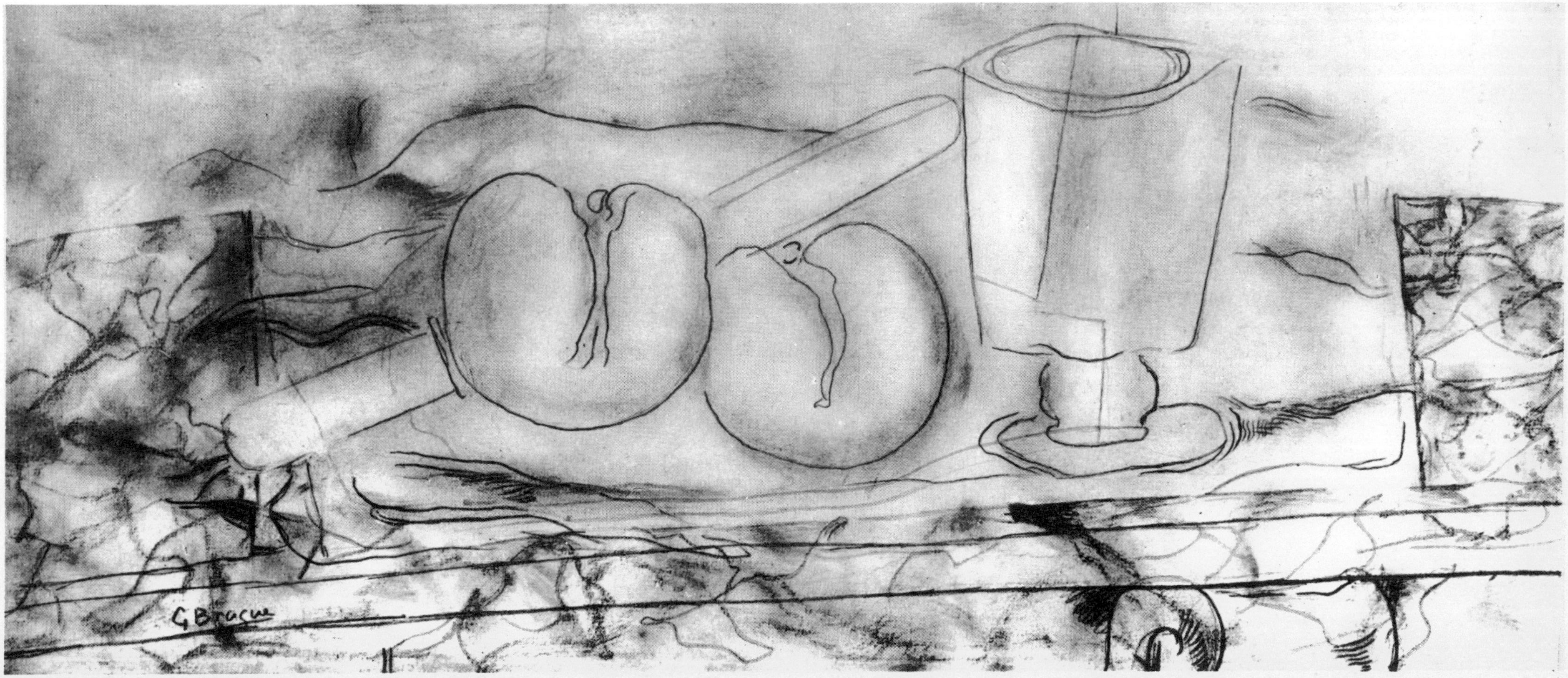
G Braque

## GEORGES BRAQUE

54 Still-life with Apples

Pencil, 17.3 × 34 cm. Marked bottom right: G. B. National Gallery, Prague (K 13 927), acquired 1923.

Like the previous drawing, this work recalls in its conception the still-lifes that Braque began to paint in about 1920 (for example, the picture *The Jug*, 1920). These two drawings must have been done before 1923.

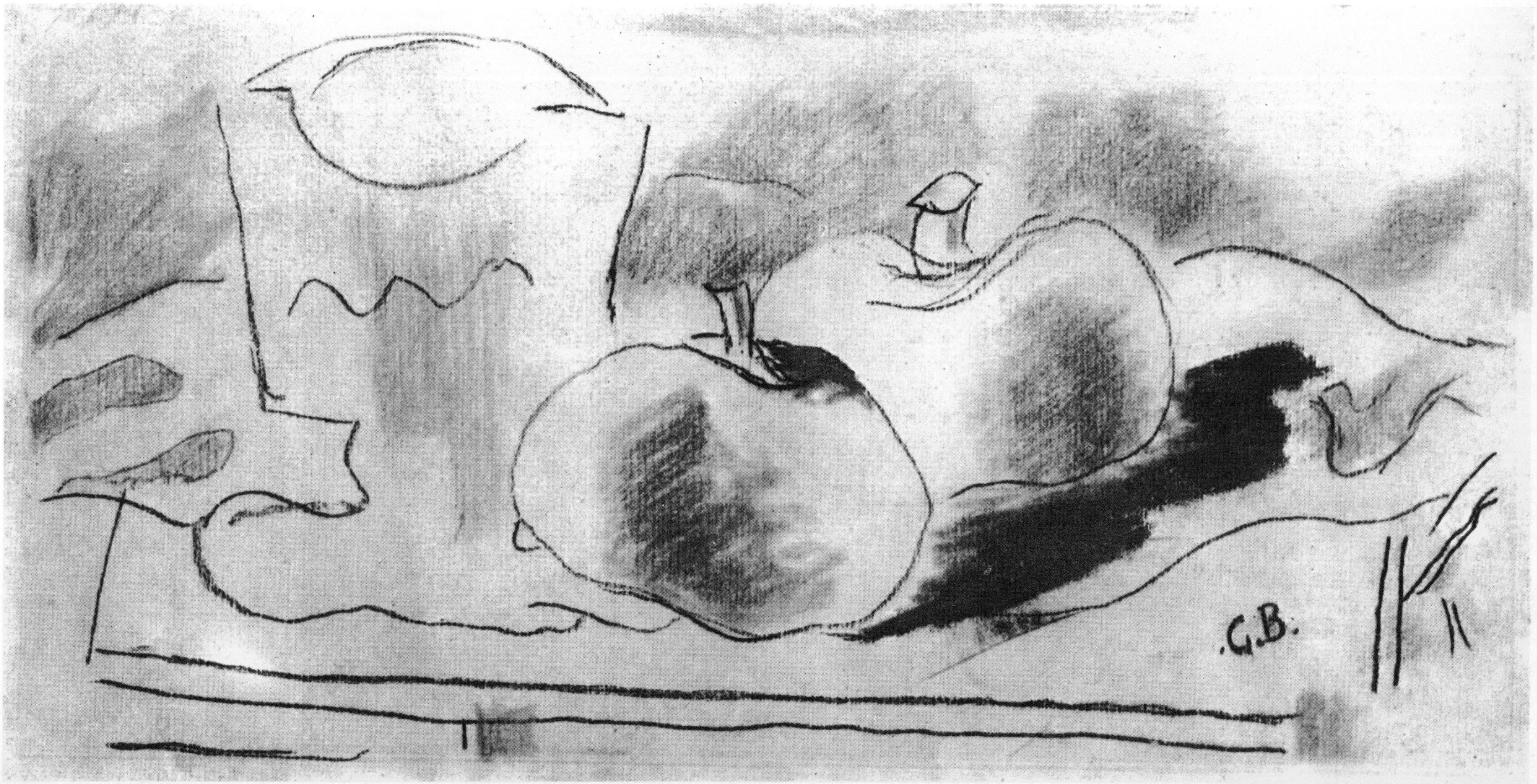
G.B.

PIERRE BONNARD

55 RECLINING NUDE

Indian ink, pen and watercolour, 31 × 24 cm. Marked top left: Mlle B. Duflos–P. Bonnard–Paris 1909. Private collection, Olomouc (Olmütz), formerly F. Venera collection, Brno.

This kind of drawing is comparatively rare in Bonnard's work; he is above all a colourist.

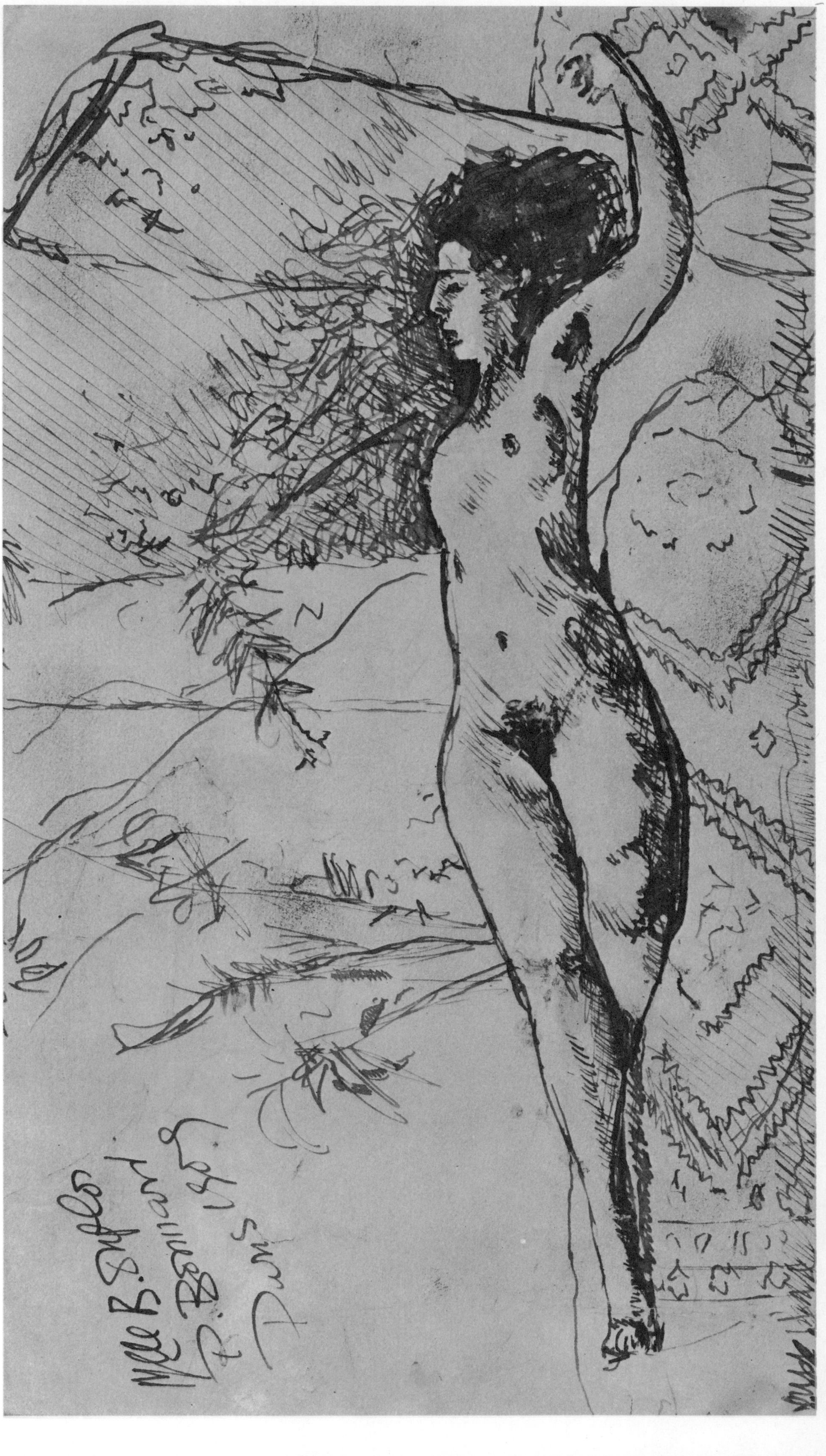

MAURICE VLAMINCK

56 LANDSCAPE WITH A BOAT

Indian ink, pen and watercolour, 21.5 × 34 cm. Marked bottom left: Vlaminck. National Gallery, Prague (K 34931), acquired 1960, formerly V. Nebeský collection.

The drawing dates from 1906–7.

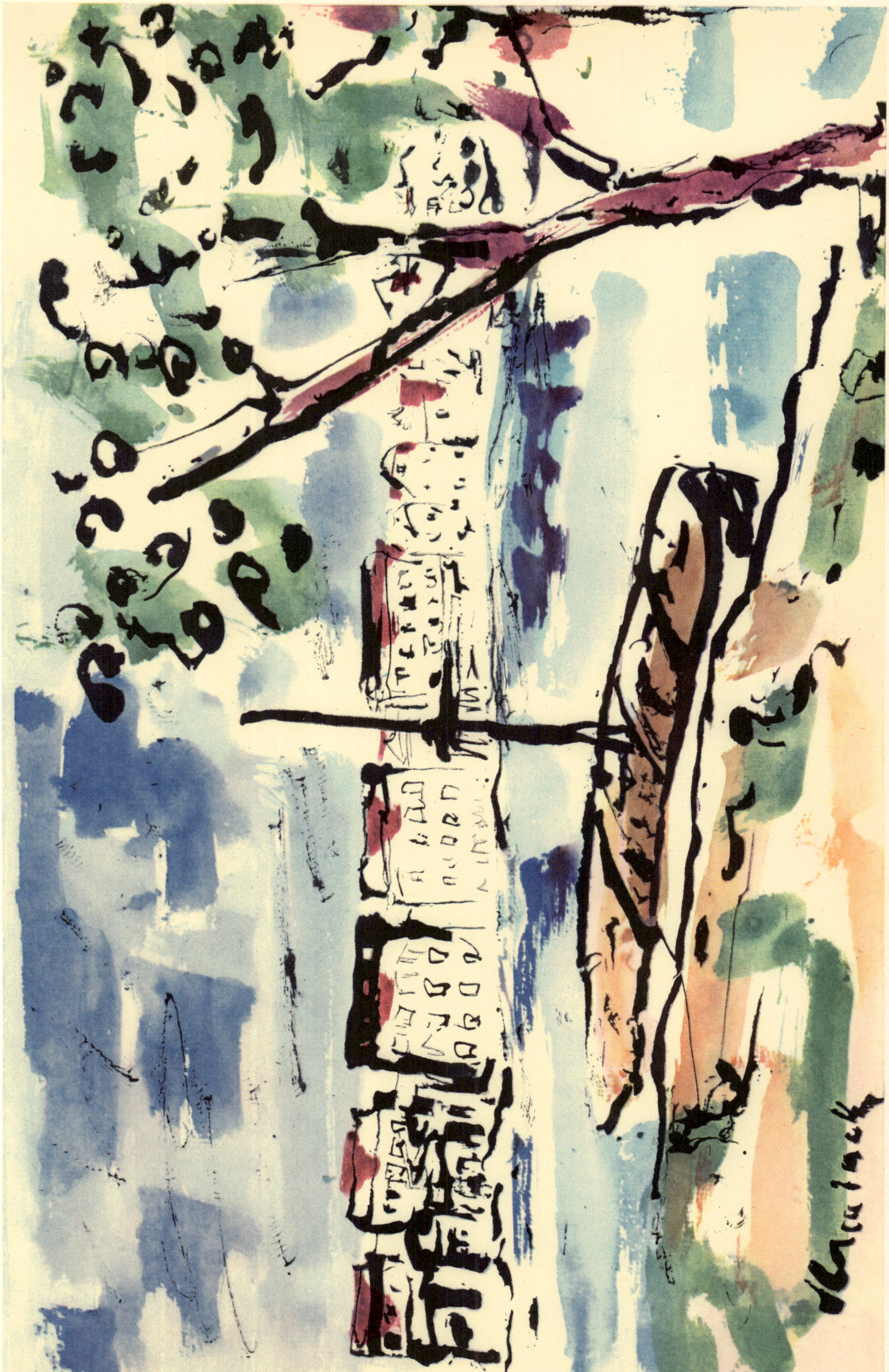

MAURICE VLAMINCK

57 HOUSES AMONG TREES

Watercolour on pen background, 29.5 × 39.5 cm. Marked bottom left: Vlaminck. National Gallery, Prague (DK 5317), acquired 1945, formerly Vildrac Gallery, Paris.

This watercolour, probably executed about 1910–15, bears clear indications of the influence of the work of Cézanne.

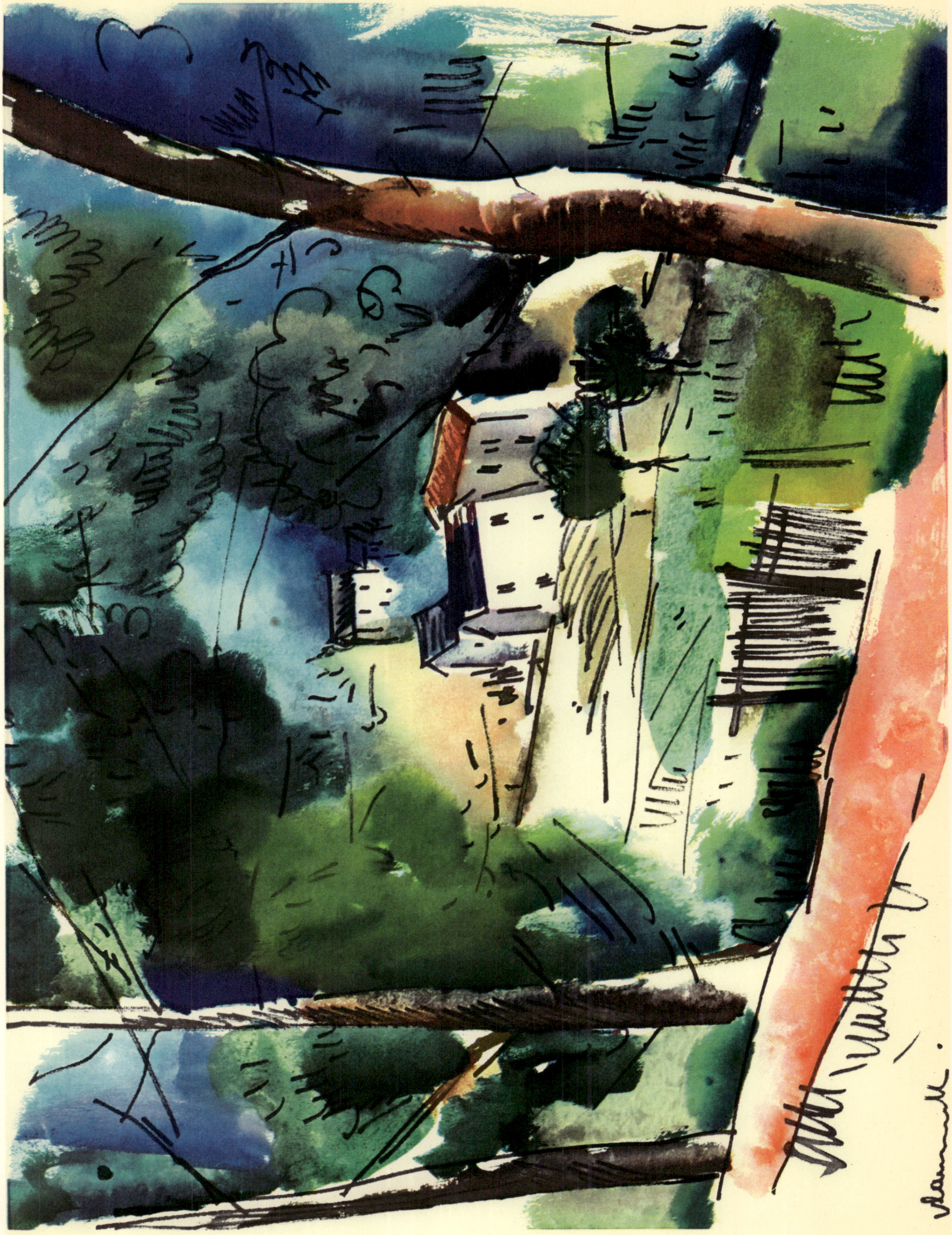

## HENRI MATISSE

58 STUDY OF A NUDE

Indian ink with quill pen, 26.4 × 20.2 cm. Marked bottom left: Henri Matisse. National Gallery, Prague (K 37 325), acquired 1963, formerly Emile Orlik collection.

Identifiable by a dramatic and animated style, characteristic of the artist's early period, this drawing must have been executed in 1909.

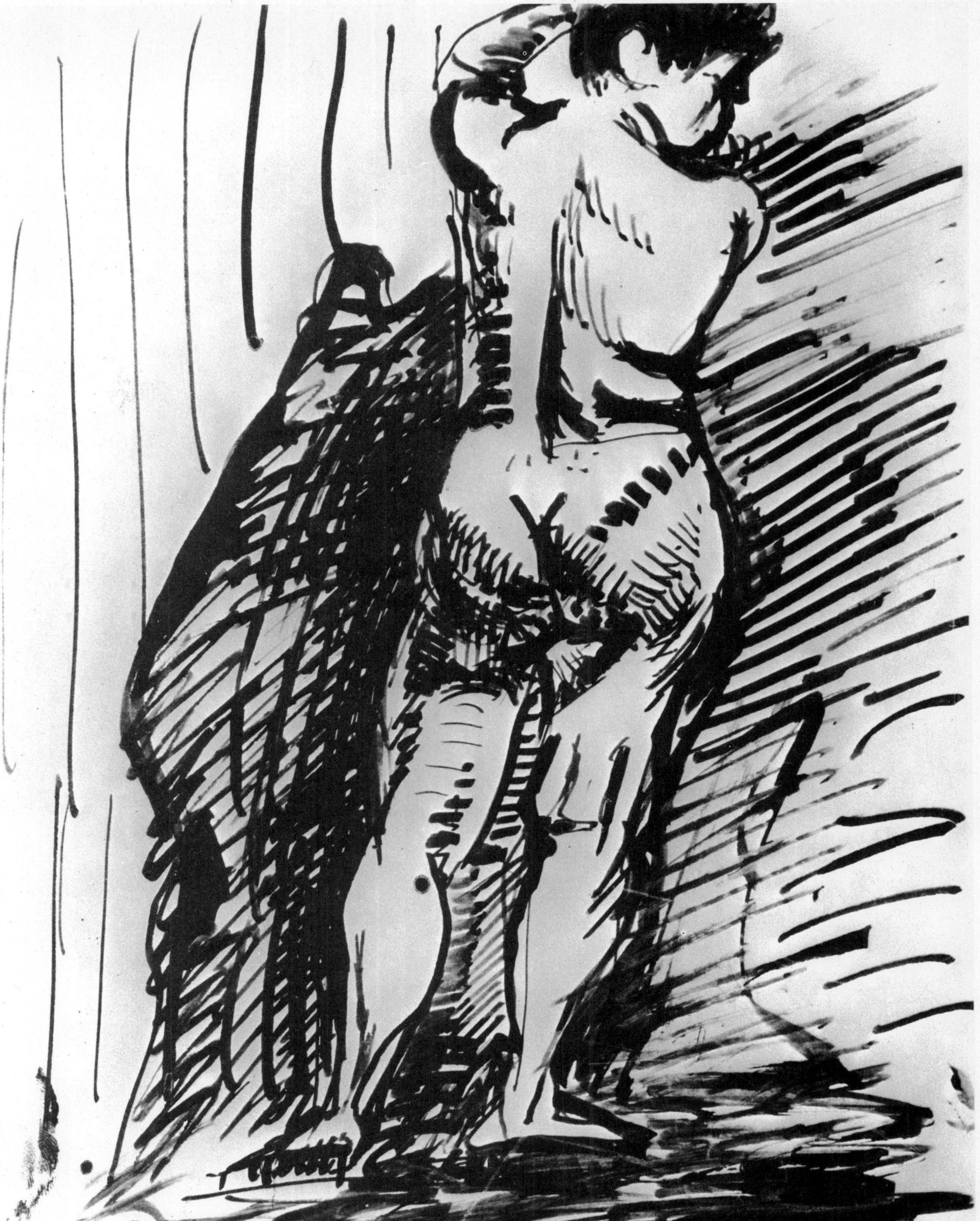
Henri-Matisse

## OTHON FRIESZ

59 ALGERIAN LANDSCAPE

Watercolour on pencil background, 39 × 53.1 cm. Marked bottom right: Othon Friesz Alger. 28. National Gallery, Prague (K 34 936), acquired 1962, formerly the Ministry of Education and Culture, earlier Vildrac Gallery, Paris.

The drawing shows the mosque in Government Square, Algiers.

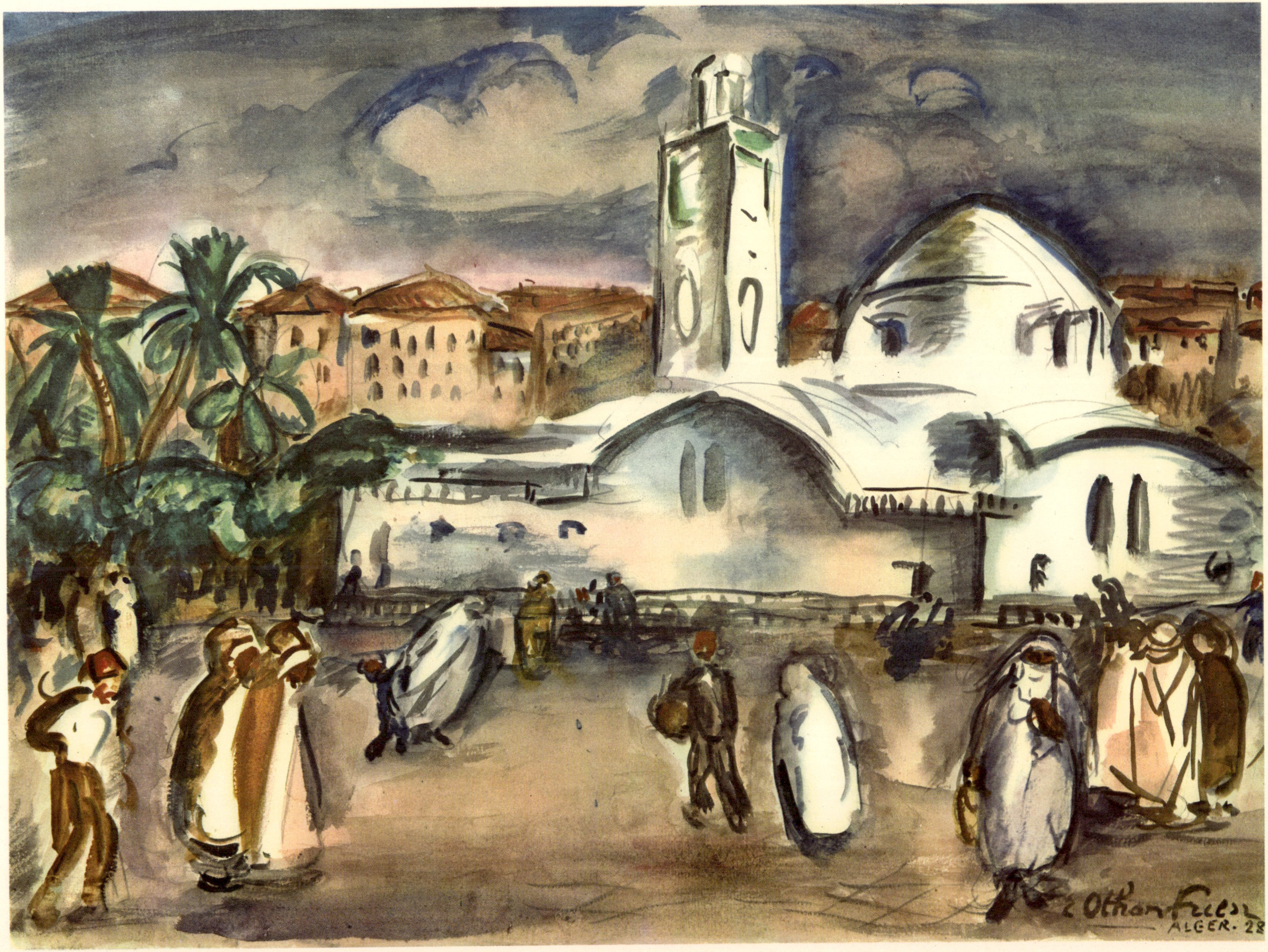
ALGER. 28

## RAOUL DUFY

60 The Bay

Pen and Indian ink, 44.5 × 56.2 cm. (inside the frame). Marked bottom right: Raoul Dufy. Private collection, Prague, from the estate of František Tichý.

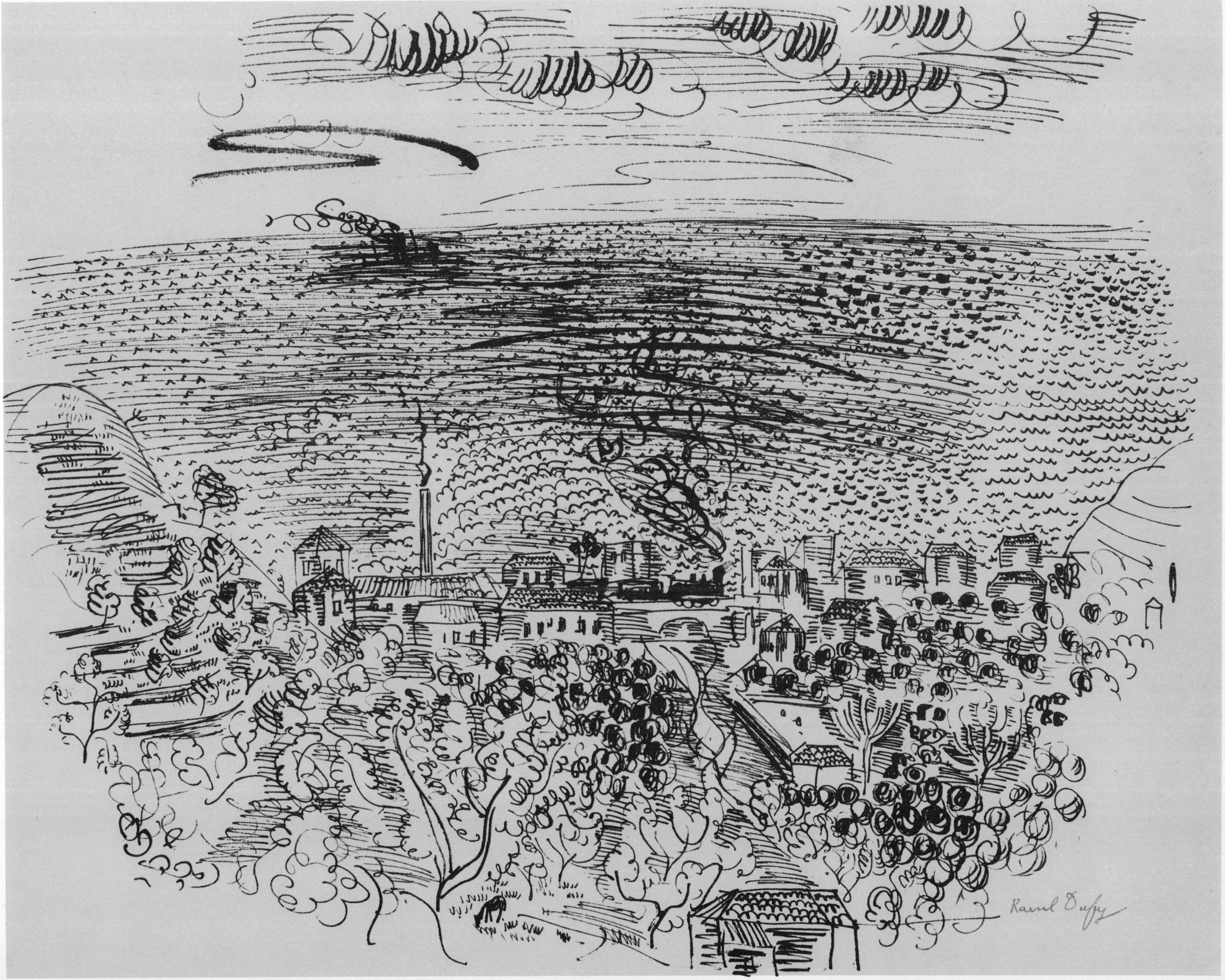
Raoul Dufy

## RAOUL DUFY

61 SEA AND BOATS

Gouache on pencil background, 49 × 62 cm. Marked bottom centre in pencil: Raoul Dufy. National Gallery, Prague (K 40 007), acquired 1965.

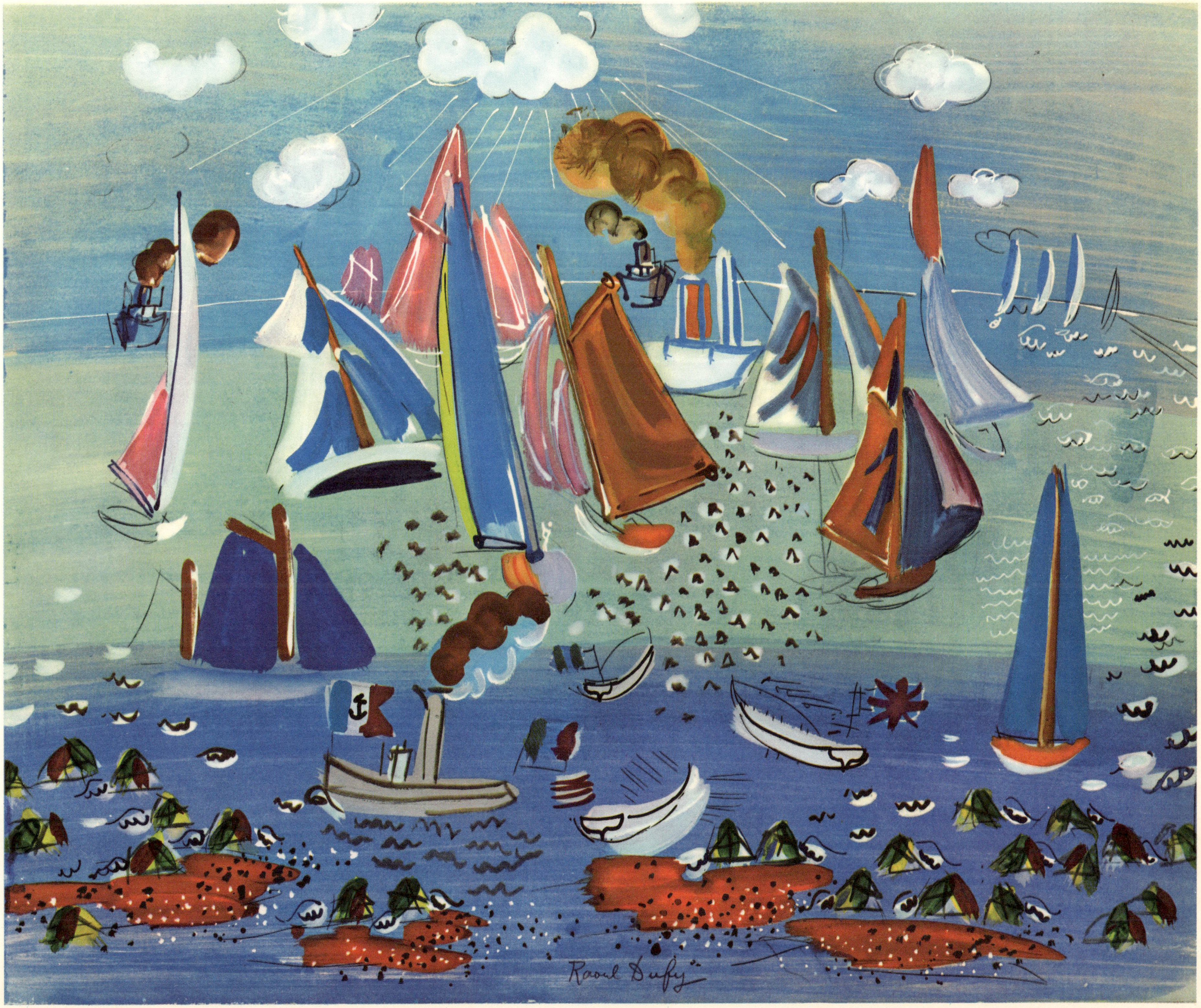
Raoul Dufy

## GEORGES ROUAULT

62 THE INN

Gouache, 56×74.5 cm. (inside the border). Marked bottom left: G. Rouault 1914. Museum of Czech Literature–Karásek Gallery, Prague, acquired 1963, formerly J. Portmann collection, Litomyšl.

The group of gouaches by Georges Rouault, all done in 1914, are among his outstanding early works. They bear witness to the expressive social-religious character of his works at this time. These gouaches arrived in Czechoslovakia through the translator, Josef Florian, who was conducting a correspondence with the painter at the time and who, in 1910, edited an album of reproductions of his works.

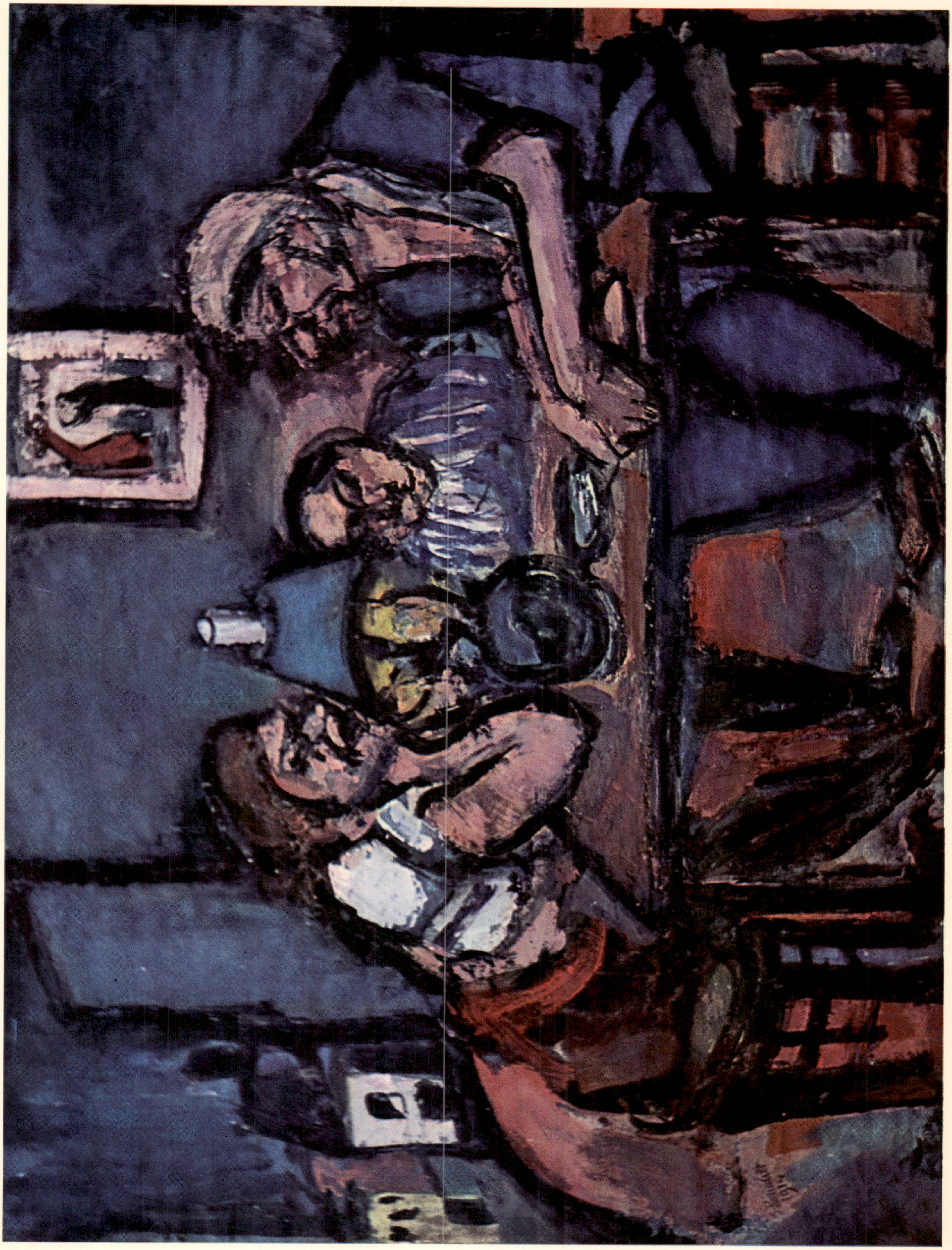

GEORGES ROUAULT

63 CRUCIFIXION

Gouache on yellowish paper, 62 × 40 cm. Marked bottom left: 1914 G. Rouault; on the back: No. 2. Private collection, Moravia, formerly Josef Florian collection, Stará Říše, Moravia.

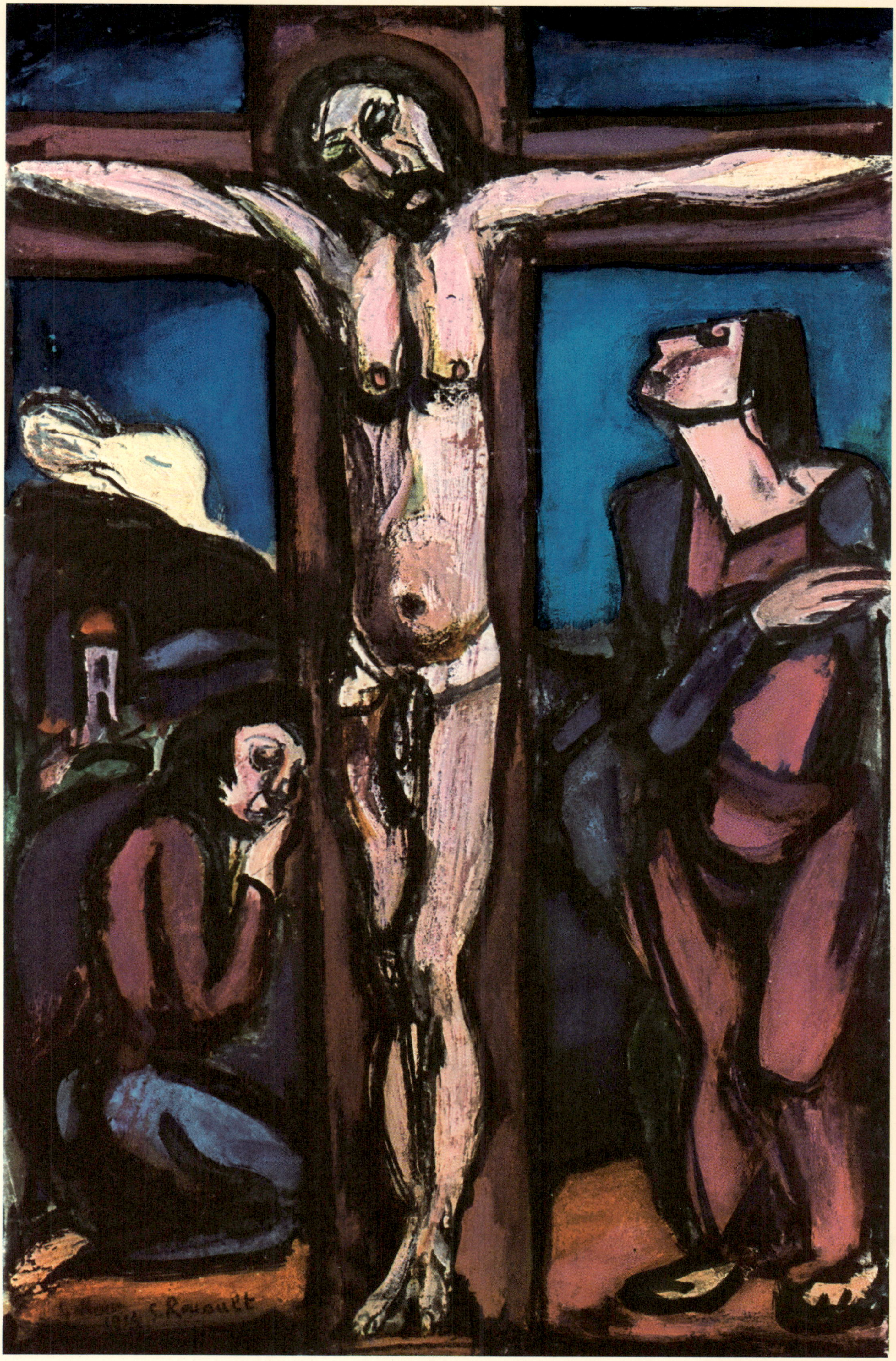
G Rouault

GEORGES ROUAULT

64 PORTRAIT OF VERLAINE

Gouache on grey paper, 75 × 51.5 cm. Marked centre left: G. Rouault 1914; added on the back: No. 14 Le Verlaine du Faubourg. Private collection, Moravia, formerly Josef Florian collection, Stará Říše, Moravia.

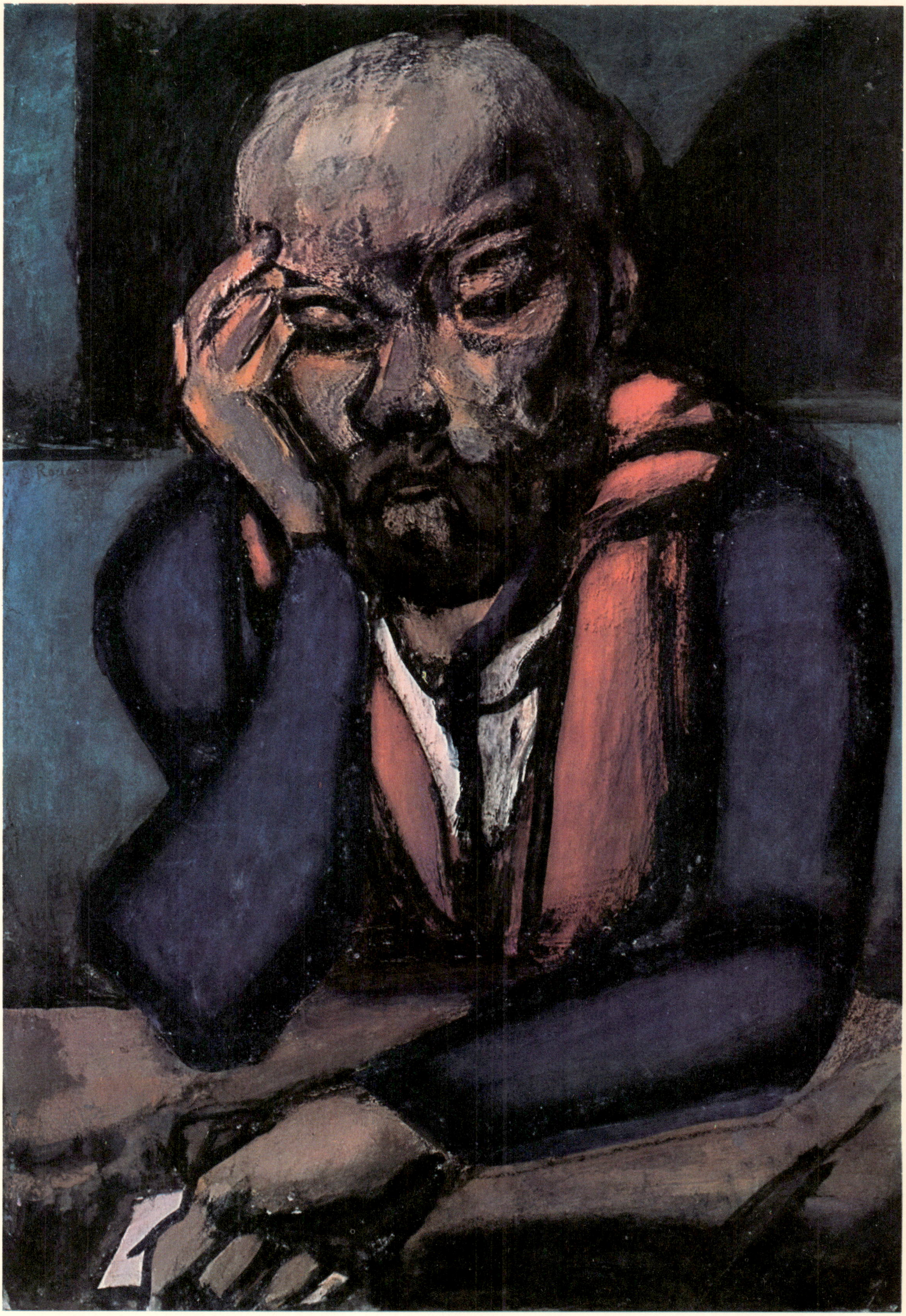

GEORGES ROUAULT

65 STILL-LIFE WITH A TABLE-LAMP

Gouache on grey paper, 57.8 × 77.3 cm. Marked bottom left: G. Rouault 1914; added on the back: No. 6. Private collection, Moravia, formerly Josef Florian collection, Stará Říše, Moravia.

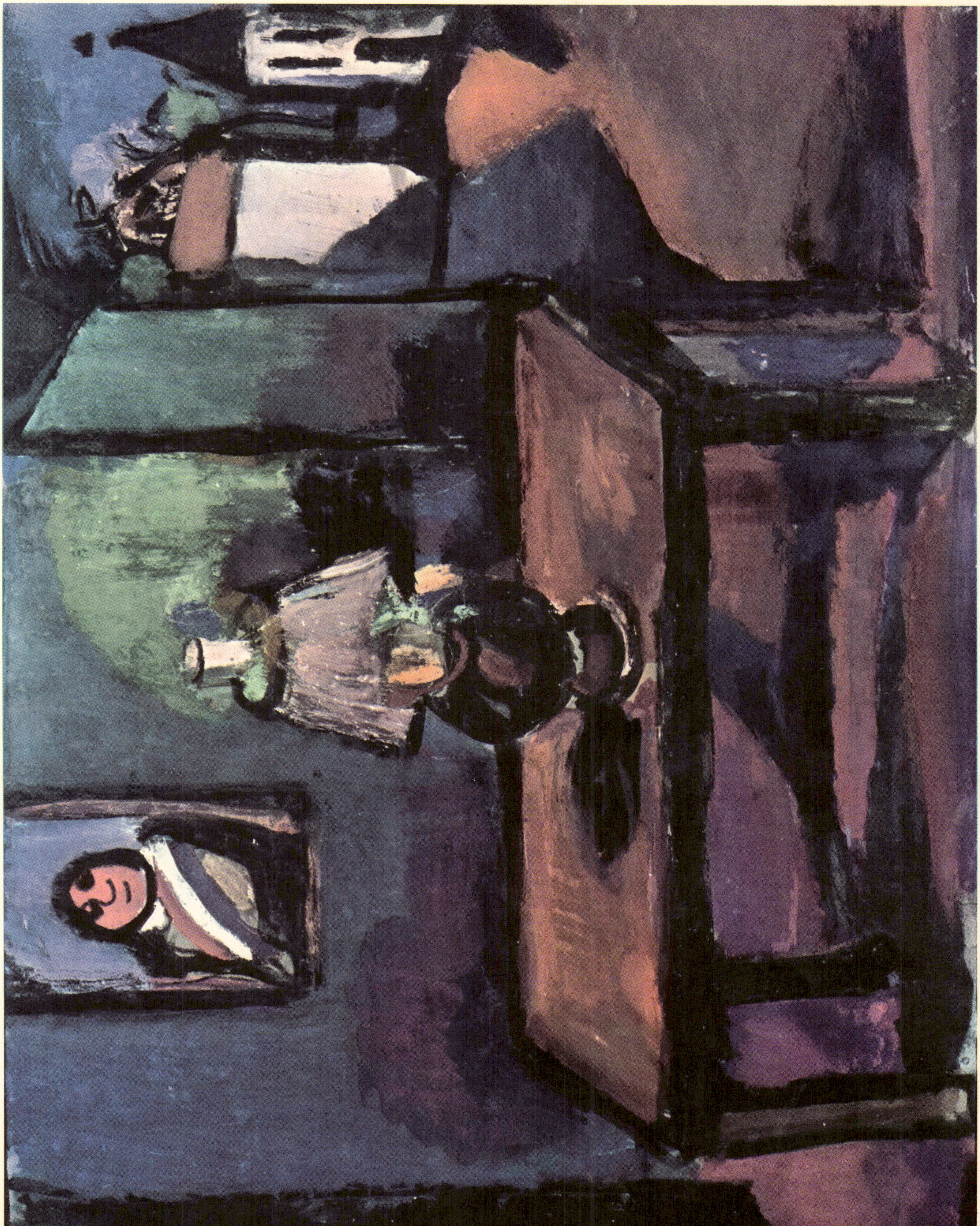

MAURICE UTRILLO

66 The Church of St Peter, Montmartre

Gouache, 50×65.5 cm. Marked bottom right: Maurice Utrillo, V, NOËL 1930; added bottom left: Église Saint-Pierre de Montmartre (à Paris). National Gallery, Prague (DK 5316), acquired 1945.

This work, dated 1930, belongs to the third, coloured period of Utrillo.

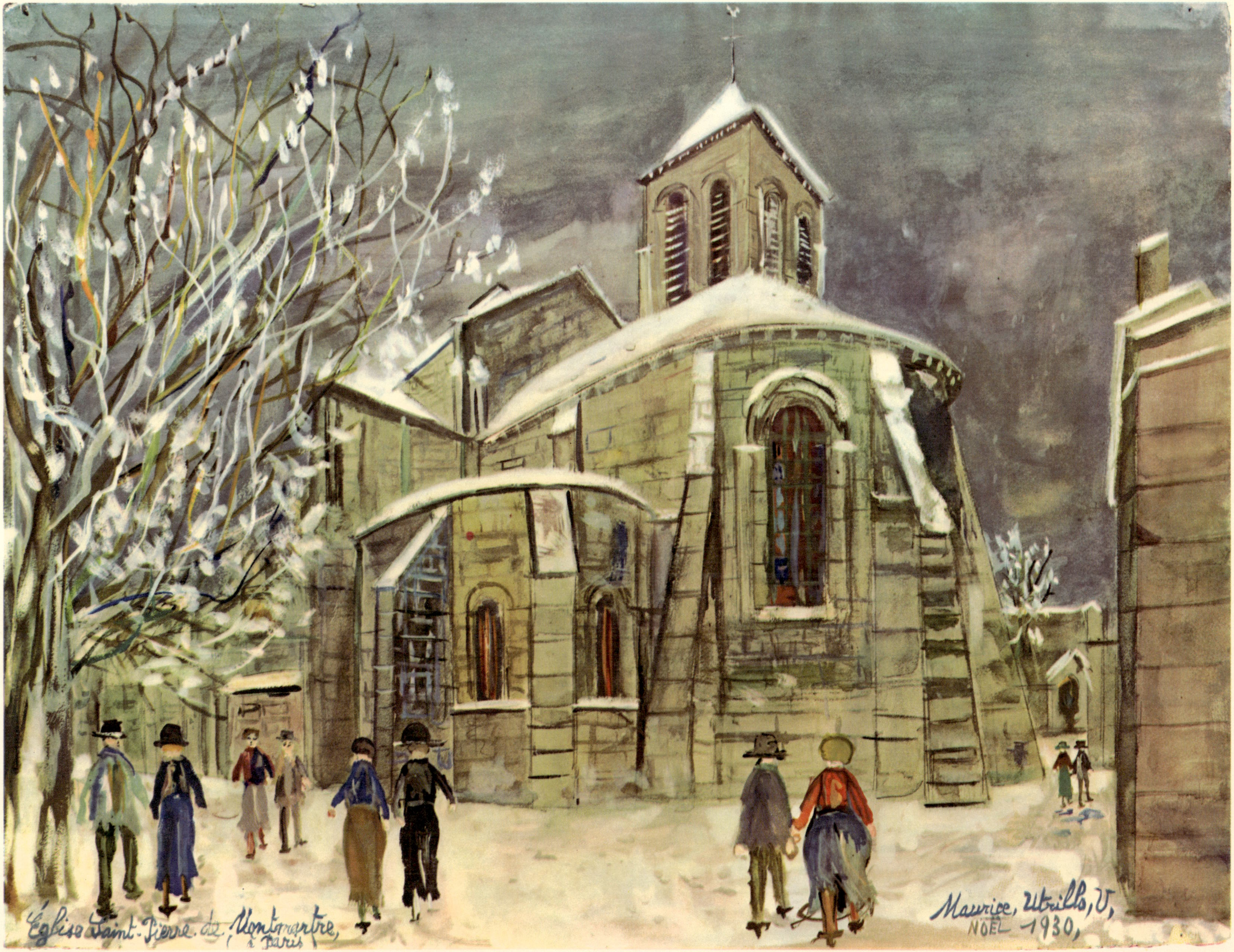
Église Saint-Pierre de Montmartre, à Paris
Maurice, Utrillo, V,
NOËL 1930,

MARC CHAGALL

67 THE WINDOW

Gouache, 49×63.5 cm (cut out from a border). Marked bottom left: Chagall. Marc. National Gallery, Prague (O 11641), acquired 1967.

This gouache is a variation of the painting *Bride and Groom with Eiffel Tower* from 1928. It, therefore, apparently originated after this date.

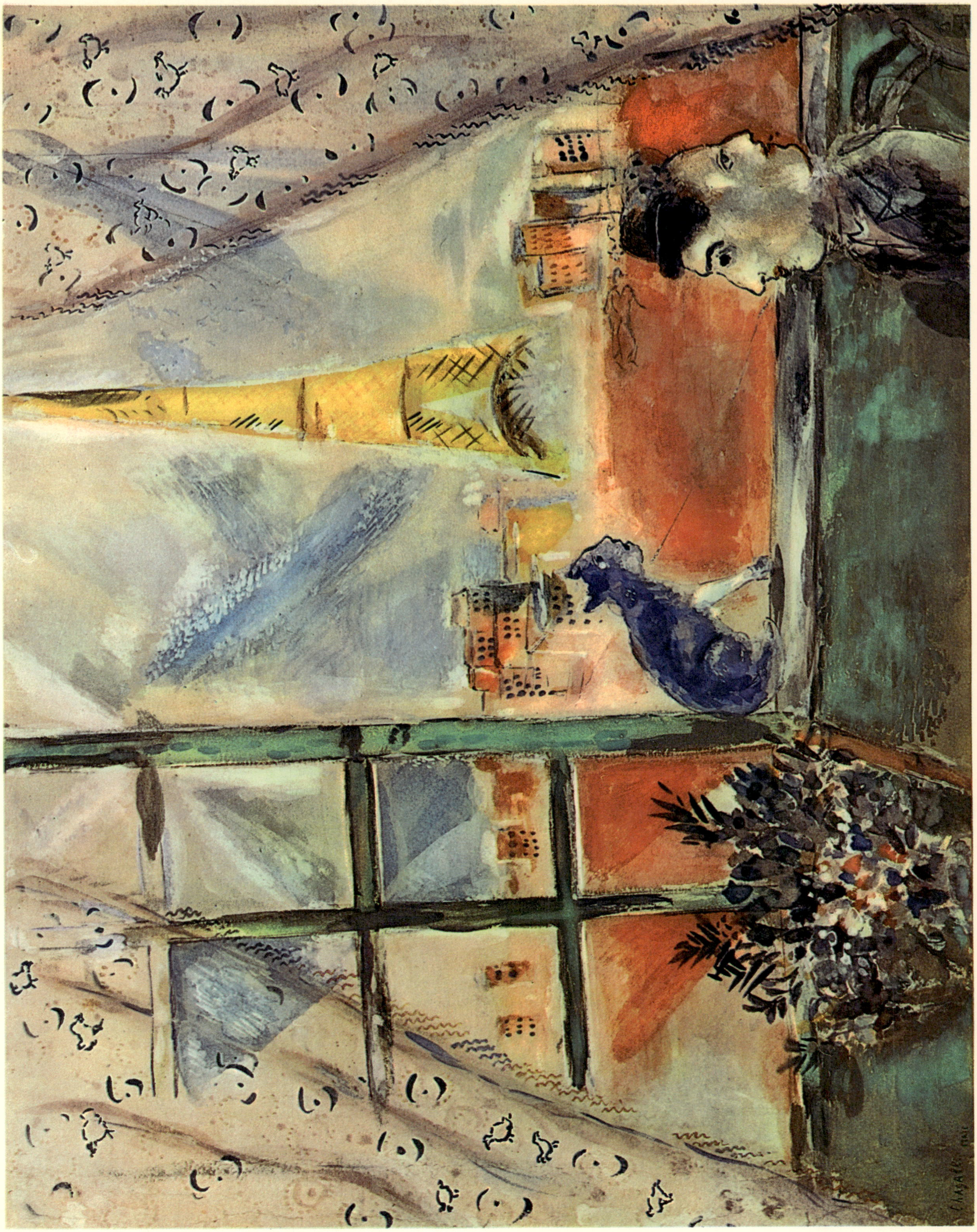

MARC CHAGALL

68 The Tailor

Indian ink, pen and brush on brown paper glued on cardboard, 23.2×18.4 cm. Marked bottom right: chagall. National Gallery, Prague (K 36 250), acquired 1963.

This drawing was done by Chagall between 1914, on his return to Russia, and 1922, year of his return to France.

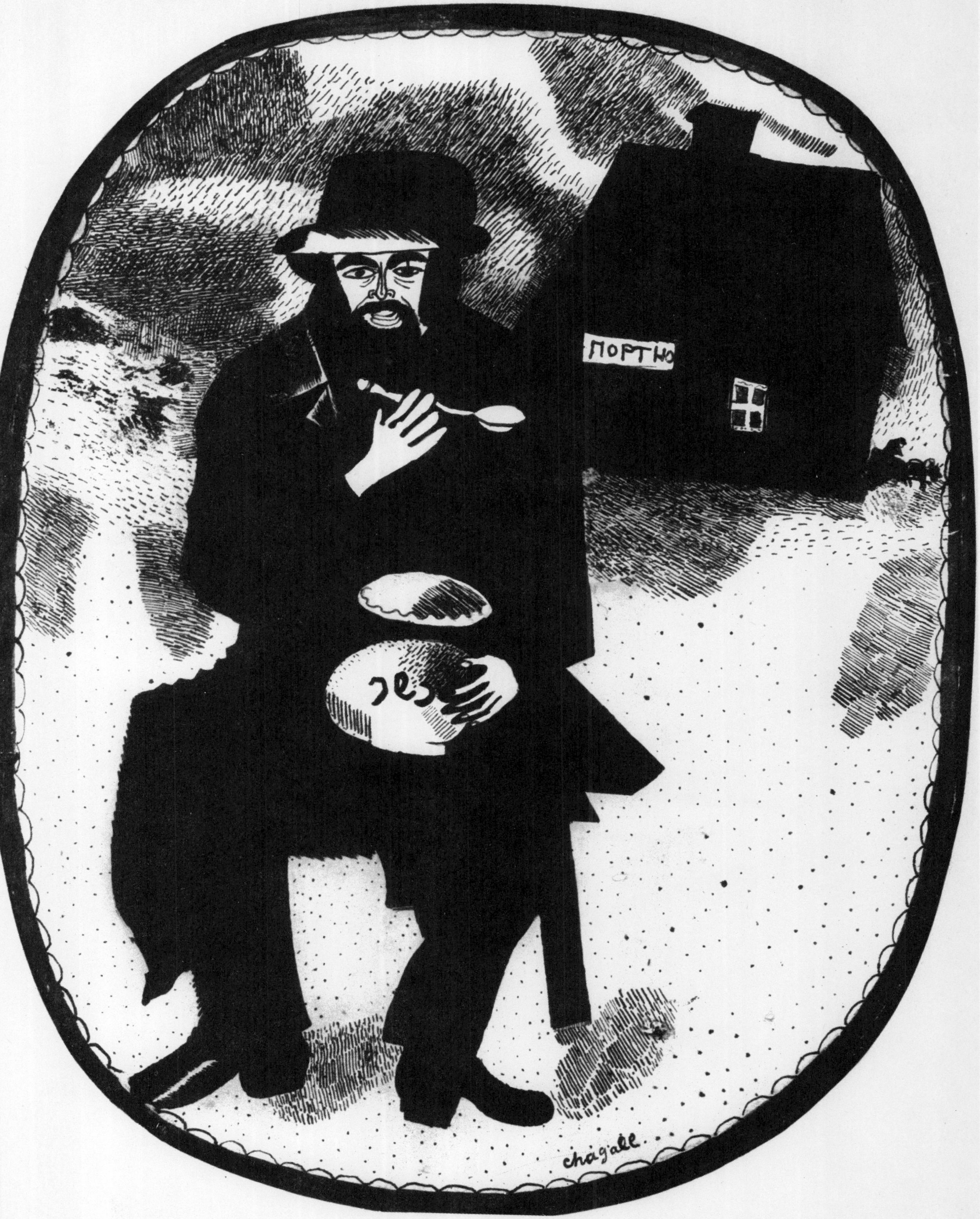
ПОРТНО
chagall

## MARC CHAGALL

69 WOMAN WITH A SCYTHE

Gouache on olive coloured paper, 50.8 × 66.2 cm. Marked bottom right: Chagall. National Gallery, Prague (K 33 822), acquired 1960, formerly Čeřovský collection, Prague.

This gouache was executed after Chagall's second return to Paris, before or immediately after 1930, the year marked on the label glued on to the back of the picture. At the end of 1932, or at the beginning of 1934, it was hung at the exhibition held by Umělecká Beseda, Aleš Room at Prague, catalogued as No. 9 as the property of Čeřovský, where the name *Woman with a Scythe* is also given.

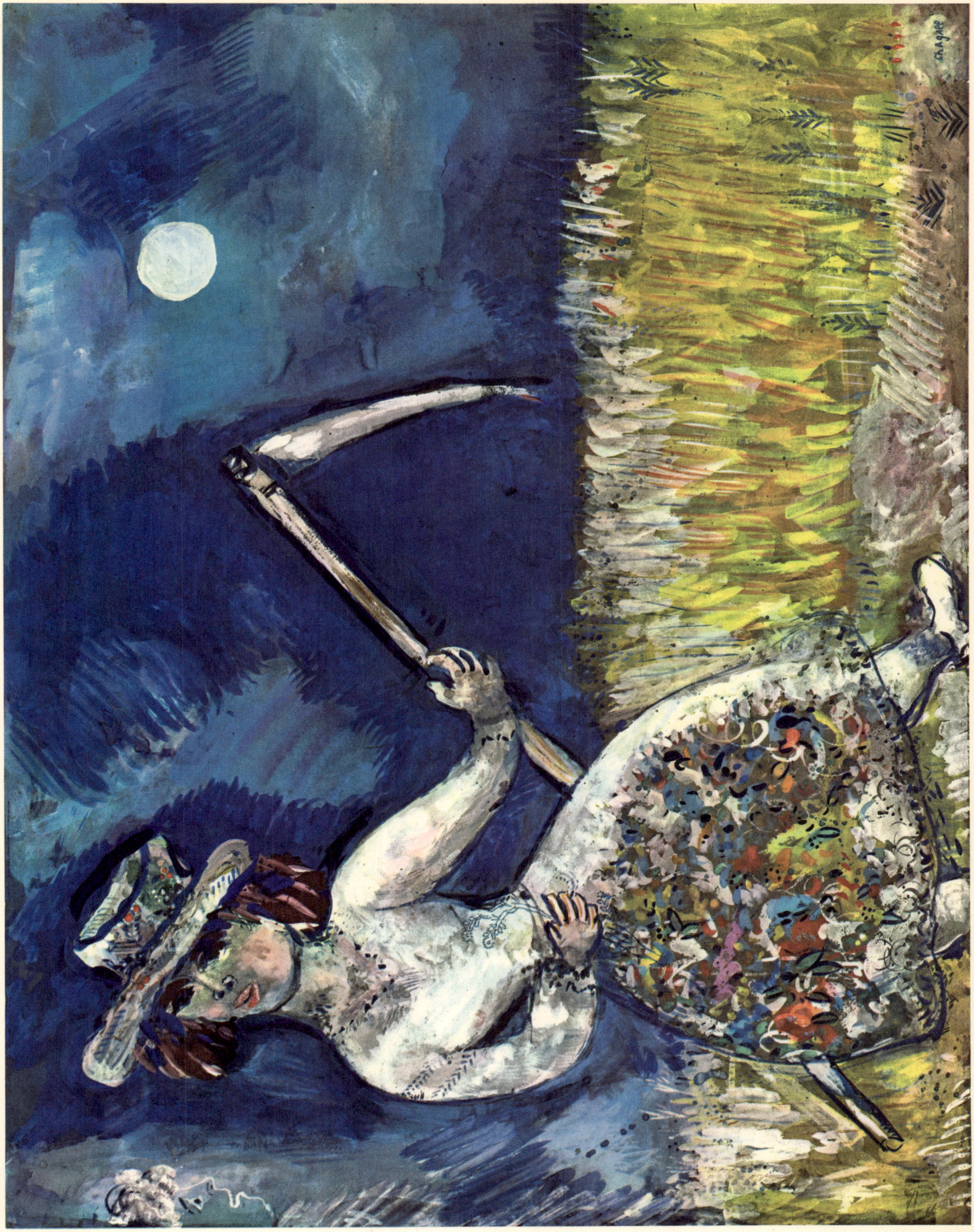

JULES PASCIN

70 ENGLISHMAN IN ARAB CAPTIVITY

Indian ink, pen and watercolour, 16.4×20.2 cm. Marked bottom right: pascin. National Gallery, Prague (K 37 318), acquired 1963, formerly Emile Orlik collection.

The drawing originates from the journey made by the artist to Africa.

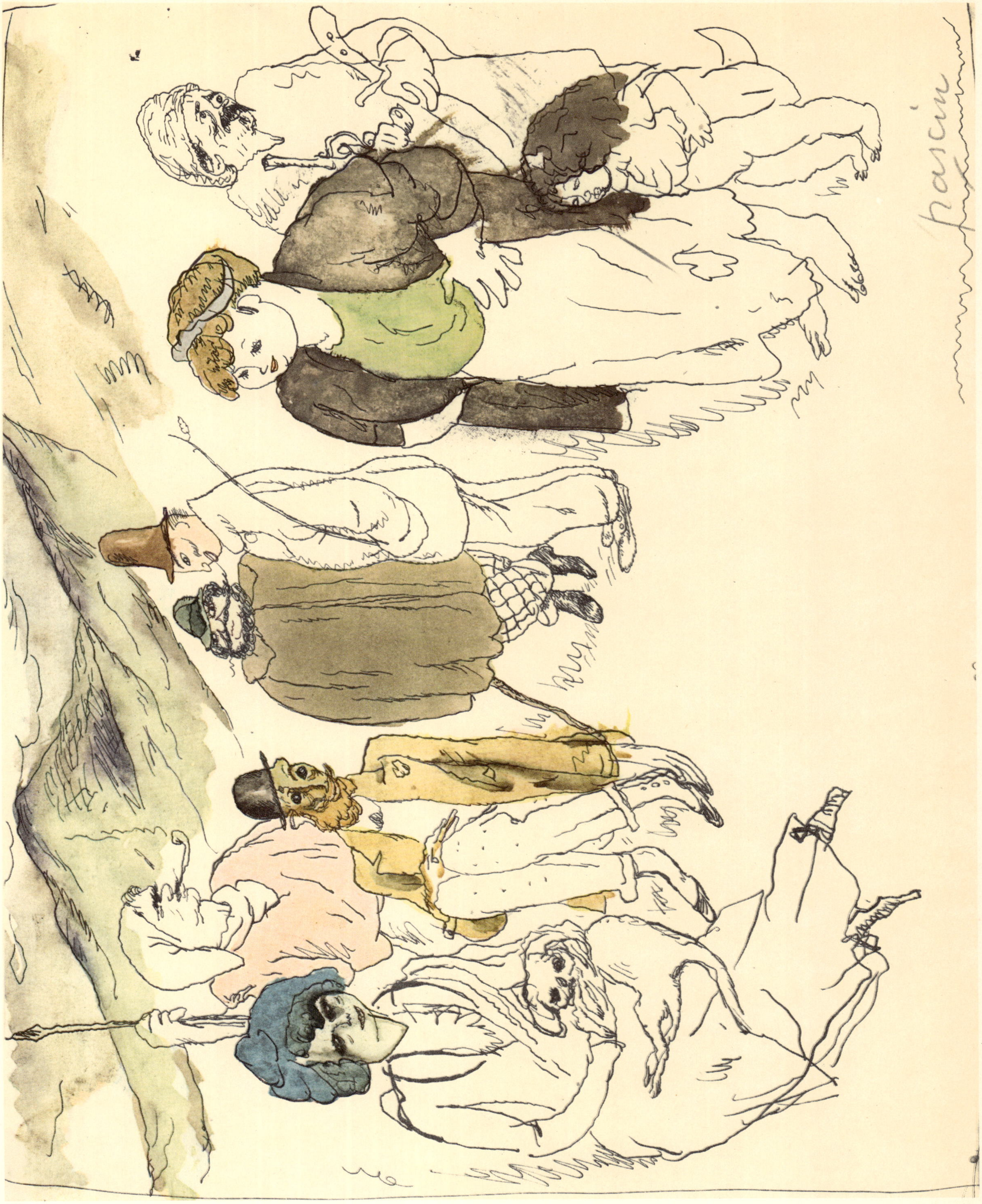

## JULES PASCIN

71 THREE YOUNG GIRLS AND A DOG

Pencil, Indian ink with pen, 18.3 × 26.5 cm. Marked bottom right: pascin. National Gallery, Prague (K 37 322), acquired 1963, formerly Emile Orlik collection.

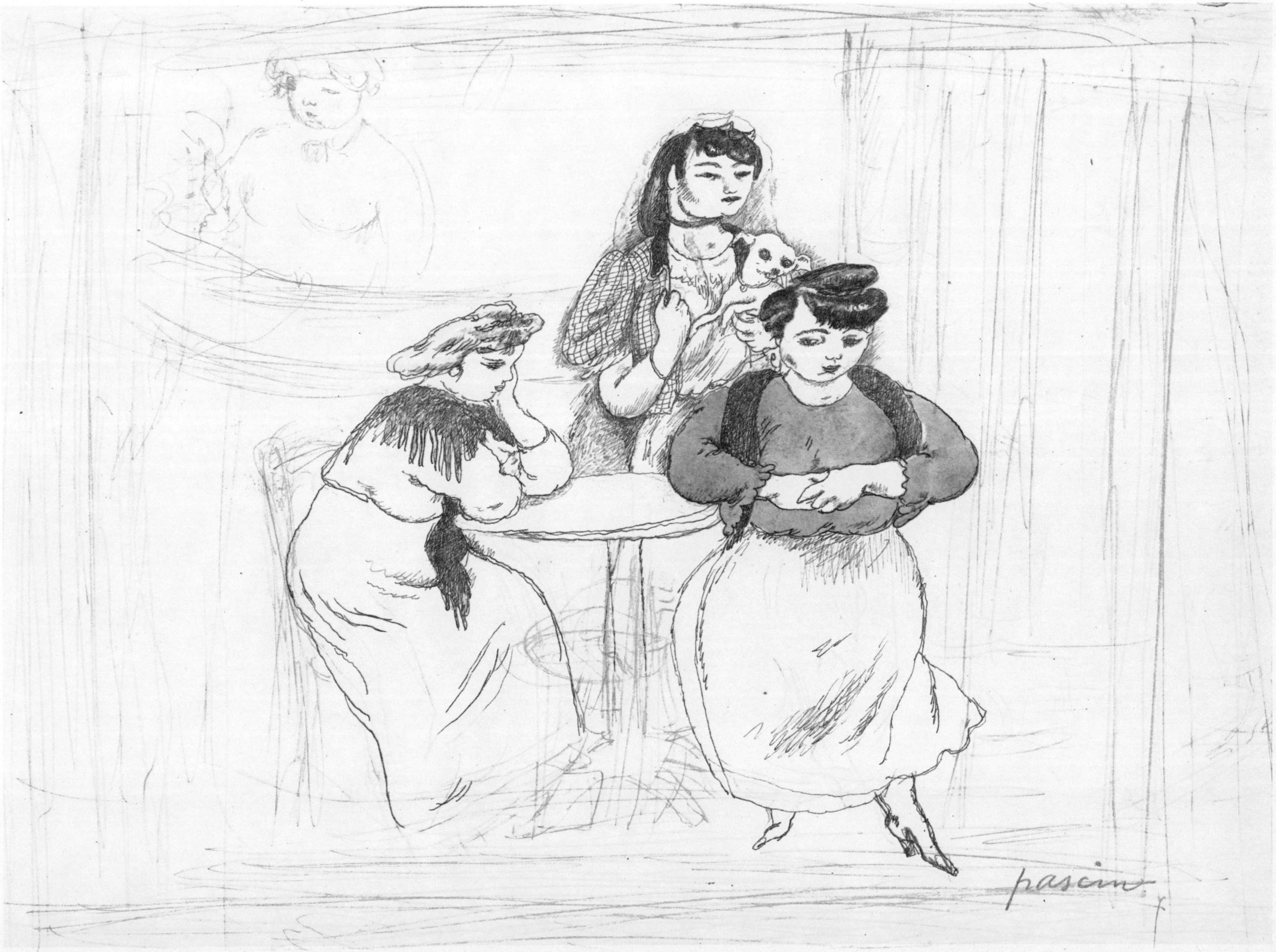
pascin

CHARLES DUFRESNE

72 THREE WOMAN IN A GARDEN

Gouache on pen background, 29.5 × 38.5 cm. Marked bottom right: dufresne. National Gallery, Prague (DK 5323), acquired 1945.

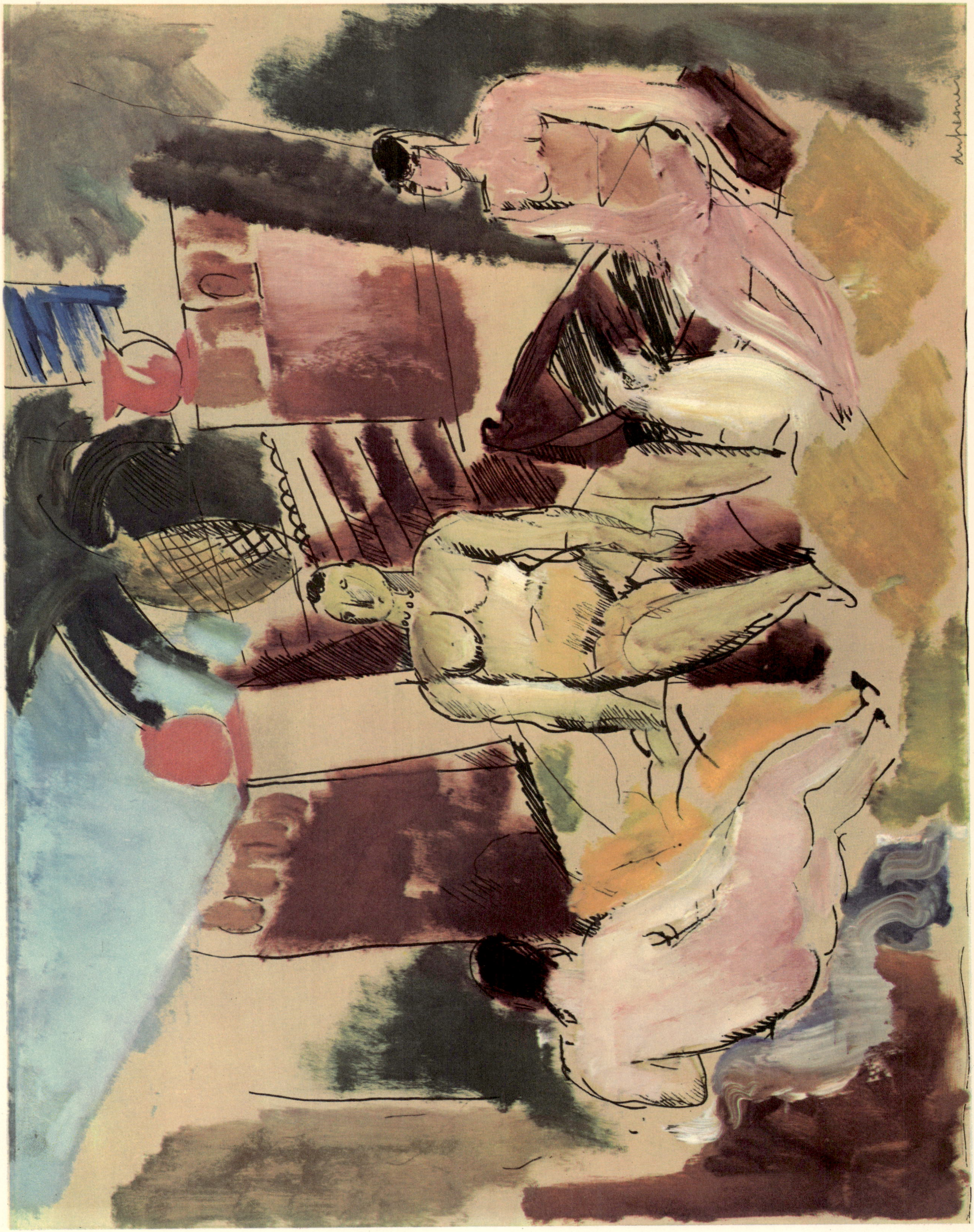

MARCEL GROMAIRE

73 WOMAN IN A FUR COAT

Indian ink with pen, 32.5 × 25 cm. Marked bottom left: Gromaire 1925. Museum of Czech Literature–Karásek Gallery, Prague.

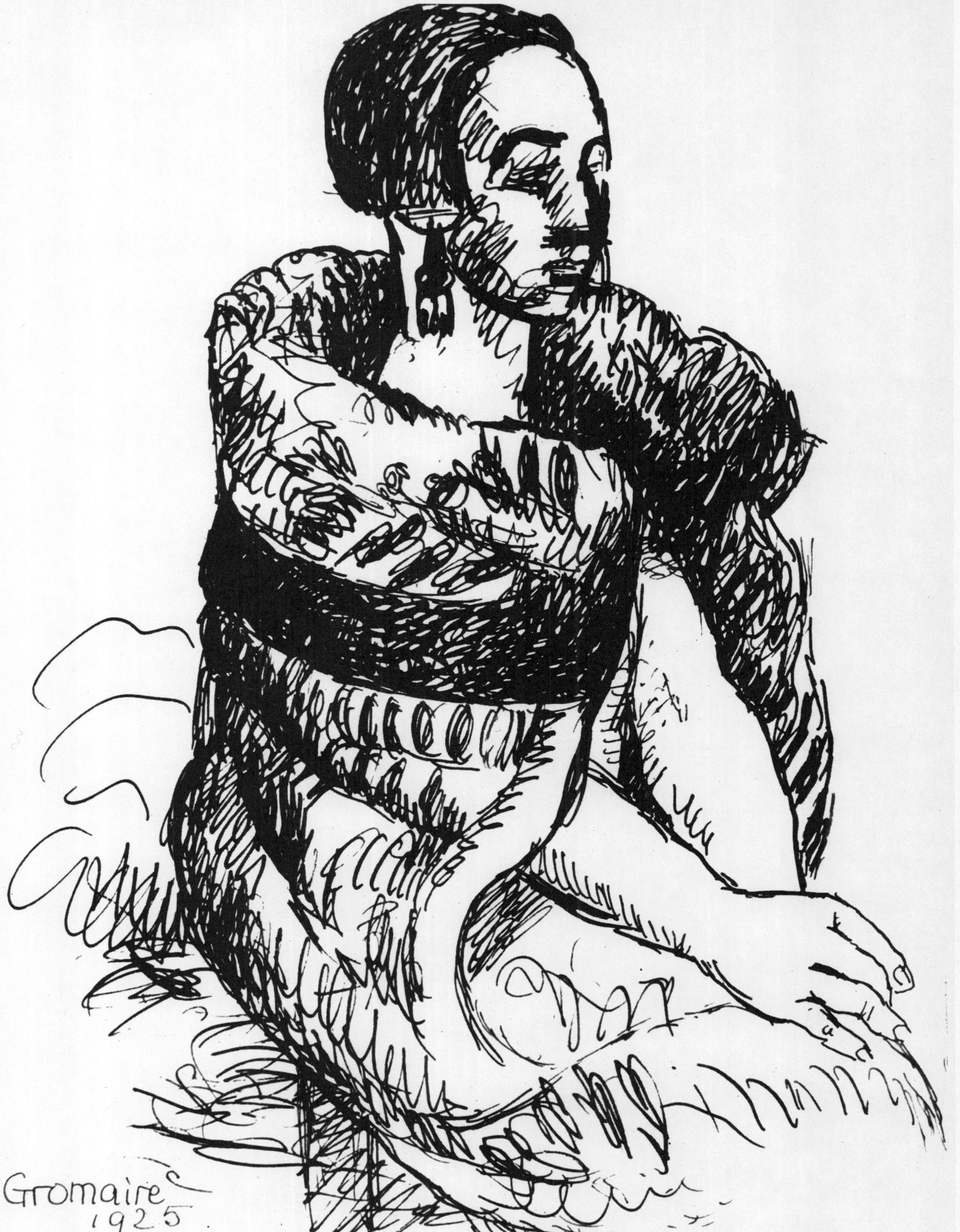
Gromaire
1925

## FERNAND LEGER

74 HEAD

Indian ink with brush, watercolour and gouache, 65 × 50 cm. Marked bottom right: A Mr. Vitezslav Nezval—Amicalement F. Leger. Private collection, Prague, formerly Vítězslav Nezval collection, Prague.

This drawing belongs to Léger's last period and was executed at the same time as the picture *The Constructors*, painted in 1950. The drawing is dedicated to the poet, Nezval, who was on friendly terms with many French artists.

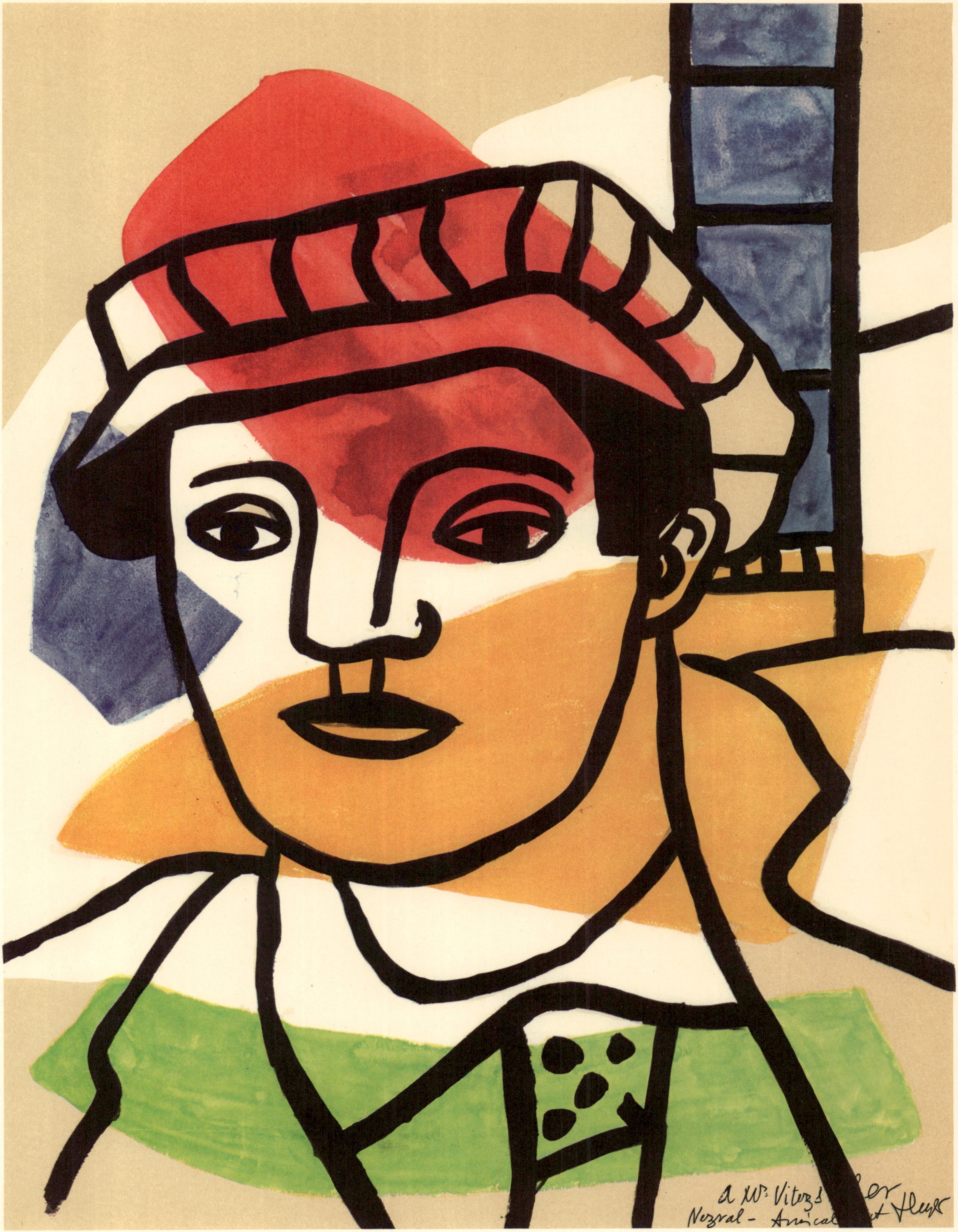

## EMILE ANTOINE BOURDELLE

75 PLATE FROM THE SERIES: THE DANCES OF ISADORA DUNCAN

Indian ink with pen and watercolour. 31.5 × 19.7 cm. Marked bottom left: EAB. National Gallery, Prague, formerly Emanuel Siblík collection (vol. 87/22).

The series is dated by the signature on the penultimate plate of the year 1909 when the artist stayed in Prague.

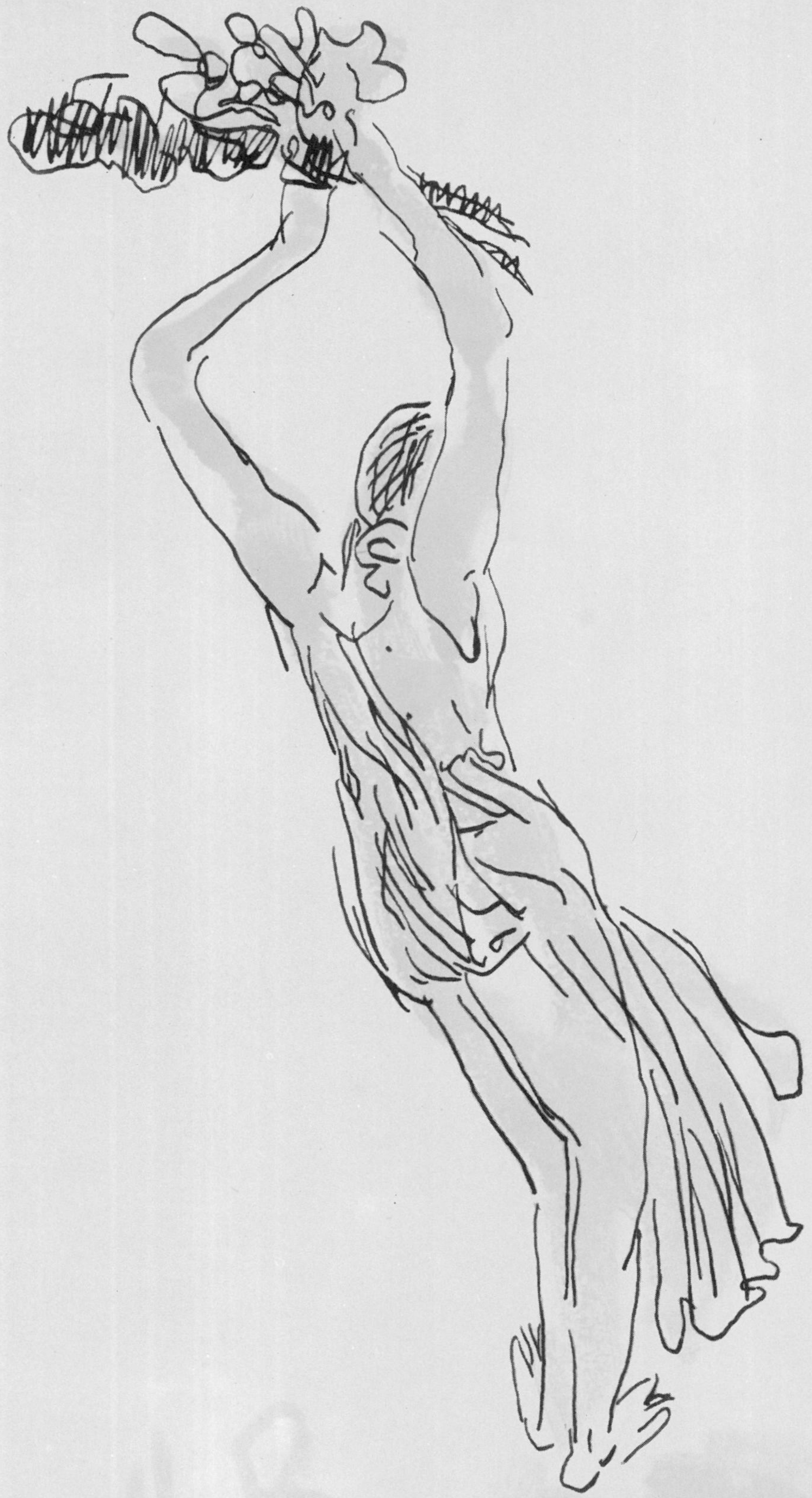

EMILE ANTOINE BOURDELLE

76 PLATE FROM THE SERIES: THE DANCES OF ISADORA DUNCAN

(Isadora in the Pathétique symphony by Tchaikovsky).

Indian ink with pen and watercolour, 31.5 × 20.3 cm. Marked bottom right in pen: Emile Antoine Bourdelle 1909. National Gallery, Prague, formerly Emanuel Siblík collection (vol. 87/28).

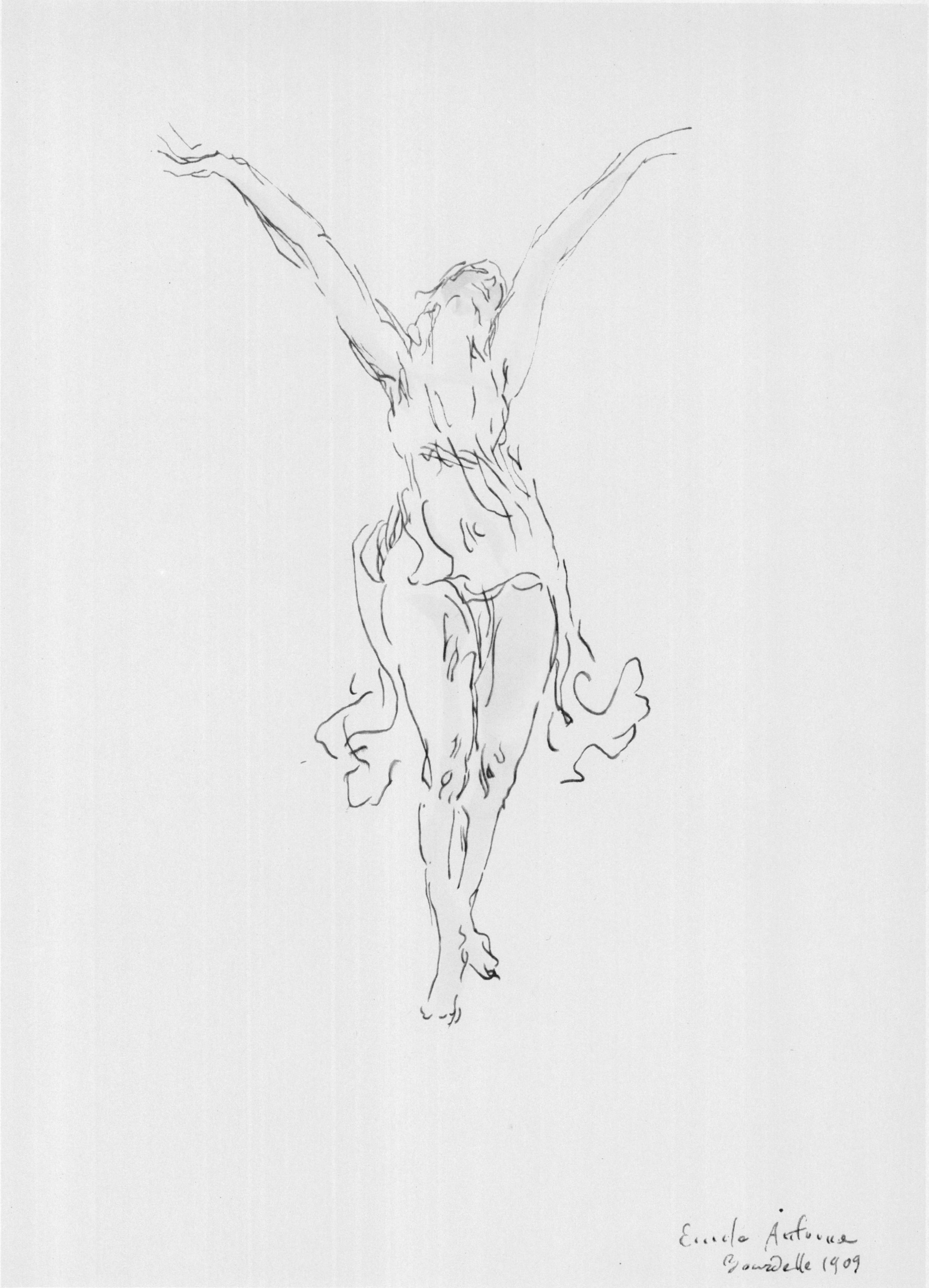
Emile Antoine
Bourdelle 1909

CHARLES DESPIAU

77 SEATED NUDE

Pencil, 30.8 × 20.2 cm. Marked bottom left: C. Despiau 1923. National Gallery, Prague (K 13 932), acquired 1923.

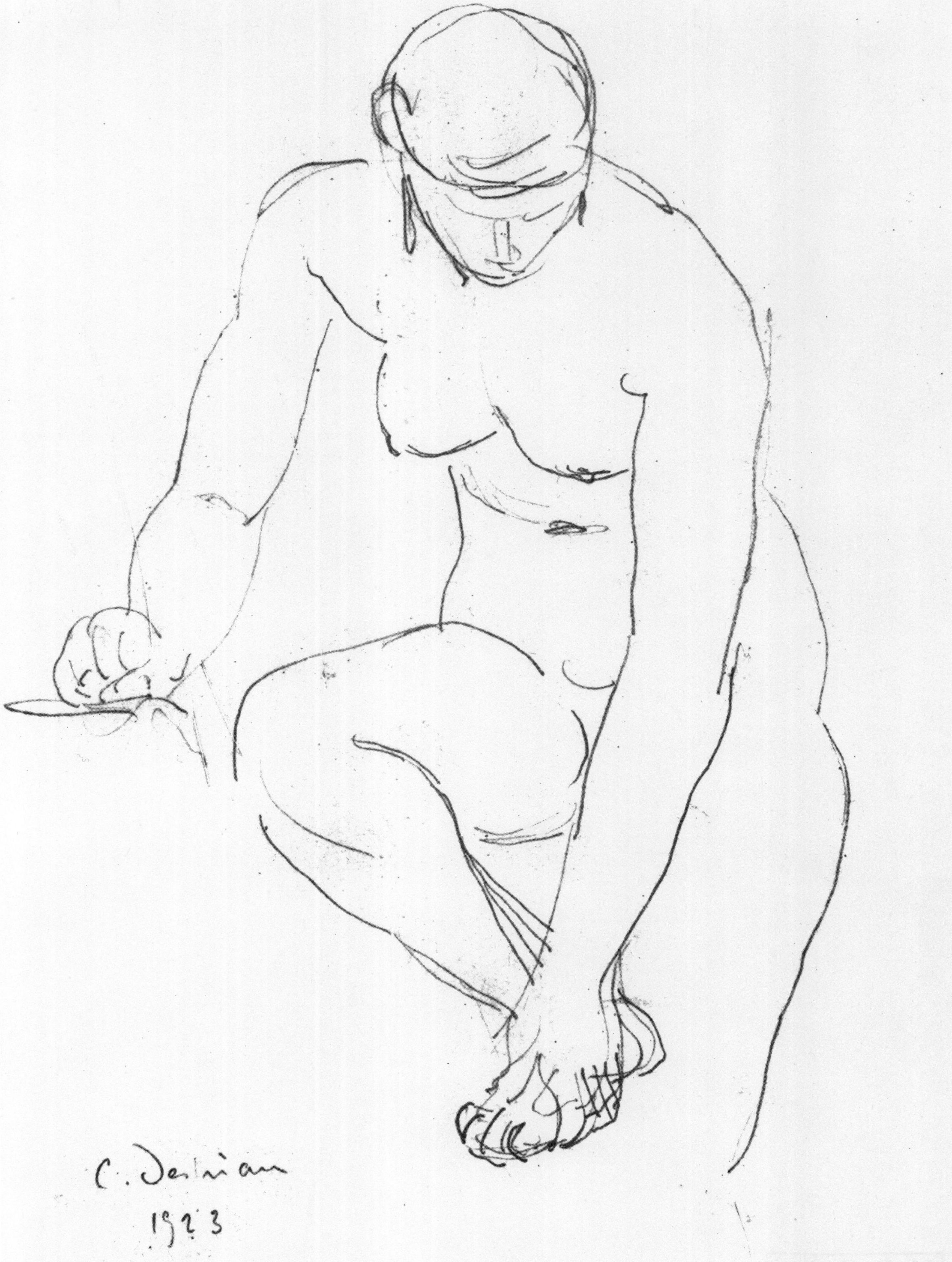
C. Despiau
1923

CHARLES DESPIAU

78 RECLINING NUDE

Drawing in red chalk, 23.2 × 36.2 cm. Marked bottom left: C. Despiau. National Gallery, Prague (K 15 883), acquired 1923.

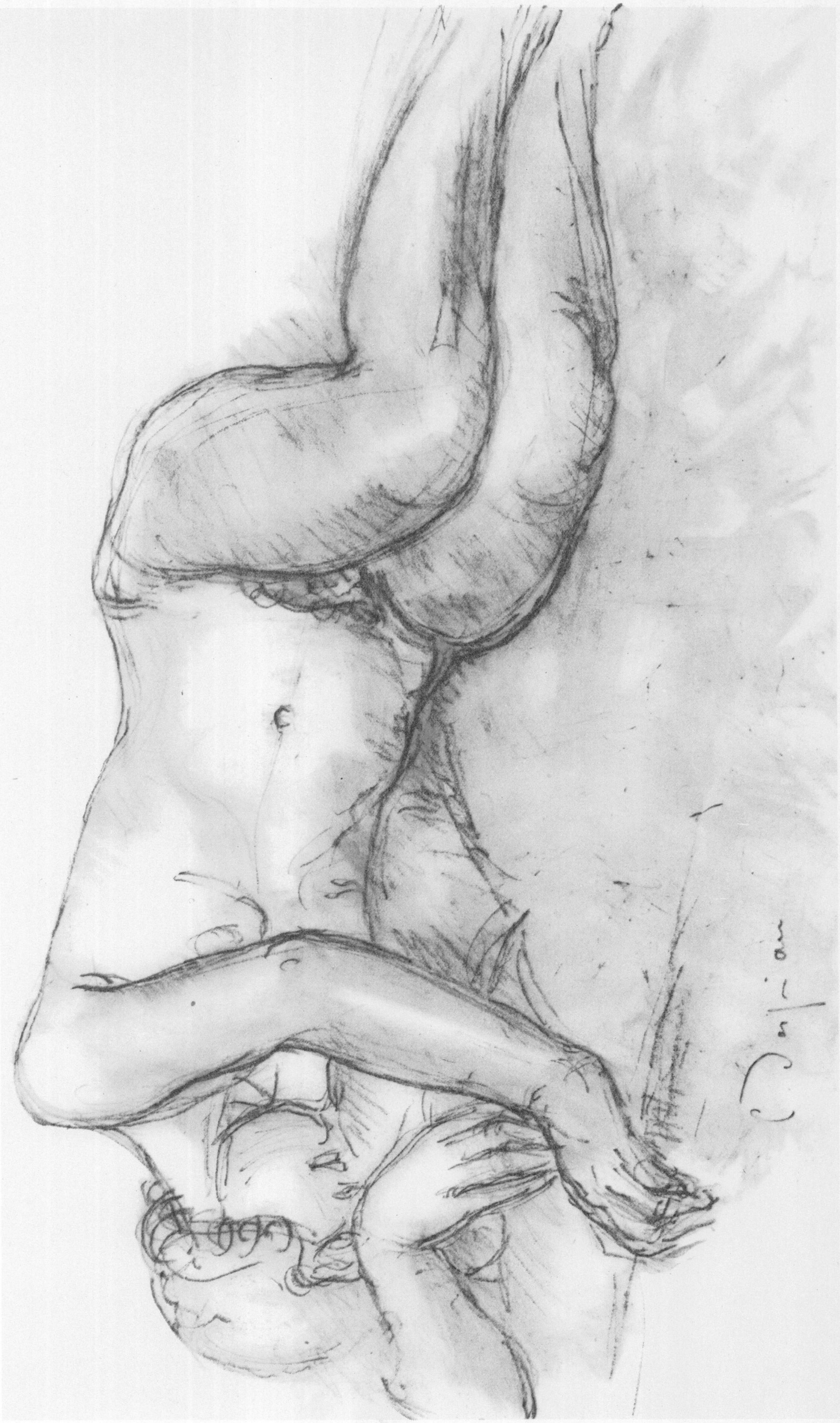

ARISTIDE MAILLOL

79 STUDY FOR THE JUDGEMENT OF PARIS

Black chalk, 15.3 × 18.3 cm. Marked bottom right: M (encircled). National Gallery, Prague (K 31 357), acquired 1932.

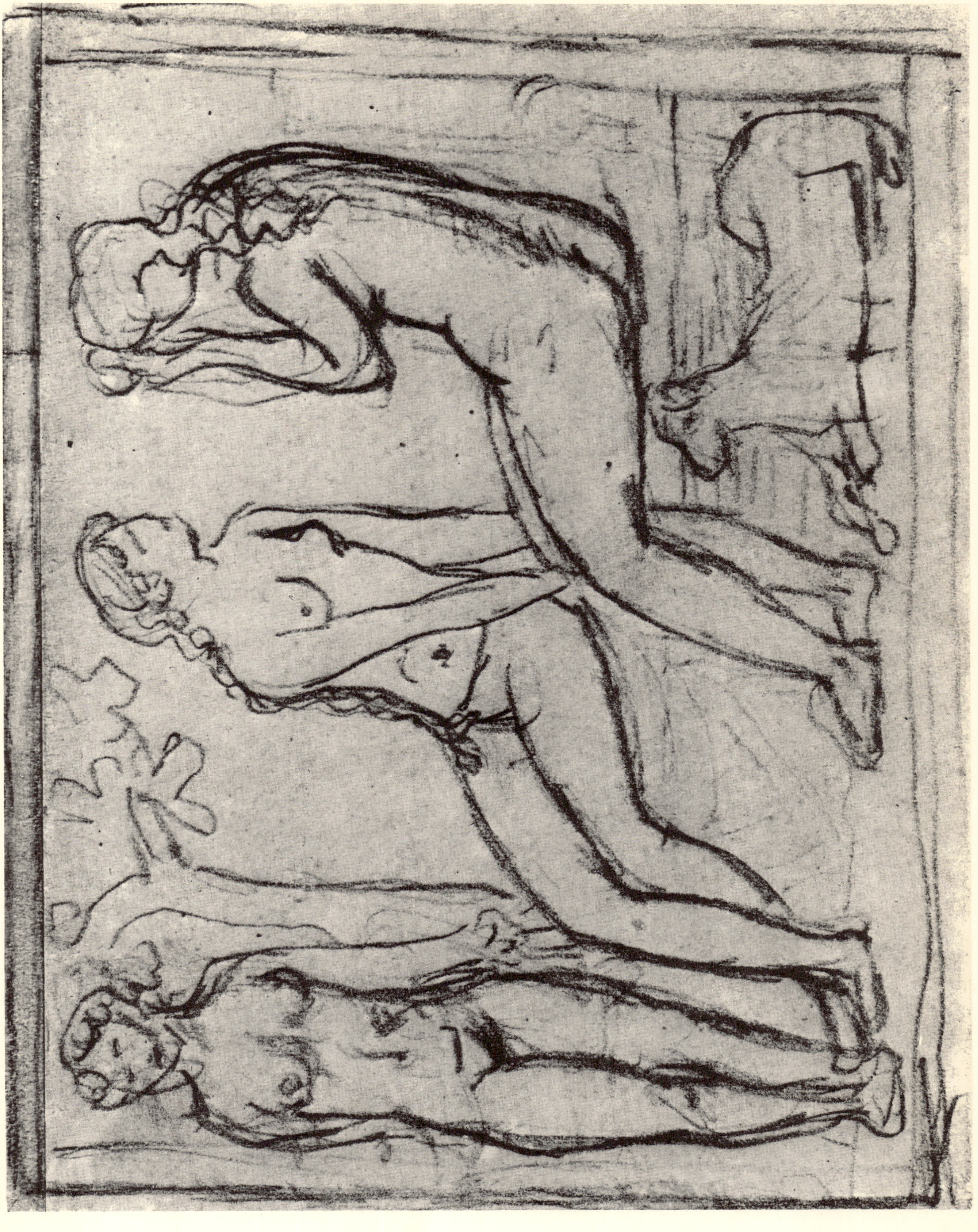

ARISTIDE MAILLOL

80 CROUCHING WOMAN

Charcoal on brown paper, 18.1 × 26.1 cm (inside border). Marked bottom right: M (encircled). National Gallery, Prague (K 38 365), acquired 1963.

This drawing recalls the statue *Night* by Maillol, done in about 1902.

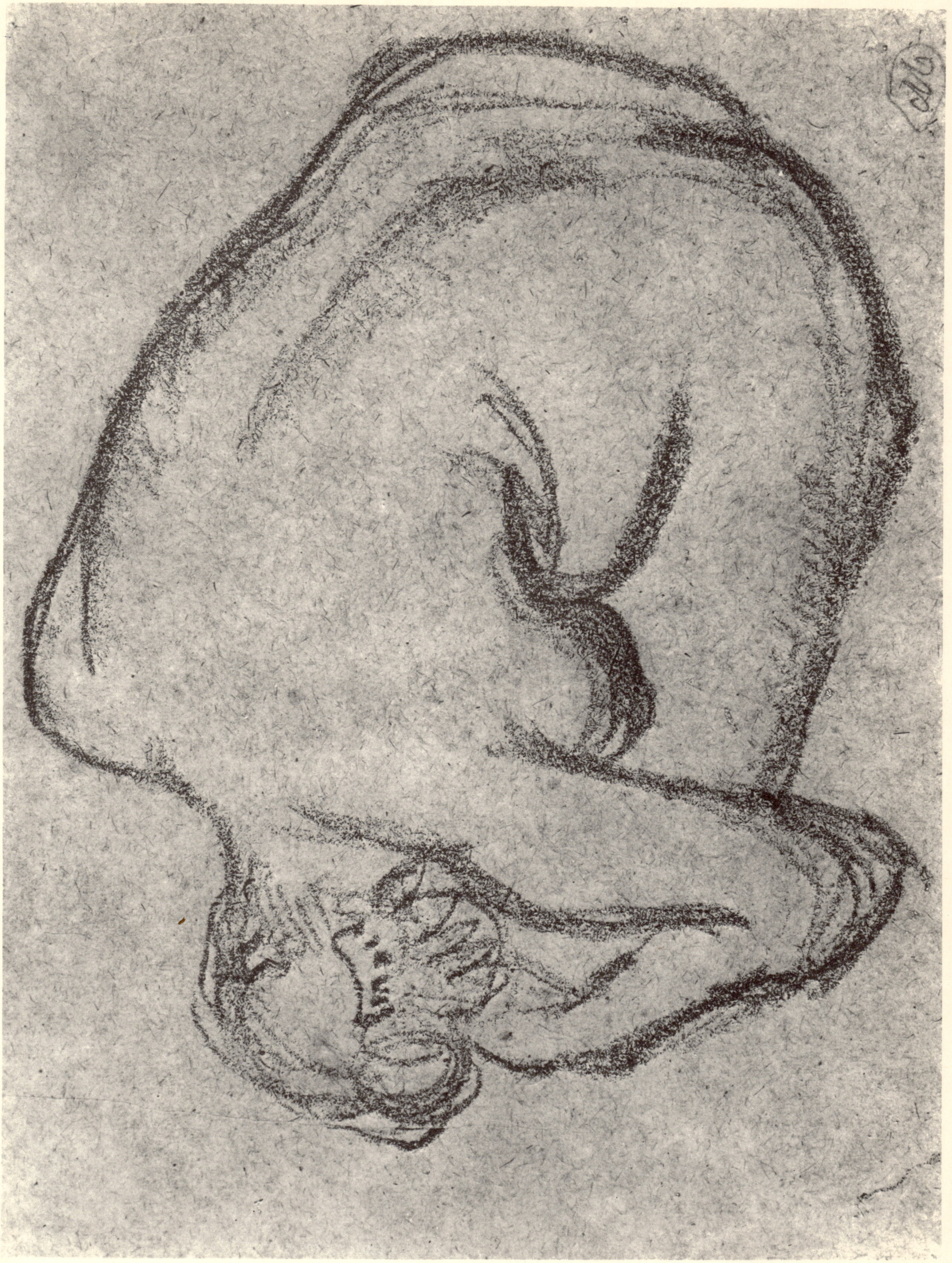